16 50

STUDIES IN RUSSIAN MUSIC

STUDIES IN
RUSSIAN MUSIC

CRITICAL ESSAYS ON THE MOST IMPORTANT OF RIMSKY-KORSAKOV'S
OPERAS, BORODIN'S "PRINCE IGOR," DARGOMIZHSKY'S "STONE
GUEST," ETC.; WITH CHAPTERS ON GLINKA, MUSSORGSKY,
BALAKIREV AND TCHAIKOVSKY

By

GERALD ABRAHAM

WILLIAM REEVES
London

Published by
WILLIAM REEVES Bookseller Ltd.,
1a Norbury Crescent, London, S.W.16

Copyright.   All Rights Reserved

Made in England

First published in 1935
Reprinted 1969

Printed in Great Britain by
Lowe & Brydone (Printers) Ltd., London

To

M. D. Calvocoressi

PREFACE

ALTHOUGH this is a book of separate essays, it is, I hope, given a certain unity by the fact that each chapter deals with some product or aspect of the "classical" period of Russian music : the music of Glinka and, more particularly, that written in the half-century following his death. I have almost ignored Mussorgsky and Tchaïkovsky, preferring to concentrate on the less discussed members of the "mighty handful," above all on Rimsky-Korsakov who has hitherto been unaccountably neglected by non-Russian critics. But in these studies of some of Korsakov's operas I have concerned myself only with certain aspects of them—perhaps too exclusively—in the attempt to investigate the working of the composer's musical mind. I have assumed that the reader has some knowledge of the plots of most of the operas discussed. After all, information of that kind has long been obtainable from such books as Rosa Newmarch's "Russian Opera" and Montagu-Nathan's "History of Russian Music." On the other hand, owing to the expensiveness of scores I have used musical examples more lavishly than would be necessary in discussing music which the reader is likely to have in his library.

My Russian spelling is a transliteration rather than a phonetic rendering, though not a *completely* consistent transliteration. It must be remembered that consistency or phonetic accuracy would necessitate "Kyui" or "Kwee" for "Cui." "Chaykovsky" may be the most sensible spelling of that composer's name, but in practice it is almost as irritating to the eye as the horrible "Tschaïkowsky." "Chaliapin" and "Scriabin" are too familiar to be superseded by the more consistent "Shalyapin" and "Skryabin." But on the whole I have followed the system recommended by the Conference of University Teachers of Russian and other Slavonic Languages. The "shch" in "Khovanshchina" looks terrifying but can be managed easily enough by anyone who can pronounce the words "English church" or "fresh cheese."

Five of these essays—the first, second, fifth, sixth and ninth—have already appeared in slightly different forms in "Music and Letters," and a sixth, that on "Prince Igor," in the New York "Musical Quarterly," and my grateful thanks are due to the Editors for their permission to reprint them. The rest are new.

I am also indebted to Messrs. Boosey and Hawkes for permission to quote extensively from works published in the Belaïev and Bessel Editions, for which they are the English agents.

G. A.

CONTENTS

STUDIES IN RUSSIAN MUSIC

I—THE ESSENCE OF RUSSIAN MUSIC.

THERE can be little doubt that the immediate and overwhelming success of Russian music when it first entered the orbit of the English concert-world in the eighteen-nineties was entirely due to its more obvious and superficial elements, its colour and general picturesqueness. As Parry said, it "naturally appealed to the awakening intelligence of the musical masses by vehement emotional spontaneity, orgiastic frenzy, dazzling effects of colour, barbaric rhythm and unrestrained abandonment to physical excitement." But if it had had no qualities other than these to recommend it we may be quite sure that the music of what we may call the "classical" Russian masters would be of as little interest and importance to-day as Grieg's or Dvorák's, equally colourful and equally pictur-esque. Qualities such as these may impress "the awakening intelligence of the musical masses," but they do not weigh very heavily with the cultured musician and fail altogether, therefore, to account for the tremendous influence of the Russians on so much of the Western European music written during the quarter of a century following Tchaïkovsky's death. These were not the qualities to impress such widely different spirits as Claude Debussy and Franz Liszt, the conservative Weingartner and the mercurial Beecham (to take only four names at random), and it is worth remarking that the one man who had no sounder elements than these in his make-up, and of whom Parry was chiefly thinking when he wrote the lines quoted, is the only important nineteenth century Russian composer whose position is weaker to-day than it was thirty years ago. Among the later men Scriabin, too, must be placed with Tchaïkovsky. Both, despite numerous affinities with their compatriots, are rather isolated figures and their most characteristic work remains outside the main current of Russian art.* This is not to be explained by

---

* Of all Russian musicians of the first rank, they are the only romantics. Their music is subjective, while all other Russian music of anything like the same value is curiously objective. But Tchaïkovsky, at any rate, was as *essentially* Russian as he was not *typically* Russian.

their attitude to conscious nationalism, with its borrowing and assimilating of folk-songs, for Tchaïkovsky, at any rate, was almost as fond of drawing on the great reservoir of peasant music as were any of the enthusiasts of the "mighty handful."* And neither Tchaïkovsky nor Scriabin was lacking in any of the colourful and emotional elements which Parry considered so characteristic of Russian music. We must go a little deeper than this, then, in our search for those qualities which are the real secret of our delight. The search for good qualities will bring to light the bad and indifferent ones at the same time, and so gradually we shall disengage the peculiarities which distinguish the Russian musical mentality so sharply from that of any of the Western peoples.

Perhaps the most valuable of all the qualities of Russian music is its compressed force and directness of expression. Its permanent intellectual appeal is almost certainly due chiefly to this conciseness. While German music has for many years, until quite recently, tended to become more and more prolix, the Russians have always been remark-

---

*"Moguchaya kuchka" is usually translated "the invincible band." But "mighty handful" is a closer equivalent to the playful Russian nickname.

able for their pointed, forceful brevity. Even Wagner and Brahms are scarcely remarkable for the simplicity and economy of their utterance, while lesser men, earnest advocates like Bruckner and Mahler, with cases of real interest to present, frequently have to be turned out of court as intolerable bores. On the other hand, if we have any complaint to make of Russian music it is usually that it is too nakedly direct, too primitive, or too sketchy. But there can be no doubt as to which is the less objectionable weakness. We may not care a snap for Mussorgsky's realism and we may be rather irritated by his continual manifestations of technical clumsiness, but there can be no contesting the breath-taking mastery of dozens of pages of " Boris " and the songs, where some subtle emotion or some intensely dramatic situation is caught up and presented to us in terms of music with astounding force and simplicity. The slightest inflection of the vocal line—and that line scarcely ever anything more than speech made musical—the sketchiest of accompaniments, and Mussorgsky has cut the heart out of some little village tragedy and brought it home to us with startling power. Think, too, of the remarkable presentation of Boris's anguish in the "Duma" scene. From the same type of mind working in the field of symphonic composition was born such a short pithy saying, like a blow straight from the shoulder, as the opening theme of Borodin's Second Symphony :—

Ex. 1

or the unison passage at the beginning of "Scheherazade," the "Schariar" theme which serves as a motto to the whole work. As early as Glinka (to whom, by the way, Parry's words scarcely apply at all) this conciseness was a striking characteristic of Russian music. His "Kamarinskaya" is splendidly to the point, and in listening to the "Ruslan and Lyudmila" Overture one is forcibly reminded of the phrase in which Bülow is said to have conveyed his impression of Berlioz's "Corsair"—"terse as a pistol shot." Even Scriabin, whatever his practice in his symphonic works, knew how to be economical in his shorter ones; many of his piano pieces are tiny masterpieces of compression, comparable only with some of Heine's lyrics.

But it is in the manner of handling the very fabric of music, and even more in the sources of inspiration, that we find men like Tchaïkovsky, Scriabin and Rachmaninov ranging themselves with Western musicians rather than with their compatriots. The impulse to create, the "jog" of inspiration, comes to all men in all countries from more or less the same sorts of things; differences in the results are usually caused by the way in which men react to the jog. It was merely because they were very self-conscious on one particular point that the Russian "nationalists" so branded themselves. Wagner, who in his way was quite as much a nationalist as any Balakirev or Rimsky-Korsakov, was self-conscious of another side of his genius—which he paraded in a similar way. But it *is* rather remarkable that hardly any of the best Russian music is inspired by erotic emotion, and less still by psychological self-analysis—commodities in which Scriabin and Tchaïkovsky, in common with the majority of Western composers, deal rather heavily. No musician has ever been a keener analyst of the human soul than Mussorgsky, but he never takes himself as his subject and his analysis is as impartial and objective as Flaubert's. Here, not for the last time, we may pause to notice a certain constancy in the working of the Russian mind in the very different spheres of music and literature. The two greatest masters of the Russian novel, Tolstoy and Dostoevsky, both intensely introspective as men, preserved almost complete detachment as artists; they were capable of drawing even themselves objectively!

In this absence of emotional appeal as in so much else, Glinka's work is the prototype. The "love interest" in "A Life for the Tsar" is as obviously manufactured as the same element in popular detective fiction, and is responsible for the worst pages of the score, just as the love-music of "Prince Igor" is the weakest part of that magnificent work. Love plays an even less important rôle in "Boris," and a merely secondary part in "Khovanshchina." In "The Golden Cockerel" it is burlesqued as Stravinsky burlesques it in "Petrushka." Surely no other artists have been so little inspired by *das Ewig-Weibliche!* When they are unable to scamp the "love-interest" altogether, Russian musicians —including even Tchaïkovsky in his stage-works as a whole—provide it perfunctorily. Except in the works of that most personal of artists, Scriabin, there is nothing in the least equivalent to "Tristan," the erotic side of Chopin, or the "Dichterliebe" in the whole range of Russian music. Indeed emotional expression of any sort is rather conspicuously lacking in Russian art. If emotion is present at all, it is usually rather curtly restrained. Patriotism, though seldom jingoism, comes fairly often to the fore, humour not infrequently, and a quick reaction to any suggestion of the grotesque is noticeable. But the excitement which Russian music manifests —and I use the word "manifests" advisedly, instead of "expresses"—is almost always physical, a direct glorification of animal joy of living and of brute strength, rather than spiritual. It is not on this account less intellectual, as might seem at first thought—but the intellectual appeal must be considered separately. Yet before we leave the emotional aspect of Russian music it is worth pointing out that the climaxes in nearly all the most remarkable symphonic works, our two notable exceptions again helping to prove the rule, are of purely musical and intellectual contrivance (for instance, the finale of "The Fire Bird") and do not arise from any emotional intensification. As the American critic, Paul Rosenfeld, says of those in "Scheherazade," they are "purely voluntary . . . . nothing other than the arbitrary thickening and distention of certain ideas."

Though Russian music differs to this extent from Western as regards emotional basis, the difference is as nothing compared with the difference in what I can only call "musical intellectuality." For real intellectual understanding of Russian music one almost needs an entirely new set of postulates. The Russian musical mind is essentially so naïve, naïve even in ingenuity. It is childlike in many other respects than its love for bright primary orchestral colours and its pure sensuous delight in sound for sound's sake. Its freedom from preconceptions opens the way to all sorts of curious triumphs. Borodin, for instance, unhampered by tradition, was able to write the scherzo of his Third Symphony in genuine quintuple time :—

Ex. 2

while the more sophisticated Chopin, trying to move in the same measure (third movement of his C minor Sonata), stumbles about uneasily in a compound duple-plus-triple time. Sometimes the extreme primitiveness of outlook gives us a ruder shock. The Russian, for one thing, seems usually to be over-concerned with the

thrill of the present moment in sound;* his mental
vision is not sufficiently broad and retentive to get
that pleasure which we derive from Brahms and
Beethoven at their best, when we feel that, in Pater's
phrase, the composer has "foreseen the end in the
beginning and never lost sight of it." Rimsky-
Korsakov, in his "Record of my Musical Life,"
that most valuable (if not always completely reli-
able) of all original documents to the student of
Russian music, tells us how in the eighteen-sixties
the members of the "mighty handful" used to form
their judgments. "For the most part a work was
criticised by its separate elements; the first four
bars were excellent, the next eight weak, the following melody was valueless, but the transition to
the next phrase was good—and so on. A composition was never considered as an æsthetic whole.
Accordingly Balakirev usually introduced new
works to his circle fragmentarily; he used to play
the end first, then the beginning . . . . "

Of the most typical Russians only Borodin, and
Balakirev in his later years, seem to have been at
all concerned with formal architecture in its

---

* Tchaïkovsky lives too intensely in this "present moment"
emotionally as Rimsky-Korsakov does *sensuously*.

broadest aspect, Tchaïkovsky and Glazunov did their best to keep to the path of orthodoxy, with unhappy results in Tchaïkovsky's case, for the mechanical symmetry of the older type of symphony becomes ridiculous in works highly charged with emotion. Even Scriabin managed better than this. But with Rimsky-Korsakov the problems of form seem to have been confined entirely to the rough "lay-out" and general arrangement of ideas, that is, to mere "design" rather than to "form" in the true sense of the word. And he is not usually very deeply concerned with that. As for Stravinsky, his big ballets are, from a strictly musical point of view, literally incoherent as wholes. The unity of works like "Svadebka" ("Les Noces") is due to their peculiarly woven texture, a texture made by the kaleidoscopic rearrangement of tiny particles—a development of Rimsky-Korsakov's so-called "miniature style" in opera, which we shall have to consider later in more detail.

The basis of modern musical construction in Western Europe, the system of logical development of germinal ideas, of which Beethoven was the first really important master, is entirely foreign to the spirit of Russian music. There have been exceptions, of course; but, broadly speaking, the most typical Russian composers have either frankly abandoned the method or used it with conspicuous want of success.   With the Russians we are never able to watch a few tiny germs unfold, showing themselves ever in new lights, till their possibilities seem almost inexhaustible and they have grown into a great and finely-wrought fabric of sound.   Such thinking in sound—*progressive* thinking—is not the Russian's way of going about things; his mental process is more akin to brooding, a continual turning over of ideas in his mind, viewing them from different angles, throwing them against strange and fantastic backgrounds, but never *evolving* anything from them. We shall see one peculiarly Russian way of developing melody—by the insertion of appoggiaturas which are afterwards broadened to form an essential part of the line—when we come to examine " Prince Igor " a little more closely. And if we want modern examples of the same thing we shall find them again in " Svadebka."   It is instructive, too, to compare the forward impulse of even a sustained Beethoven melody like " In des Lebens Frühlingstagen," in " Fidelio," with the static nature of the opening melody of " The Rite of Spring " :—

Ex. 3

It is almost like putting a Rodin against a Grecian frieze. And in this respect it is easy to find plenty of folk-song counterparts for the Stravinsky example.

When we turn to the field of opera this inability to think progressively, this mental trait of making the most of the subject by showing it passively in fresh circumstances instead of by setting it in active conflict with something else, produces even more curious results. Contrast and conflict, and through them progressive development, are the essence of drama, as we conceive it, just as they are the essence of sonata-form. The lack of them is far more obvious on the stage than in a symphonic movement, and though apparently a more serious defect—from our point of view—it has this advantage that it is the much more easily grasped. There can be no quibbling about the facts in opera; the presence or absence of this element of conflict is hardly demonstrable in pure music, but in opera it is so obvious that it needs no demonstration. In the finest and most characteristic Russian operas, "Igor," "Boris," "Sadko," even in the earliest of them all, "A Life for the Tsar," we find only the sketchiest outline of a plot, no drama of development, but a brilliant series of stage-pictures, sometimes highly dramatic in themselves, sometimes not at all so, detached and apparently almost disconnected yet cumulatively most effective in their presentation of an exuberantly vital whole. And it is significant that this is particularly true of the masterpieces, while some of the less important Russian operas— for instance, Rimsky-Korsakov's "Tsar's Bride" and "Pan Voevoda"—approach much more nearly the Western idea of theatrical effectiveness. It may be said that this is due simply to the composers' lack of stage-sense, but as it happens we only need turn to the work of non-musical dramatists to realise that this inability to see an action or a conflict of wills as the complete and rounded thing *we* call drama must spring from something deeply rooted in the Slav nature. Prince D. S. Mirsky has pointed out that "Tolstoy's dramatic method was not dramatic—his plays (as he has explained himself) are a succession of peep-show slides, rather than a dynamically unfolded action. So that a play by Tolstoy has more in common with a picture-series like 'The Rake's Progress' of Hogarth than with a real drama." Might not the same be said of Tolstoy's "War and Peace"? As for "Boris," Mussorgsky's opera is actually less diffuse than the play by Pushkin on which it is based.* The important thing is to remember that this lack of dramatic interest, a serious weakness in Western eyes, is no weakness to a Russian. He is aware of it, but it does not worry him. Rimsky-Korsakov himself described "Sadko" as an "opera-epic" consisting of "seven tableaux of a fabulous and epic nature."

In more purely musical matters—harmony, counterpoint and modulation—the working of the Russian mind differs quite as essentially from that of the Western. Harmonic thought is a personal

---

* Maurice Baring says of Pushkin's "Boris": "The play is constructed on the model of Shakespeare's chronicle plays, but in a still more disjointed fashion, without a definite beginning or end. . . . . Pushkin had not the power of conceiving and executing a drama which should move round one idea to an inevitable close. . . . . A subject from which a drama might be written is taken, but the drama is left unwritten. . . . It is not a play, but a chronicle; and it would be foolish to blame Pushkin for not accomplishing what he never attempted. As a chronicle, a series of detached scenes, it is supremely successful."

affair, at any rate in the case of a mature master. Many of Rimsky-Korsakov's harmonic idiosyncrasies, for instance, are peculiar to himself and certain harmonic progressions stamp a work as his quite as definitely as some of his favourite melodic shapes. But one can say without hesitation that, generally, harmony forms as inessential a part of a Russian composer's original conception as colour did of Brahms's.* To put it in another way : the bulk of Russian music is as clearly "harmonised" as Brahms's is "orchestrated." The music is conceived in terms of melody and colour; the harmony is a support, a filling-out, a spice—anything but a living organism. And much the same may be said of Russian counterpoint. Genuine contrapuntal feeling, the production of the musical texture by the natural flowing together of parallel, simultaneous streams of thought, is practically unknown in Russian music. On the other hand, some of the Russians have been very fond of using contrapuntal means in constructing their music, a fundamentally different matter. Borodin, in particular, frequently shows great ingenuity in juggling with combinations

---

* On the other hand, Tchaïkovsky told Mme. von Meck that "every melodic idea brings its own inevitable harmony."

of themes, but the themes (as in the well-known "On the Steppes of Central Asia") are only fitted together; they have not *grown* together. There is nothing forced or unnatural about the fitting, but the resulting musical texture is, as the composer himself, being a chemist, might have put it, a "mixture," not a "compound." Rimsky-Korsakov was another good theoretical contrapuntist; his Sextet, his String Quartet and his Third Symphony are monuments—one might almost say, tombstones—of academic counterpoint. But in his most characteristic works he never achieves anything like the living woof of parts which men like Wagner and Strauss manage so well. At its best, as in the magnificent finale of the fourth tableau of "Sadko," his counterpoint amounts to nothing more than ingenious dovetailing. More often it is a mere loose patchwork of themes like this example from "Scheherazade" :—

Ex. 4

Yet another typical idiosyncrasy of the Russian

musician is his habit of suddenly "pivoting" on one
or two notes common to two chords, a sort of right-
angled turn of thought which has either the piquant
quality of an epigram or the disconcerting effect of
a logical *non sequitur*, according to the skill with
which it is managed.   A simple, and very delightful, example is the trumpet fanfare which opens
each part of "Tsar Saltan" :—

Ex. 5

There is a more elaborate one in the second movement of "Scheherazade" :—

Ex. 6

and it is characteristic of Rimsky-Korsakov that,
having discovered this little trick of harmonic
sleight-of-hand, he amuses himself with it at great
length in sheer childish delight at the fun of the
thing.   The first time we hear it we accept it as a

piece of genuine wit, wit being a matter of unexpected juxtapositions, but the joke becomes tiresome when the point is put in italics. The same trait shows itself in the general fondness for what we may call "enharmonic puns," not only as modulatory short cuts but for their own sakes. There is a startling instance in Balakirev's First Symphony, where, taking F sharp as G flat, he pivots suddenly from E minor to E flat minor, stays in the new key for four bars and then returns almost as abruptly.

One could multiply examples of similar tricks of musical thought almost indefinitely. Some, of course, are peculiar to individual composers, but many are common to practically all Russians and are the tokens of a far more essential "Russianness" than that which finds expression in the borrowing or imitation of folk-songs. The folk-song element is immensely important—both in symphonic music and in opera—but it offers no difficulty to the Western musical mind. Rather the reverse, for Russian folk-song is generally very attractive. It is the entire freshness of viewpoint—so delightful to anyone with an open mind—which has led to so much misunderstanding of Russian music on the part of those who put no very high value on its more superficial qualities. We are so accustomed to logical development in a symphony and to a particular kind of architecture in the drama that we have the greatest difficulty in appreciating any other ways of building a musical or theatrical fabric. We condemn as a "weakness" the absence of what we are accustomed to find, forgetting that it is as natural for a Russian to think episodically as for a Frenchman to think logically. There are plenty of real weaknesses in Russian music, as we soon find when we come to look more closely at individual works, but it is most important to distinguish between these and what are only peculiarly Russian ways of doing things. Mere freedom from prejudice is not enough; one must arm oneself with active will-to-understand. That need not preclude open-eyed criticism.

II—GLINKA AND HIS ACHIEVEMENT

SOME knowledge of the conditions under which work is produced must obviously be helpful, if not essential, to its complete understanding in any circumstances, but in few cases is it so absolutely necessary as in Glinka's. Only with the fullest realisation of his environment can one estimate with justice the extent of his achievement; that is, of his achievement considered positively as a thing valuable in itself, as apart from the value of its influence in determining the direction and methods of the later nationalist movement. One can talk glibly enough about this latter aspect of Glinka's work without even troubling to make its acquaintance, for his name has long since become petrified into a landmark of musical history. We perfunctorily touch our hats to it in passing and do not bother to examine it more closely.

In the case of the average composer, education, social position, immediate intellectual environment

and the general state of national culture certainly
modify his work, but they can scarcely be said actually to condition it, to define and limit it on all
sides. Yet this was so with Glinka. Indeed, one
may go further and say that the force of surrounding
circumstances was a generating as well as a con-
trolling one. Glinka was no Beethoven or Wagner
imposing himself on circumstances, moulding them
to his will and hacking a way through difficulties.
Nor was he a Bach, a Mozart or a Haydn mutely
accepting conditions as he found them, yet working
such miracles within those limits that one is unconscious of them. His part was almost a passive one.
His enthusiasms were like those of any dilettante
and his triumphs of real artistic insight seem to be
lucky hits rather than fruits of harnessed inspiration.
A wealthy amateur, amiable, modest, gifted, highly
strung (as witness Lenz's well-known anecdote of
his behaviour on hearing the Chòral Symphony),*
almost always ill, either in fact or in imagination,
playing the violin indifferently well and the piano
better, as became a pupil of Field and Charles
Mayer, dabbling in composition, though with the

---

* In " Beethoven et ses trois styles," and quoted by Grove
(" Beethoven and his Nine Symphonies," p. 362).

scantiest technical equipment, his only serious, systematic study of the technique of composition was
made in the five months he spent with Siegfried
Dehn in Berlin in 1833, when he was twenty-nine—
and twenty-three years later, the year before his
death, he went back to Dehn and studied "Das
Wohltemperirte Klavier." Yet this rather simple-
minded avoider of unpleasant sensations was the
initiator of a movement which exercised a fertilising
influence on music during the last century second in
importance only to that of Wagner himself. One
can hardly say that he was unconscious of what he
was doing, but his consciousness was much less definite than that of his immediate followers. As
Fouque remarks, "It was only after his death that
he became a reformer and innovator; in his life-time
his ambition was not so far-reaching." Of ambition
he had, indeed, as little as any creative artist can
have. From such a man it is obvious that no great
personal message could have come. His music is
as nearly impersonal as music can be. The light
which shines through it scarcely ever comes from his
own rather colourless personality but is generated
by the excitement of external circumstances. It is
to the force of these surrounding influences that we

owe alike the power, the colour and the weakness
of Glinka's art. From the days of the pampered,
coddled childhood to the journey to Italy made in
1830, nothing occurred to lay bare the real artist
concealed beneath the dilettante exterior. His education completed, there was nothing for him to do
but to write variations for harp and piano, to fall
mildly in love and to travel for health's sake in the
Ukraine and the Caucasian provinces. At home, at
Novospasskoe, he certainly gained useful knowledge both of the orchestral classics and of the
mechanism of the instruments from a little band
kept by a wealthy uncle and, beside a number of
trifles, he even produced a cantata for the accession
of Nicholas I, of which he speaks complacently in
his memoirs. But of exceptional gifts there was
yet no sign. At St. Petersburg where, as in cultured circles all over Europe at that time, Italian
opera was at the height of its glory, "he plunged
for some time into a half-artistic, half-worldly life
among a number of wealthy young fellows of good
birth, fond of fêtes and serenades and theatrical
performances."*

It was the long holiday in Italy (1830-1833) and

---

* M. D. Calvocoressi : "Glinka : biographie critique."

the consequent home-sickness which revealed the
real Glinka, even to himself. The brilliant super-
ficialities of Bellini and Donizetti repelled him at
the same time that they fascinated him, and
although they left marks on his style which he could
never quite remove they now irritated his nostalgic
melancholy. In this mood was born the resolve to
"write music in Russian" and it was not long before
opera suggested itself as the medium. Then came
the five months with Dehn in Berlin, and by the time
he reached home again he had already composed
fragments of what was later to be "A Life for the
Tsar," though, curiously enough, he had as yet a
different subject in mind. Even when the new subject was suggested to him by Zhukovsky, his musical thought was independent of any consideration
but the broad outline of the drama; at times he was
actually in advance of the librettist (Rosen, the
German secretary of the Tsarevich). Nothing
could prove more clearly the absolutely musical
genesis of "A Life for the Tsar"—though, musically, the progenitors of the work were an ill-as-
sorted couple, Italian opera and Russian folk-song,
the one the environment of his childhood, the other
that of his maturer years. Yet the thing succeeded.

The first performance was on November 27 (December 9), 1836, and the success was both immediate and lasting. Only a few aristocrats sneered at the "coachman's music." But the Tsar was favourable, accepted the dedication, nominated the composer Master of the Imperial Chapel, and hailed Glinka as "a great master." Encouraged by this initial triumph, Glinka now turned to Pushkin's "Ruslan and Lyudmila" for a new libretto and, but for the author's tragic death, might have had his assistance in redrafting the work for a musical setting. He worked at "Ruslan" from 1837 to 1842, producing also the incidental music to Kukolnik's tragedy, "Prince Kholmsky," during the same period. Calvocoressi remarks that this is to be considered the period during which the composer's artistic development reached maturity and that not only is "Ruslan" incomparably finer than "A Life for the Tsar," but in itself shows a great advance on its first sketches. Such an advance has quite a different significance in Glinka's case from that which, thanks to Nottebohm, we can trace in the development of many of Beethoven's ideas. With Beethoven it shows only the operation of the technical process of refinement; with Glinka it is the token of the composer's increasingly sure grip on his whole means of expression. Yet "Ruslan," much farther removed from Italianism than "A Life for the Tsar," had only a moderate success and Glinka, discouraged, wrote no more for six years.

To opera he never returned. The output of his later years consists entirely of those "picturesque fantasias" with which he hoped to please "equally the connoisseurs and the general public," compromises between "the exigencies of .art and those of the time," to use the composer's own words.* The material for two of these, the "Capriccio on the Jota Aragonesa" and "Summer Night in Madrid," was provided by the realisation of a "far-off dream of youth," a visit to Spain (1845-47), in the course of which he made considerable, if not very scientific, researches into the nature and origin of Spanish folk-music. He was particularly struck by the Oriental flavour of much of it—attributable apparently to Moorish elements. In 1848 we find him again in Warsaw after a brief stay at home. Here he wrote another of his orchestral fantasias, the well-known "Kamarinskaya," based on two Russian folk-tunes, one of which he had already turned to

---

* Letter to Kukolnik.

account in a piano piece.   Again in 1852 his love
of travel led him through Berlin and Paris to the
south of France and then back to Paris, where he
composed a fragment of a " Ukrainian Symphony."
This was a programmatic work based on Gogol's
"Taras Bulba," but it was soon abandoned on account of "the impossibilty of getting out of the
German   rut   in   the   development"—significant
phrase and explanatory of what many would take
for weaknesses in Glinka's work.   This fragment
really marks the end of Glinka's creative career, if
career it can be called, though he wrote an orchestral polonaise for the coronation of Tsar Alexander II in 1855.   Glinka had been driven home
by the outbreak of the Crimean War and, except for
the Berlin visit of 1856, spent the last three years of
his life in complete quiet.   He studied church music
and toyed with a new libretto but, though still a
middle-aged man, he did not rouse himself to any
creative effort.   It was at this time that he met the
critic-composer Serov and Alexander Dargomïzhsky, who without Glinka's richer qualities was yet
able to accomplish those reforms in the nature of
Russian opera in which the other had only partly
succeeded.   And then there was the young Bala-

kirev (introduced to him by that Ulibishev whom
we remember chiefly as an authority on Mozart and
as the antagonist of von Lenz as a Beethoven critic),
Balakirev who was to become the leader of that
"mighty handful" who soon trod Glinka's little
footpath into a broad and noble road. Glinka recognised the boy of nineteen as his natural suc-
cessor : "He alone has ideas so like my own about
everything concerned with music . . . . In time he
will be the second Glinka."

For all critical purposes Glinka's work may be
considered as consisting only of the two operas, the
"Prince Kholmsky" music and the orchestral fantasias. With the exception of one or two effective
songs, such as Chaliapin's favourite battle-steed,
"The Midnight Review," and one or two *salon*
pieces for piano, the remainder of his output "does
not even," as Calvocoressi says, "reveal a temperament." Such a handful of works, for none of which
(except "Ruslan") any but the most enthusiastic
admirer* could claim artistic perfection, extraordinary beauty or very uncommon imaginative
power, seems to offer but small ground on which to

---

* There have been many such in Russia, however—Tchaïkovsky,
Anton Rubinstein and Rimsky-Korsakov among the rest.

build any substantial claim for respecting Glinka as
anything but a pioneer.   Yet I should like to show
if I can that Glinka deserves admiration for something more than the fact of his being the first to
"write Russian music," that, within the limits imposed on him by the special conditions I have outlined, he produced some really remarkable work
and that this work is, in any case, specially worthy of
study on account of those unique conditions.   By
far the most interesting and important of these is
Glinka's technical "incompetence."

It is easy enough to laugh at his awkward modulations and his naïve solutions of the problems of
symphonic architecture—and to miss the point completely.   After all, how otherwise could he have
managed things?   This Russian musical language
had to grow from itself, or rather (if I may mix
metaphors) to form its own channel.   Traditional
methods would have corrupted the purity of the
young growth and perhaps even stifled it altogether.
Better almost any weaknesses and severe growing
pains than that.   Glinka himself recognised this
very clearly; "Taras Bulba" was thrown over
because of "the impossibility of getting out of the
German rut," and elsewhere he says that "severe

German counterpoint is not always in accord with imaginative fire." It is easy to say that his was a short-sighted view, that he ignored the fact that "those move easiest who have learn'd to dance." But surely he was right in preferring natural awkwardness to the dancing-master correctness of deportment of the academic product who says next to nothing in the nicest possible way. Learning is like fuel; it feeds the fire, yet too much will put it out. Too much counterpoint nearly extinguished Rimsky-Korsakov and the same accident might have befallen Glinka. On the other hand, given something new and vital to express, that something will, in spite of every disadvantage, find a natural outlet through which to express itself. (Your illiterate tinker of Bedford will, in his earnestness, turn you out noble prose, while the Great Cham of English literary scholarship could write only a laboured jargon.) So we may imagine Glinka facing these rough ashlars of popular melody, feeling instinctively that there must be some way of hewing them into fine and vital shapes. The tools that every craftsman uses are ready to his hand, but they are designed to work in other material than this, even if he could use them less awkwardly. So he struggles—and sometimes flounders helplessly enough—as every man must struggle who sets out to make something in a new way, without model or precedent and without the skill of the long-practised craftsman. Hence the loose, almost amorphous designs of the symphonic fantasias, for instance, "A Summer Night in Madrid," in which one theme is merely taken up after another, without coherence, till at the very end the two most important are picked up again and brilliantly dismissed in the brief coda. Only the fleeting later references to the "Punto Moruno" tune show that the composer is aiming at anything more organic than a piece of patchwork. The "Capriccio on the Jota Aragonesa" hangs together better only because of the economy of material. But it is in "Kamarinskaya," the most interesting in every way, that the difficulty of spinning a more or less sophisticated art-work out of popular material is displayed most clearly and grappled with, if by no means solved, most successfully. Here, more truly than anywhere else in Glinka, we may say that the form has grown round the substance and "corresponds to the real nature and purport of it." It is admittedly crude and amateurish but, despite its

looseness, it is in this respect a more notable
achievement than the "Ruslan" Overture. The
Overture, by far the best thing Glinka ever wrote
on classical lines, is concise, well organised, bearing
no marks of technical incompetence, and giving an
impression of striking vigour and confidence, even
of great power (in the famous passage near the end
where the trombones play a descending whole-tone
scale *fortissimo*) :—

Ex. 7

The problem of fitting the material into a given
design is satisfactorily solved, but one can hardly
say that the form has arisen naturally from the
material or is conditioned by it in any way. But
"Kamarinskaya" is a natural growth.

'Kamarinskaya" also raises, and to some extent
answers, a question of fundamental principle in the
treatment of folk-song material in sophisticated
music. We must remember what a folk-song is—
and how much it is that. A man's music is the

manifestation of a something which is the sum of many things—thoughts, emotions, and purely musical feelings and ideas. In the music of a competent composer that "something," complicated as it may be, is expressed more or less completely and satisfactorily; in folk-music, although the "something" is usually simple, it frequently is not. In the majority of cases a folk-tune, divorced from the words, gives only an imperfect idea of the spirit of which it is the outward manifestation. Its beauty is the beauty of a body without a soul, which is perhaps the explanation of its peculiar charm. When he sets such a tune a composer may be content merely to dress up the body to the best advantage or he may try to breathe into it again the spirit which gave it life in the first place. To do the first skilfully is good and useful work, but craftsman-work; the artist can be content with nothing less than a re-creation of the vital spirit. To take familiar examples : this is precisely what Delius has done in "Brigg Fair" and what Grainger has failed to do in his choral setting of the same tune, true and beautiful though his treatment is.

Now this is what Glinka attempted, but did not quite achieve, in "Kamarinskaya," if not in the two

Spanish fantasias. He failed—or only partially succeeded—because his material was not thoroughly digested. It was not seen through a personality, as the "Brigg Fair" tune is seen through Delius's, and so the easiest way of recreating the feeling at the back of the thing was missed. Time after time we do realise the dim presence of the real soul recreated, only to be baffled again by patches of what is only a brilliantly scored "setting" of the tune. Even so, it is far in advance of its time—in advance, too, of the methods of the Smetanas and Liszts and Griegs and Dvoraks of later years.*

For Glinka had the root of the matter in him. He had the right method of approach, realisation of the fundamental fact that what folk-melody needs, if it is to be used in art-music, is to be displayed against fresh backgrounds. That is to say, the tune, in whatever fresh lights and relationships it may be shown, must not be mangled by subjecting it to the largely mechanical processes of "development"

---

* Tchaïkovsky thought "Kamarinskaya" "astonishingly original," and said that "from it all the Russian composers who followed Glinka (including myself) continue to this day to borrow contrapuntal and harmonic combinations directly they have to develop a Russian dance-tune. . . . . Glinka managed to concentrate in one short work what a dozen second-rate talents would only have invented with the entire expenditure of their powers."

which have been devised to exploit quite a different kind of material. The method of "fresh backgrounds" is peculiarly congenial to the Russian mind and was long employed exclusively by the Russians, but as a formula for folk-song treatment it is popular with modern composers of every nationality. (Among the latter one may be pardoned for referring once more to Delius, and incidentally for pointing out the curious parallel between his social position and haphazard manner of drifting into the world of music and Glinka's.) Perhaps the most serious objection to Glinka's method is the glaring light it throws on the poverty of a composer's inventive resources and on any weaknesses in the material. Glinka nowhere works with really first-rate material, but whether here in "Kamarinskaya," where it is quite weak :—

Ex. 8

in the Spanish "Capriccio," or in the best pages of "Ruslan" (for instance, the chorus that opens Act III and the splendid dances of Act IV), he is

seldom at a loss for ideas for original and often
daring treatment. This is particularly noticeable in
the "Ruslan" dances.

It will perhaps be objected that Glinka, for all his
care in avoiding the Charybdis of German thought
and methods, crashed heedlessly on to the Scylla of
Italianism in opera—apparently the worse evil.
This is true, above all, of "A Life for the Tsar."
But since it was almost inevitable that at first some
foreign matter should mingle with the pure metal,
it was really fortunate that the other component
should be Italian rather than German, seeing that
the former was far easier to eliminate afterwards.
And though Glinka never entirely threw off this
weakening influence, its power over him was at its
worst confined almost entirely to manner and
method. His essential thought was but little corrupted by it, and in the crucible of his mind the very
clichés of the Italians became as Russianised as the
Spanish tunes in the "Summer Night in Madrid."
When, as in Finn's and Ruslan's songs in the
Second Act of "Ruslan," both thought and expression are altogether native, the result is strikingly
fine. The march in the "Prince Kholmsky" music
is an instance of a triumph over, or rather *through*,

another kind of commonplace. Naïve and square-
cut as it is, there is a certain dignity in its rude
strength and it admirably expresses what it is intended to express—an outburst of popular feeling
at a national crisis. Glinka is not to be compared
with Mussorgsky or even Rimsky-Korsakov as an
interpreter of mass-feeling, but, like so many Russian intellectuals, he drew power from his sympathy
with the people. Even Mussorgsky never sur·
passed the "Slavsya" chorus in "A Life for the
Tsar."

Glinka's strength—and one feels that it is never
the man's own force of character, but some outward
exciting circumstance that is the driving power—

Ex. 9

nearly always finds expression in the roughest way. It is better controlled in the "Ruslan" Overture than in anything else he did. But it scarcely ever finds an outlet in those barbaric outbursts to which Russian orchestral music owes so much of its superficial attractiveness. Yet even of these we get a foretaste in the *lezginka* of "Ruslan" and the Prelude to Act V of "Prince Kholmsky" (Ex. 9). One gets a keener thrill of sensuous pleasure from this than from most of Glinka's work, but the naïve, healthy vigour of almost all the things really worthy of him is extremely refreshing. The thought is always simple, usually individual (though not, as I have tried to show, very personal) and often extremely beautiful. And though its expression is not always completely free, it is probably little more hampered by the medium than is the essential thought of many composers of far greater reputation. After all the number of composers who have entirely subdued their means of expression to the supple instrument of their thought, to the natural ease of a limb rather than of a skilfully handled tool, is surprisingly small.

Glinka, of course, was often clumsy enough in quite elementary matters of craftsmanship. To the end he remained too much the dilettante to master the tricks that every Mus.Doc. in England has at his fingr-tips. But in one branch of workmanship he was always conspicuously successful and his mastery is overlooked only because of the still more remarkable triumphs of his younger fellow-countrymen in the same line. As an orchestrator he deserves a very high place indeed. In his attitude to the orchestra, as in his treatment of folksong in " Kamarinskaya," Glinka is very nearly abreast of the composer of the present day, in that the instrumental colour forms an essential part of his original conception. Though Glinka never arrived at that point where the exigencies of instrumental colour begin to influence the line itself one never feels, as one does with nearly all his Western contemporaries, that the colour is merely a more or less happy afterthought. To whatever source he owed it, the experiments with his uncle's little orchestra or the contact with Berlioz (only made, however, when " Ruslan" was finished), his sureness of touch was remarkable. As the French master himself wrote in the " Journal des Débats," Glinka handled the instruments "with understanding of their most secret resources." Rimsky-Korsakov never tired of singing the praises of Glinka's "enchanting scoring" and its "lightness and transparency." His own style of orchestration was for many years deliberately modelled on Glinka's; right up to 1888, that is until after the composition of "Scheherazade," the "Capriccio Espagnol" and the "Easter Festival" Overture, his method of scoring was simply a development of Glinka's. It was only after the "Ring" performances in St. Petersburg in the winter of that year, that he came under Wagner's influence. It is easy to see how the percussion writing in the "Capriccio" and "'Scheherazade" is modelled on that in "A Summer Night in Madrid," but the similarity of orchestral handling goes much deeper than that.

One hardly knows which to admire the more in Glinka, his mastery of the orchestral palette as a whole or his treatment of the individual instruments. In both the Spanish fantasias the handling of the broad masses of colour is exceedingly rich and brilliant; "Kamarinskaya," less rich, has a hard, transparent brilliance of its own. The clarinet solo in the latter work is perfectly suited to the instrument and the clarinet is again treated with fine insight in "Ruslan." One passage in particular is

so essentially "clarinettish" that I must qualify my
observation that Glinka "never" derived his
melodic line from the nature of an instrument :—

Ex. 10

But to point out little technical points of this kind
would lead one into a boundless wilderness of
praise. One can only mention their presence as
some sort of compensation for the awkward harmonies and floundering modulations which offend
the ear accustomed to a more polished style of
utterance.

III — THE FOLK-SONG ELEMENT

THE problem of the use of folk-song material in symphonic music presented itself to Glinka's successors in a different and more difficult form than it had done to Glinka himself. He had been concerned with nothing more than the stringing together of folk-tunes into frankly popular fantasias, harmonising them and orchestrating them so as to complete the spiritual pictures for which they were only rough sketches. Dargomïzhsky, in his "Fantasia on Finnish Themes," and the young Balakirev, in his "Overture on Three Russian Themes," seem to have been content to do no more. But as the younger Russians developed, these rather naïve forms no longer satisfied them. They began to write more elaborate orchestral compositions still very largely based on folk-melodies, and found themselves faced with the extraordinary difficulty of fusing into the most complicated of musical organisms—sonata-form on the symphonic scale—the simplest of all natural forms of musical organism. For a folk-song is a complete entity, not a mere cell as a motif is, and therein lies the difficulty. Being already a fully developed whole, it contains no growing power. Nor, without vandalism, can it be decomposed into its constituent parts and these parts treated as germ-cells. Glinka's instinct in rejecting conventional development was sound, but his successors found it almost impossible to go further than he had done without it.

Of course, when we speak of particular artistic "problems" and "difficulties" we do not necessarily imply that the artists themselves were specially conscious of them. Rimsky-Korsakov and Tchaïkovsky and the rest of them were probably quite unaware how their problem differed from Glinka's. There is no reason to suppose that they were aware of a definite "problem" at all; it was simply that they admired these melodies and wanted to weave them into their compositions. They were still obsessed with the idea that, as Glinka had put it, "the people were the composers; *they* were only the arrangers." But the problem, akin to that of the novelist who borrows characters from history, existed all the same and we can get a great deal of insight into each composer's mind if we can see how he solved it.

The composer's difficulties begin even in such an apparently simple matter as the harmonisation of a folk-tune. The ideal method, no doubt, would be to employ only such harmonies as are implied by the melodic line; but, like so many ideals, it is hardly practicable or even desirable. The way of the purist is seldom that of the creative artist; he finds more congenial society among critics. But one can sympathise with Rimsky-Korsakov's anxiety about the harmonisation of his two well-known collections, the "Hundred Russian Folk-Songs," Op. 24, and the smaller collection of forty songs taken down from the singing of T. I. Filippov. He continually remodelled his settings before he was satisfied that his harmonisations were "simple and Russian enough." Yet for all his pains, he was not preserving the purity of peasant art as he imagined, for like Balakirev, Lyadov and all the other supposedly "sympathetic" folk-song arrangers of his circle, he was on a wrong scent altogether. Their fundamentally wrong conception of Russian folk-music as homophonic was pointed out

in their own lifetime by Y. N. Melgunov, who died
as long ago as 1893, but his discovery of the poly-
phonic nature of a great deal of Russian folk-music
came just too late to influence the development of
Russian art-music.*   In the whole of the Russian
classics there is only one genuine example of folk-
harmony—the unaccompanied peasants' chorus in
the last act of "Prince Igor."   In its simplest form
this folk-polyphony is produced by "under voices"
(*podgoloski*) branching out from the chief melody,
after an opening usually in unison, and rejoining it
in the final cadence.   But in many songs the poly-
phony has in the course of time become more and
more elaborate, often producing bold and interesting harmonies.   How completely this true folk-
harmony differs from the harmonic idiom of the
most sympathetic arrangers of the last century has
been graphically shown by A. D. Kastalsky in his
"Peculiarities of the Russian Folk Music System,"
in which he gives parallel examples of folk-har-
monisations collected by Melgunov and Palchikov
and harmonisations of the same melodies by

---

* The first part of his "Russian Songs" appeared in 1879, the
second in 1885—and Rimsky-Korsakov condemned them as "bar-
barous"!

Glinka, Lyadov, Mussorgsky, Balakirev, Rimsky-Korsakov and Tchaïkovsky.*

This point is not very important. It is of no consequence that these composers harmonised folk-melodies in their own way when they used them in their own compositions. They were artists, not archæologists. But it does dispose once and for all of the commonly held view that the "Kuchkisti" and their followers knew very much more about peasant music than Tchaïkovsky did and treated it in a very different spirit. As a matter of fact, even in points of notation, he and they constantly tended to think along the same lines. In the familiar *andante cantabile* of his first String Quartet, for instance. Tchaïkovsky has written out the melody, "Sidel Vanya," with a key-signature of two flats as if it were in B flat major, although it is clearly in the mixolydian mode (i.e., in F, but with the E flattened). At the same time he has harmonised it throughout in the normal F major, with E natural. It might be said that he has not been very "sympathetic." Yet when Rimsky-Korsakov included the song in his "Hundred Folk-

---

* Some of these were reproduced in Victor Belaev's article on Kastalsky in "Music and Letters," Vol. X, No. 4.

Songs," five or six years later, his so-called arrangement consisted simply of a trifling modification of Tchaïkovsky's treatment of the tune when it returns later in the movement on the three upper strings in unison, though he omitted to acknowledge his obligation clearly in a foot-note. And although he thought it necessary to alter Tchaïkovsky's time-notation from four bars (2/4, 2/4, 3/4, 2/4) to two (4/4, 5/4), he adopted his key-notation, a much more important matter, just as it stands. In fact, Tchaïkovsky's bass is just such as Glinka might have written. It is only when we study his bigger (and later) orchestral works that we begin to see what differentiates Tchaïkovsky from the avowed nationalists.

It is particularly interesting to compare the treatment of the same tune by different composers; for example, Balakirev's handling of the song, "Vo pole bereza stoyala" ("In the plain stood a birch-tree") in his B minor "Overture on Three Russian Themes," with Tchaïkovsky's in the finale of his F minor Symphony, or Rimsky-Korsakov's use of a certain dance-tune from the Nizhny-Novgorod Government in *his* "Overture on Russian Themes" with Tchaïkovsky's in "1812." Such comparison is not easy. We have to take into account the fact that the Balakirev Overture was written in 1858, the year after Glinka's death, by a twenty-one year old composer, while the Tchaïkovsky Symphony was composed nineteen years later by a man of thirty-seven. And we have to guard against facile generalisations suggested by knowledge derived from outside sources—saying, for instance, that Balakirev tries to identify himself with the popular spirit of the tune, while Tchaïkovsky only treats it as the symbol of something of which he remains a detached, if not unsympathetic, observer. That is true enough, but it has little or nothing to do with the purely musical treatment of the melody. When we come to examine that we can hardly avoid being struck more by the resemblances than by the differences. Tchaïkovsky uses a more primitive form of the tune, in which each of the two short phrases is exactly repeated, while Balakirev prefers one in which the repeated phrase is varied (the version given by Rimsky-Korsakov in his Op. 24). Balakirev, Rimsky-Korsakov and Tchaïkovsky agree in giving the melody a pedal bass. Balakirev treats the theme sometimes in close imitation, sometimes with creeping chromatic counter-themes; sometimes he intersperses it with rushing passage-work. Tchaïkovsky does all three. Tchaïkovsky, it may be objected, also uses the tune in diminution, distorting it in the "German manner" of development which Glinka had set his face against. But Balakirev's Overture opens with a passage in which precisely the same thing happens as in the working-out of Tchaïkovsky's finale; the theme in diminution is thrown quickly from one group of instruments to another and whirled into flights of rushing semiquaver octaves. Tchaïkovsky's "unsympathetic" treatment of the tune itself appears only in his obliteration of the three-bar rhythm and in the sensational showiness of the orchestration. Here Tchaïkovsky does seem to forget the origin of his material, to be thinking of its possibilities as an occasion for orchestral fireworks in the abstract. (But Rimsky-Korsakov came nearer than he thought to doing the same thing in his "Easter Festival" Overture.) Yet after all, the impression we get that the "Birch Tree" tune is, so to speak, indigenous in the Balakirev piece but merely a foreign substance embedded in the Tchaïkovsky, is due more to the nature of the rest of the music than to the handling of the theme itself. Whereas in the Balakirev it is surrounded with music entirely based on other folk-material, in the Tchaïkovsky it is set in the middle of a good deal of gaudy stuff of the composer's own. Because Tchaïkovsky, despite his fairly numerous experiments with folk-music, never really absorbed its idiom, hardly even tinctured his style with it, he can never make his borrowings sound natural. When he quotes a folk-song the quotation never seems inevitable; it seldom matches his own ideas; it sounds as if it had been dragged in by the heels. He quotes like a headmaster showing off to the parents on a speech-day rather than like Elia.

When we turn to the attempts to grow symphonic music entirely from the seed of folk-song we have to leave Tchaïkovsky behind altogether. Cases like his Second Symphony and the finale of his popular String Serenade, Op. 48 (in which both the theme of the introduction and the principal subject of the *allegro con spirito* are folk-tunes), are quite exceptional in Tchaïkovsky's music. And even in these the subsidiary material is his own. He must have seen that these attempts of Balakirev and Rimsky-Korsakov were foredoomed to failure, or at any rate to failure directly they went beyond certain clearly defined limits. Indeed, when one considers the difficulty of the problem, it is astonishing that Balakirev and Korsakov achieved as much as they did either in quantity or quality. There is little to be said of Balakirev's early works, the overtures "on a Spanish March," "on Czech Themes," and the youthful B minor "on Russian Themes" already mentioned. They combine Glinka's methods with a surer mastery of musical architecture than Glinka showed. But in spite of their clearness of outline they remain essentially "fantasias." The themes are delightfully treated but they do not take root in the composer's mind and grow. The symphonic poem, "A Thousand Years," composed in 1862 to commemorate the tenth centenary of the foundation of the Russian state by Rurik, reorchestrated in 1887 and published under the title, "Russia," is on a different level. The three folk-tunes which provide the whole of the material (Nos. 1, 2 and 22 of Balakirev's own folk-song collection) are intended to symbolise "the three principal elements of our history : paganism, the Muscovite state, and the quasi-democracy of ancient Russia," and the struggle between these elements, terminated by Peter the

Great's "Westernising" reforms (which Balakirev, as a Slavophile, regarded as a national disaster), is supposed to be depicted in what the composer himself called an "instrumental drama." Actually the musical form and substance of "Russia" are much more like those of the earlier B minor Overture than a Lisztian symphonic poem. In essence it is glorified Glinka. It is certainly not programme-music in the usual sense of the word. Its superiority to the B minor Overture is due simply to the extraordinary quality of the musical imagination playing on the material. It towers above all other fantasias and overtures on Russian folk-themes not because the given melodies are handled with greater technical skill or because the composer has used them to a definite end, but because they clearly fired his imagination as another composer's imagination might have been fired by the act of conceiving themes of his own. Balakirev has *made* these his own by right of artistic conquest. Though almost every bar of the piece is based directly on the material (and there is hardly any conventional development) one completely forgets that the composer is "treating" themes. The process has altogether ceased to be an external one; it is the spon-

taneous chemistry of a creative mind working freely
on perfectly congenial ideas. " Russia " is just as
much "inspired" as if Balakirev had invented his
own themes instead of borrowing them. It demonstrates beyond cavil what can be done with folk-
material by a composer of genius. But it stands
alone.

Of Balakirev's circle only Rimsky-Korsakov
attempted to emulate him in this field. And of his
handful of works we may neglect the early " Fantasia on Serbian Themes," Op. 6, a clever attempt
to make bricks without straw, the Piano Concerto,
Op. 30, and the Fantasia for Violin and Orchestra,
Op. 33, a loosely-put-together occasional piece,
almost redeemed by the beauty of its chief subject.
The well-known "Easter Festival" Overture,
Op. 36, is certainly based on traditional church-
melodies but it seems to belong to a different genre.
Like the Spanish themes of the "Capriccio
Espagnol," the liturgical melodies of the Overture
give one the impression, despite the composer's intention, of being little more than a pretext for the
unloosing of a riot of gorgeous orchestral colour.
The early D major " Overture on Russian Themes "
was frankly modelled on Balakirev's B minor

Overture and "Russia," and may be ranked in achievement somewhere between these two works. It is a more effective piece of work than Balakirev's B minor but not to be compared with "Russia." Rimsky-Korsakov adopts Balakirev's pian without modification, an *allegro* on two themes with a slow introduction and coda based on a third, in this case, the familiar "Slava" melody used by Beethoven in the trio of the second "Razumovsky" Quartet and by Mussorgsky in the coronation scene of "Boris."* The opening theme of the *allegro* has been made equally well-known to Western audiences through Tchaïkovsky's "1812" Overture (the dance-tune in E flat minor). Though Rimsky-Korsakov's overture is dated 1880, when it was re-written and re-scored, and is numbered Op. 28, it was actually composed, and played at one of Balakirev's Free School Concerts, in 1866. It is therefore one of the earliest of all Rimsky-Korsakov's compositions and would have been more properly numbered Op. 2, Opus 1 being the First Symphony. The Sinfonietta, Op. 31, based on the first three movements of an unpublished string quartet written

---

* Rimsky-Korsakov also employed it again in a cantata, Op. 21, and as the leit-motif of Ivan the Terrible in "The Tsar's Bride."

in 1879, is a more important work, probably the biggest composition entirely based on folk-tunes ever written.* The first movement, autumnal in mood (it is based on a song, "Over the field creeps the mist"), is a particularly interesting attempt to solve this problem of folk-song treatment on symphonic lines. Roughly speaking it consists of a compromise between Glinka's methods and conventional development. There is development of a kind but, instead of a motif of three or four notes, two or four bars of melody are generally taken as the smallest unit. Balakirev had done something the same in his "Russia," but Korsakov's music is warmed by no corresponding play of imagination. He is more methodical; one can easily watch the working of his mind from bar to bar; and the themes are not very attractive. So an interesting point of view results in rather dull music. Again, the beautiful horn melody of the slow movement is spoiled by unimaginative harmonisation; at least, is spoiled for those who remember the simple harp chords with which Stravinsky supports the same tune in the *khorovod* of the captive princesses in "The Fire

---

* The score contains eight altogether, Nos. 12, 51, 68, 70, 75, 79 and 90 from his own Op. 24, and No. 31 of Balakirev's "Forty Russian Folk Songs."

Bird" or Rimsky-Korsakov's own arrangement of it in his Op. 24. Nor does the jolly, bustling scherzo-finale throw any fresh light on the problem. On the whole, then, Rimsky-Korsakov's essays in this field can be considered only moderately successful. He never digested the given material completely. It remained with him always some-

Ex. 11

thing to be worked *on* rather than worked *with*. And so he was unlikely to hit on such a master-touch as the penultimate bar of Balakirev's "Russia," for instance. At the end of this poem the symbol of the old, pagan Russia creeps back on the lower strings, muted; the picture fades away in harp arpeggios; but the first violins float down, not to a final chord, but to die out into silence with a last fluttering reference to the chief theme* of the *allegro* (Ex. 11) surely one of the most imaginative endings in all music.

The only moral one can draw from "Russia" is the rather obvious one that success in the symphonic handling of folk-tunes is purely and simply a matter of genius corrected by good taste—"good taste" being shown here in the avoidance of virtuosity in the treatment of the material and in not making it an excuse for talking about oneself. But a genius capable of spinning a masterpiece from given material is far more likely to prefer to work with material of his own invention, which will not tie his hands at every turn by compelling him always to respect its original nature. It is significant that

---

* A melody which left its mark on a theme in **Borodin's B minor Symphony (Ex. 26).**

Balakirev used only one folk-theme (with a snatch of an Oriental melody) in his First Symphony (finished in 1898) and only two in his Second (completed ten years later). They are set out in a masterly way. In the context they sound like natural ebullitions of the composer's own high spirits. But he had definitely abandoned the ideas embodied in the overtures of forty years earlier, the attempt to create an instrumental art purely folkish in origin.

It is in the field of opera that folk-song has made its presence in Russian art-music most effectively felt. In opera folk-song no longer has to be self-sufficient. It finds itself in surroundings which support it, so to speak, and where it sounds more natural. The composer is no longer involved in a struggle to reconcile irreconcilables, the very simple and natural with the very complex and, in a sense, artificial. There is no temptation to develop something which by its nature obstinately refuses to develop, which is complete in itself and which cannot be subjected to ordinary symphonic methods without barbarously torturing it. Folk-song can be effectively turned to account in opera in half-a-dozen ways : as aria (Olga's " Stay with Me, my Love " in " Pskovityanka "), chorus (the last scene of

" Boris,"), leit-motif (Ivan the Terrible's theme in
" The Tsar's Bride "), orchestral interlude (prelude
to Act III of " Snegurochka ") or ballet music (the
" Cleopatra " scene of " Mlada "). It was a favourite device of Rimsky-Korsakov's to employ a
folk-song sung by the chorus or in the orchestral
accompaniment, as a background to dialogue-recita-
tive. But on the whole the use of folk-song in
Russian opera is more effective than interesting to
the student. It gives a delightful flavour to the
scores of the classical Russian masters, but throws
no light on the composers themselves.

But in their operas, even more easily than in their
symphonic music, we can trace their evolution of a
natural folk-idiom of their own. If it is difficult
to make up one's mind as to the æsthetic value of
genuine folk-song as an element in art-music, it is
twenty times more so in the case of imitated folk-
song. It would appear at a first glance to be
simpler; we are rid of borrowings; we no longer
have to balance subtle differences of method of
treatment; we do not need to consider whether a
composer has been faithful to letter and spirit of an
original, to decide whether or not he has done right
in putting in or leaving out so much of himself, and

so on. If the music is entirely his own we have to take into consideration nothing but its own merit. No doubt that _is_ ultimately all that matters. But the difficulty is that folk-songish music, as distinct from genuine folk-music, is of two kinds, one perfectly natural, the other unpleasantly artificial—and that it is hardly possible to distinguish one from the other. Musical ideas naturally occur to a composer —or, as the romantic phrase has it, he is _inspired_— in terms of the musical idiom to which he is accustomed. If he is used to hearing tunes with certain well-marked tonal and melodic and rhythmical peculiarities, especially if he has heard a lot of them during the impressionable years of childhood, the themes which spontaneously occur to him will probably have the same peculiarities.* This, one feels sure, was what happened in Mussorgsky's case. He wrote in the folk-song idiom as naturally as Burns wrote in the Lowland Scottish dialect. The other essential elements of his musical

---

* This is more particularly likely to occur in his earlier work. He reproduces _with a difference,_ and as he grows older he will, if he is a genuinely fertile composer, listen more and more to himself and less to outside influences. The maturing of a composer, the development of his musical personality, is probably nothing more than this—the reproduction of melodic, rhythmic and harmonic formulæ with ever greater modifications.

language were realistic, descriptive, imitative, ex-
pressionistic—anything but purely musical. Except
a few altogether unimportant trifles,* the equivalents
of Burns's unfortunate English poetry, everything
Mussorgsky wrote is expressed in an idiom of which
the only *musical* root is folk-song—however far, as
for example in the clarinet melody at the end of "A
Night on the Bare Mountain":—

Ex. 12

it has grown from that root. Indeed Mussorgsky
made the folk-idiom his own instrument so completely that it is rather easier to detect the quotation of an actual folk-melody in his music than in
Rimsky-Korsakov's—which is less paradoxical than
it at first seems to be.

The same, with modifications, may be said of
Borodin. There were other elements in Borodin's

---

* "Il vecchio castello" in the "Exhibition Pictures" is the
first example which springs to the mind, and is probably the best
known.

musical make-up—reflected Schumann, reflected
Balakirev, a natural oriental strain, and some remarkable streaks of absolute originality which give
him a place apart.   But in so far as he derives from
Great Russian folk-music he seems to stand with
Mussorgsky.   But about Rimsky-Korsakov one
cannot feel nearly as sure.   As we have seen, he was
second to no one in his appreciation of native folk-
music and in conscientious desire to turn it to account in art-music.   Though he went further than
any other composer in the embodiment of actual
folk-songs in his compositions, he was no more
satisfied with this than Mussorgsky was.   Even
more literally than Glinka, he wished to "write
music in Russian"—and we must concede at once
that he did naturally absorb a great deal of the
idiom.   No musician, preoccupied with popular
music as he was, could have failed to do so.   But
as one so often notices in Rimsky-Korsakov's work,
the coldly intellectual element intervenes; beside
this natural absorption there is a large proportion
of artificial imitation.   In other words, it is clear
that Rimsky-Korsakov was sometimes guilty of
the cold-blooded concoction of synthetic pseudo-
folk-songs.   There can be no doubt on this point;

he admits it in his memoirs, amusingly enough, in
defending himself against the charge of having
used too many actual folk-melodies in his early
operas, an accusation brought forward by contemporary critics as evidence of the poverty of his
melodic invention.   It is curious that he failed to
see how his defence went to prove that there was
more than a grain of truth in the hostile criticisms.
"As regards the invention of folk-songish melodies," he says, "they must naturally be based on
the curves and motives of genuine folk-songs."
And he goes on to ask naïvely, if with irrefragable
logic, "how two things can resemble each other as
wholes, if they do not resemble each other in any
single detail?   Hence : how can any melody be
'folk-songish' if its separate curves are not copied
from those of genuine folk-songs?"   The real
point at issue seems to have escaped him as completely as it escaped his critics.

If, however, a defender of Rimsky-Korsakov
should come forward and say, " Here are two folk-
songish melodies, not genuine folk-songs.   One is
the spontaneous invention of a composer soaked in
the folk-idiom, the other has been artificially imitated by an expert who also happens to be an artist.

Be good enough to tell me which is which," he might put the critic in a quandary. Superficially the natural tune might seem inferior to the artificial one; and in all probability it would be the less like a genuine folk-melody. The more fertile the composer, the less likely he would be to reproduce without adding something of his own. That is one of the tests by which we can sometimes detect the conscious imitator; he keeps too closely to his original. It never really becomes a living part of his own musical mind; it decorates his musical thought externally (and the decoration is "fixed," unchanging), but is not a part of its living, changing tissue. And so the artificiality betrays itself in his work as a whole, though melody for melody he may be able to turn out something which even the expert cannot distinguish from the genuine article. Apart altogether from Rimsky-Korsakov's implied admission, it is obvious that his creative faculty was never impregnated with the folk-idiom as thoroughly as Mussorgsky's was or he would never have been able to purge it away as he did in works like "Pan Voevoda" and "Servilia," to say nothing of dozens of pages of some of his most characteristic scores.

But the curious problems presented by the working of Rimsky-Korsakov's peculiar creative intelligence must be considered later in other aspects. For the present we must be content to sum up the results of his contact with folk-music as mainly superficial. In the best pages of his work—above all in "Sadko" and "Kitezh"—its influence has gone deeper, really saturating his thought. And before we dismiss the rest as "merely" decorative, it is only fair to remember its charm as decoration. One need not enjoy "Snegurochka" a jot the less because some of it is rather of the nature of musical patchwork. If Rimsky-Korsakov is here so much the less a creator, he is a particularly delightful compiler and arranger. There is no feeling of patchwork about the style of the work as a whole. No composer has ever known better than he how to make the most of given material of this nature. I emphasise the artificiality of his folk-song reproductions only because of the light it throws on his musical mind and in order to measure him in relation to an absolute standard of musical values.

And we may sum up the value of the folk-song element in classical Russian music as a whole in much the same way. The actual substance of folk-song embedded in it in one way or another is very considerable in bulk. Directly and indirectly, popular music has salted it through and through with simple, homely beauty, though not with that remote, mysterious beauty-with-authority which sets whatever possesses it on a plane apart. It is easy for the unfriendly critic to say that the path of folk-song led these composers nowhere. But they were not travelling to arrive—except at home like the man in Chesterton's story. They had something fresh to say and folk-song gave them the words to say it in. To one—Mussorgsky—it gave almost all the language he needed, and in varying degrees it enriched the vocabularies of all the others.

IV — THE STONE GUEST

DARGOMÏZHSKY'S "Kamennïy Gost" ("The Stone Guest") has a curious place in the history of Russian music. It is one of those works which are landmarks without being master-pieces. One cannot read half-a-dozen pages about classical Russian opera without coming across some reference to it. Yet hardly anyone outside Russia knows it, and even in Russia itself it has never been more than a museum piece. It is true that it is con-stituted the operatic "Gospel" of the "mighty handful" and that, according to Cui, it was "the keystone of the new Russian operatic school." But even the Kuchkisti did not carry their admiration to the point of imitation. Mussorgsky, of all the younger men the most in sympathy with Dar-gomïzhsky's longing for "the expression of truth. . . truth and realism . . . the note as the direct equiva-lent of the word," attempted only one music drama on the lines of "The Stone Guest," his setting of

Gogol's "Marriage." And he lost interest in that after a month's work on it.* In Mussorgsky's later operas the element of Dargomïzhskian "truth" is mingled with others, lyrical and epic, and it is significant that there is less of it in "Khovansh-china" than in "Boris," while the fragmentary "Fair of Sorochintsi" was apparently to have been almost wholly lyrical. Rimsky-Korsakov flirted with Dargomïzhsky's style and methods throughout his career, as he did with Glinka's and, later, with Wagner's. Borodin did not even pay lip-service to Dargomïzhsky's principles. In short, this "recitative in three acts," as Lenz called "The Stone Guest," served the younger men less as a model than as a standard of reference. There it stood, a fixed point by which they could steer; but none of them cared to make straight for it. But since it has this historical importance and a sort of reputation at second-hand, it is worth at least cursory study.

"The Stone Guest" was the third and last opera of a composer even more the dilettante than his friend, Glinka. His first opera, "Esmeralda"

---

* It is only fair to admit that such an authority as Calvocoressi attributes the abandonment of "Marriage" to Mussorgsky's growing interest in "Boris."

(finished in 1839, but not produced till 1847) was, on his own confession, "weak and often trivial, in the style of Halévy and Meyerbeer," though he felt that "the most dramatic scenes already show some traces of that realistic style I have since tried to develop in my Russian music." His next, if we neglect an opera-ballet *manqué*, "The Triumph of Bacchus," was "The Russalka" (1856), which still keeps a place in the Russian repertoire, thanks to the vehicle it offers to Chaliapin's art in the rôle of the miller. In "The Russalka" Dargomïzhsky's lyric gifts are seen to be so conspicuously weak that a hostile critic might suggest that, in turning his back on pure melody in "The Stone Guest," he was merely making a virtue of necessity. But that would be definitely unfair. Dargomïzhsky's leaning toward the dramatic was natural, not the result of his lyrical weakness—except in so far as every artist is compelled by his weaknesses to concentrate on his strengths. Some of his songs of the late 'forties and early 'fifties show strongly dramatic tendencies. And even while he was writing "The Russalka," very much under Glinka's influence, he protested to a correspondent that Glinka understood only the lyrical element of Russian folk-music and had neglected its humorous and dramatic sides.

But Dargomïzhsky suffered from his environment. However individual an artist may be, he needs understanding friends as a plant needs soil. Even a Wagner needs encouragement, and Dargomïzhsky was no Wagner. Except Glinka, Dargomïzhsky for the greater part of his life mixed only with his artistic inferiors. His admirers were amateurs who must have praised his music for its weaknesses and who could hardly have been capable of sympathy with the progressive tendencies which have won Dargomïzhsky his place in the history books. It was not till the beginning of 1868, at the age of fifty-five, that he found the right sympathetic environment among his juniors, Balakirev, Stassov and their circle. And then it was too late; he was to be granted only another year of life—and that clouded by ill-health.

There is a certain pathos about Dargomïzhsky's gathering the younger men about him and writing his swan-song before their eyes. They met regularly at his house and Rimsky-Korsakov has told how "The Stone Guest" grew from week to week

and how it was tried out, the composer singing Don
Juan in his "hoarse tenor,"* Mussorgsky taking
Leporello and Don Carlos, General Velyaminov (a
keen amateur) the Monk and the Commander, and
Alexandra Purgold, Laura and Donna Anna—with
Nadezhda Purgold (afterwards Mme. Rimsky-
Korsakov) at the piano. One fact is curious : Dargomïzhsky had thought of setting Pushkin's "little
tragedy" as early as 1863 but, dilettante that he
was, had been frightened by the magnitude of the
task, though he was in perfectly good health. Now,
early in 1868, a sick man, he composed three-
quarters of the opera in two and a half months. He
wrote to the singer, Karmalina, that his nervous
condition seemed to generate one idea after another.
" I have scarcely any physical strength left. . . . It is
not I who write but some unknown force of which I
am the instrument." A curious statement from a
composer, never very spontaneous, about a work
which has every appearance of having been calculated rather than created. However, the "unknown
force" failed him in the autumn and, during the
last few months of his life, Dargomïzhsky never

---

* Glinka speaks of Dargomizhsky, when he first met him in 1834,
as " a little man with a sharp, piercing voice."

had sufficient strength to finish the first scene of Act
I. It remained for Cui to add the last sixty bars or
so, and for Rimsky-Korsakov, in scoring the work,
to fill out some passages which the composer had
merely sketched.*

The plan of Pushkin's "little tragedy" or "essay
in dramatic investigation," "The Stone Guest," is
very simple. The first scene of the first act is played
before a monastery in Madrid. Don Juan, banished
for the murder of the Commander (who in Pushkin's version is the husband, not the father, of
Donna Anna), has returned to Madrid in disguise.
He is speaking to Leporello of a dead love, Inez,
when a monk appears and asks them if they are
waiting for Donna Anna, who comes every day to
pray for her dead husband's soul. She appears
momentarily and piques Juan's curiosity. In the
second scene we meet another lady, the actress
Laura, whose part in the drama seems to be quite inessential; she is introduced, apparently, only to sing
a couple of Spanish songs and to give Don Juan a
further opportunity of demonstrating his power over

---

* "The Stone Guest" had its first performance at the Maryin-
sky Theatre, Petersburg, on February 16, (O.S.), 1872. Theodore
Komissarzhevsky the elder, father of the famous producer and of
Vera Komissarzhevsky, was the Don Juan.

the other sex. Laura, a former love of Juan's, is
entertaining guests, one of whom, Don Carlos, she
keeps back when the others go. But Don Carlos's
pleasant evening is interrupted by the appearance
of Don Juan. He and Carlos fight, the latter is
killed, and the fickle Laura easily consoles herself
once more with Juan. In the second act we see Don
Juan, disguised as a monk, waiting by the Commander's statue for Donna Anna. When she comes
he first addresses her respectfully in character with
his dress, then makes love to her as "Don Diego."
Finally she gives him an appointment for the following day, and when she has gone he mockingly
invites the statue to come too, to stand sentinel at
his widow's door. The third act consists of the
scene in Anna's room, with the coming of the statue
to exact vengeance.

Dargomïzhsky's way of going to work was really
breath-taking in its daring simplicity. He simply
set Pushkin's text, just as it stands, to what he accurately claimed to be "melodic recitative," declamation to definite musical rhythms and preserving some sense of melodic contour. As Calvocoressi
has pointed out, the only parallel to such an under-
taking (except Rimsky-Korsakov's "Mozart and

Salieri" and Mussorgsky's fragment of "Marriage") is Debussy's "Pelleas and Melisande" of more than thirty years later. But "melodic recitative," to be of any value, must be written by a man whose faculty of musical creation works in a peculiar way, to whom words naturally suggest music (living music, not a mere formula for declamation), yet with whom the music never takes the bit in its mouth, so to speak, and runs away with things. Mussorgsky, Borodin, Rimsky-Korsakov could all do this intermittently, but probably no composer has yet lived who could do it continuously. Dargomïzhsky certainly does not convince one that he had a peculiar genius for this species of composition. Try as he will to avoid the stereotyped, he cannot keep his recitative genuinely melodic. There are frequent lapses into dry declamation and too few compensating slips into genuine living melody. Except Laura's two songs (the first, by the way, preluded by a snatch of that *jota aragonesa* on which Glinka based his orchestral "Capriccio"), the vocal line is infused with genuine musical life and warmth only for a few bars here and there, as in Juan's love-making to Anna or in some of the monk's phrases. The monk's music has a character of its own, broad and unfolding for the most part in notes of even value. But, generally speaking, Dargomïzhsky failed to achieve *characterisation* in recitative as Mussorgsky, and even Rimsky-Korsakov frequently did. Dargomïzhsky's note for word translation of Pushkin into music is "true" in declamation, never emotionally false and sometimes very graphic—as in Leporello's gasping invitation to the statue. But though the notes may be the "direct expression of the speech," they only occasionally express the nature of the person who utters it. The feeling expressed by the vocal line is not only weak but generally impersonal, a curious result of such longing for *drama.*

Nor does the orchestra help the voices much. There is no question of the orchestra's expressing, or attempting to express, "that emotion which the spoken word cannot express,"* as with Wagner. The orchestra supplies an unobtrusive accompaniment, occasionally a commentary, hardly anything more. There is no prelude, though Rimsky-Korsakov thought it necessary to write one, based on material from the opera, for his

---

* Wagner: "Opera and Drama."

second edition of the score. Eight bars of introduction, which may mean anything or nothing, and Don Juan is speaking. And it is typical of Dargomïzhsky's score that these few bars of "marking time," a mere musical commonplace, recur here and there throughout the first scene, not to make a dramatic point, but simply as padding cut from the same piece of musical material. A hardly more significant figure seems to be always associated with Don Juan's memories of his "poor Inez":

Ex. 13

And yet both these apparently platitudinous fragments are worth noting, since they show Dargomïzhsky's fondness for the sharpened fifth of the scale, for the augmented triad which is, so to speak, the "common chord" of the whole-tone scale which plays such an important part later in the work. Dargomïzhsky toys with the leit-motif: a little figure of four chords associated with Donna Anna :

Ex. 14

another chord-progression associated first with the
true monk, later with Don Juan in his monkish disguise; and so on. But his motives are mere inex-
pressive tags. They have no character. They do
not cling about one's memory, calling up the past
to enrich the present whenever we hear them. Dargomïzhsky sees *how* to make some extremely effective point but he is not good enough a musician
actually to bring it off. There is an instance at the
end of the first act. Juan and Laura embrace and
go into another room, but the orchestra adds a
significant last word before the curtain falls slowly
on the empty stage. Now this stormy, passionate
epilogue is based on the phrases to which Carlos has
sung the words, " I, Don Carlos," and in which he
has reminded Laura that she will enjoy only a few
more years of youth, and the music to which he died
in the duel; the idea was a stroke of dramatic

genius. Yet it fails because of the sheer inadequacy of the music. In fact, Dargomïzhsky fails here in a dramatic moment for precisely the same reason that he fails earlier in the same scene to catch the glamour of the moonlit night in the love scene between Carlos and Laura; the music is dry and almost lifeless. But there are some striking dramatic details in "The Stone Guest": the very "modern" chromatic side-slipping of diminished sevenths at Anna's anxious "Diego, what is it?" as Juan gradually admits his identity in the last act, and an incessant chromatic quintuplet figure which admirably expresses their emotional agitation.

The most striking fruit of Dargomïzhsky's intellectualism is, of course, his devising of themes in the whole-tone scale, apparently symbolising the stoniness of the statue. As we have seen, Glinka had used the scale *as a scale* in "Ruslan," and the younger men were, for the most part, content to do no more. Rimsky-Korsakov introduces a descending whole-tone scale for expressive purposes in "May Night" and, with diatonic trimmings, in "Scheherazade" (the opening theme associated with the harsh Sultan Schariar). Borodin does the same in the accompaniment to his song, "Falshi-

vaya Nota." Dargomïzhsky must be given whatever
credit attaches to the distinction of having been the
first to use, not the scale itself, but whole-tone
themes. And even he, a man bold enough to write
a whole opera without a single key-signature,*
tackled the harmonic implications of the system
very half-heartedly. We first hear the "statue"
theme in Act II, between Leporello's anxious:
" But the Commander? . . . . What will he say about
it?" :

Ex. 15

Later, at the point where the statue nods acceptance,
Dargomïzhsky does actually manage to write
entirely in the whole-tone mode (see Ex. 16).
The appearance of the statue in the last act is
accompanied by a whole-tone chord (A flat, B flat,
D, F sharp) held for two bars *fortissimo*, and as it

---

* **Dargomïzhsky** might almost be hailed as the pioneer of aton-
alism. But he would have saved himself trouble on a good many
pages of "The Stone Guest" if he had followed the normal practice as regards notation.

steps into the room there is a terrific outburst with a triplet bass moving in whole-tones. All this was

Ex. 16

very bold for the 'sixties; Dargomïzhsky went a long way farther than Glinka had done. But, like him, he only used the whole-tone scale in passing, for a definite and limited expressive purpose. He could never have imagined, as Debussy seems to have done, that it might be employed as a self-sufficient, though limited, musical vocabulary in itself.

Apart altogether from the intrinsic value of " The Stone Guest" itself, apart from Dargomïzhsky's sheer musical incapacity to realise his own ideals, one cannot help doubting the value of a theory

which leads to such a result when carried to its
logical conclusion.   Even when practised by a
musician of far greater power, as in "Boris," this
kind of realism cannot be kept up for long.   Mere
"literal translation" of words into music is not
enough.   It is no more likely to produce music
worth calling such than literal translation of poetry
into another language is likely to produce poetry.
And verse wedded to music of this kind is, on the
whole, less effective than spoken verse.   It loses
more than it gains.   Tchaïkovsky was not so very
far wrong when he spoke of the "unsuccessful attempt to drag *truth* into this sphere of art, in which
everything is based upon falsehood, and 'truth,' in
the everyday sense of the word, is not required at
all."   A play of any kind demands our acceptance
of conventions.   Poetic drama asks us to accept a
great deal, and even the most realistic forms of
music-drama still more than that.   And since we
must accept a convention of some kind, it surely
does not matter very much what the convention is.
All we ask is that the composer shall make the best
of it.   And if the history of opera teaches him anything at all, it is that the only way to succeed is, not
by striving for "truth," but by exerting his musical

power so as to make us forget the "lie." The striving for an illusory "truth" which is a recurrent feature of the history of opera (Rameau, Gluck, Wagner, Dargomïzhsky and Mussorgsky) is more valuable as a corrective to extreme artificiality than for its own sake.

It is, of course, impossible to discuss Dargomïzh-sky's theories without thinking of Wagner's. The obvious idea that must occur to everyone—it occurred to Serov and other hostile critics in Dar-gomïzhsky's own lifetime—is that Dargomïzhsky was merely a disingenuous disciple of Wagner. And it must be admitted that there is evidence for, as well as against, that view of him. His use of the leit-motif cannot be allowed to count for much; he is just as likely to have taken the hint from Glinka. But it is absurd to point out, as some of Dargomïzhsky's apologists have done, that as Wag-ner's music was very little known in Russia at this time Dargomïzhsky must have been almost wholly ignorant of it. In any case it is Wagner's theories, rather than his scores, which are in question. But in 1864-5 Dargomïzhsky was in Western Europe—Leipzig, Paris, Brussels, London—and must have had ample opportunities of discussing Wagner, if

not of seeing his operas. Wagner was then the
most talked of musician in Europe. Is it likely
that anyone so deeply interested in operatic
problems as Dargomïzhsky was, neglected any
chance of finding out all he could about him? After
all, the piano score of " Das Rheingold " had been
available since 1861. And we know that Dargomïzhsky was acquainted with " Tannhäuser " as
early as 1856, for in that year we find him writing
to Serov, " I have not returned your score of ' Tannhäuser,' as I have not yet had time to look through
the whole of it. You are right; there is a great deal
of poetry in the scenario and also in the music. But
the spicy melodies are unnatural, and although the
harmonies are sometimes very interesting, one is
conscious of the effort—*will und kann nicht!* Truth
—truth before all—but we have a right to expect
good taste as well,"—a criticism which might be
applied even more fittingly to his own " Stone
Guest " !

We have Rimsky-Korsakov's word for it that
when Dargomïzhsky attended the first Petersburg
performance of " Lohengrin," only two or three
months before his death, he " poured out on it his
inexhaustible store of humour, mockery and venom-

ous comment." There is no reason to accuse Dargomïzhsky of jealousy or moral dishonesty on that account, however, though the story does leave a nasty taste in the mouth. He may have genuinely disliked Wagner's music, and he must have delighted in the consciousness that his own "Stone Guest" was far more "advanced" and unconventional than this very lyrical work of Wagner's. But, however many hints he may have taken from Wagner's theories, Dargomïzhsky's operatic style has hardly more in common with Wagner's than the Russian language with the German. His subordination of the orchestra to the voice is alone sufficient to mark a vital difference caused by something more than the musical inequality of the two composers. Musically, of course, Dargomïzhsky owed nothing, or next to nothing, to Wagner. In the whole of "The Stone Guest" there are only two passages that even remotely suggest Wagnerian influence : Don Juan's cry, "Alas! A victim of hopeless passion," in Act III (Ex. 17), and the orchestral passage, pallidly Wagnerian in both its sequential treatment and its rising chromatic excitement, when,

thinking of the dead Inez, Juan recalls "the curious
charm of her pale lips and serious eyes."

Ex. 17

V—TOLSTOY AND MUSSORGSKY

EVER since Plutarch men have amused themselves by drawing parallels between the great. It is at bottom merely a pastime, an intellectual game which at the same time allows scope —too much—for the play of the imagination. But it is not quite an empty sport; like other games it is a discipline and an education. To change the metaphor : if our travelling leads us nowhere, we at least see many things on the way. But one danger above all is to be guarded against. " It is," says Bacon, "the vice of high and discursive intellects "—and others, maybe—" to attach too much importance to slight resemblances; when this is indulged to excess it leads men to catch at shadows instead of substances." Moreover, in comparing two such men as Tolstoy and Mussorgsky, who were not only compatriots but contemporaries,* there is always the

---

* Tolstoy was about ten years older than Mussorgsky, though he survived him by nearly thirty years.

risk of attributing to individuals ideas and beliefs
generally current and belonging to the common
stock.* Here, common sense and one's more or less
defective knowledge of the period are one's only
safeguards.

The coincidence of Mussorgsky's conception of
art and his methods of artistic procedure with Tolstoy's may be partially due to the circumstances in
which both lived, but even if it were wholly so, the
identity of ideas between Russia's greatest novelist
and her greatest dramatic musician would be hardly
less interesting. The agreement is not limited to
one or two striking points; it is extraordinarily complete. Insistence on the unimportance of beauty in
art; the conception of the function of art as "a
means of conversing with one's fellow-men"; contempt for technique, even as a means; a strong leaning toward realism; a tendency to make the masses
more important than individual characters or to
value individuals in proportion as they are representative of the masses; over-valuation of the
peasant-type—all these are equally characteristic of

---

* No doubt both were influenced by the theories of the critics
Chernyshevsky (1828-1889) and Dobrolyubov (1836-1861), cham-
pions of artistic realism.

Tolstoy and Mussorgsky. It is true that all these heterogeneous theories, instincts and prejudices are (or, at least, can be shown to be) more or less logically connected. But, man being the illogical animal he is, that hardly makes the coincidence less striking.

Let us take these points one by one; first the contempt for beauty as the end and aim of the serious artist. When the seventy-year-old Tolstoy wrote "What is Art?" he took this as his starting-point. His method was simple enough. He catalogued all the known definitions of beauty, from Baumgarten's to those of contemporary æstheticians, and pointed out that they might be boiled down to two fundamental conceptions, "the one objective, mystical, that beauty is one of the manifestations of the absolutely Perfect, of the Idea, of the Spirit, of Will, or of God—a fantastic definition, founded on nothing; the other, on the contrary, a very simple, and intelligible, subjective one, which considers beauty to be that which pleases." And he concluded that "to see the aim and purpose of art in the pleasure we get from it, is like assuming that the purpose and aim of food is the pleasure derived when consuming it." Mussorgsky had, by whatever chain of reasoning (or none), come to the same conclusion a quarter of a century earlier, for we find him writing to Stassov in 1872 that "the artistic representation of mere beauty, in the material sense of the word, is sheer childishness, a rudimentary form of art." His conception of the artist's business, outlined in this letter and later ones to the same correspondent, is not that of the Tolstoy of "What is Art?" but it exactly describes the attitude of the earlier Tolstoy of the great novels: "Life, wherever it manifests itself; truth, however unpleasant; daring, plain-speaking before everyone *à bout portant*—that is what I aim at." Again: "The masses, like individuals, present subtle traits, difficult to fathom, not yet grasped. To distinguish them, to learn to read them at sight, by observation and hypothesis, to study their inmost recesses, to feed mankind with them as with an as-yet-unknown health-giving food—that is the task, the supreme joy!" And in his brief autobiography Mussorgsky states his "profession of artistic faith" as the belief that "art is a means of conversing with men, and not an end in itself," which exactly anticipates Tolstoy's conclusion in "What is Art?"

Now this view of art is essentially that of phil-

osophical optimism—probably unconscious in Mussorgsky's case, all too self-conscious in Tolstoy's.
Life is real; life is earnest; and everything which in
no way helps humanity toward its goal is mere
child's play. Carlyle said something to the same
effect about the Waverley novels. It was the old
Puritan view. And the pessimistic view harmonises
curiously with it. In the very year that Mussorgsky finished " Boris," the young Nietzsche—not yet
out of his Schopenhauerian-Wagnerian leading-strings—had written his first book, " The Birth of
Tragedy," to prove that great art (that is, *beautiful*
art) springs only from the soil of pessimism. Confronted with a real world of imperfection, contradiction and ultimate chaos, man is compelled to
make something whole and perfect and harmonious
for himself.* Nietzsche traces the decline of Greek
art from the appearance of Socrates, the "theoretical optimist." Once the universe could be shown
to admit of a logical explanation, art was no longer
regarded as a necessity but as mere child's play.

In various notes and sketches dating from the

---

* " My melancholy seeks repose in the hiding-places and abysses
of *perfection*; for that purpose I need music," he wrote years
afterwards.

same period.* Nietzsche makes his position still clearer. He, too, concludes that beauty exists only in our own "consciousness of pleasure." But, far from beauty being truth, truth beauty, the sole function of the beautiful (hence, the sole object of art) is to cover reality, the terrible truth, with a veil of illusion.† "The further a thing is from real existence, the more pure, beautiful and good it is. . . . It is not possible to live with truth; the Will to Truth is a symptom of degeneracy." Incidentally, Nietzsche attributes classic art to the "pessimism of strength," the artist rejoicing in the knowledge that he alone can create perfection, and traces romantic art from the "pessimism of weakness," the artist brooding sentimentally over an imperfect world. So, if we like, we can reconcile Nietzsche with Tolstoy to our own satisfaction by assuming that great

---

* Published in Vols. IX and XIV of the German edition of his complete works.

† Compare with this one of Rimsky-Korsakov's most self-revealing remarks, reported by Yastrebtsev: "You would scarcely find anyone in the world who believes less in everything supernatural, fantastic or lying beyond the boundaries of death than I do—yet as an artist I love this sort of thing above all else. And religious ceremonial—what could be more intolerable? . . . . And yet with what love I have expressed such ceremonial customs in music! No, I am actually of the opinion that art is essentially the most enchanting, intoxicating lie." Nothing could show more clearly the difference between Rimsky-Korsakov's outlook and Mussorgsky's.

art may be either classic, romantic, or optimistic in origin.

So much for theorising. But the important point is that contempt for beauty as the end of art, and striving after "truth" or "realism," are shown to be logical consequences of an optimistic *Weltanschauung*. We have seen that Mussorgsky, like Zola, wanted to take for his subjects "life, wherever it manifests itself, and truth, however unpleasant," and we know that Tolstoy did so, achieving his effects by minute observation and analysis and the accumulation of an infinite number of accurately rendered details. But the musical realist cannot go about things in quite the same way. There *is* a kind of musical realism, which Mussorgsky exploited to the full in several of the "Exhibition Pictures" for piano, in some of his songs, and in a few passages of "Boris Godunov" and "Khovanshchina," but depending as it does so largely on arbitrary association of musical with non-musical ideas, we can only smile at it as we do at Haydn's "sinuous worm" and Strauss's windmill. Mussorgsky's genuine realism is revealed in his choice of subjects and in his handling of his artistic materials. As he claimed, he took all life for his province, not

merely those facets of it which tradition and convention have marked out as peculiarly suitable for
artistic treatment.   He wrote songs about children,
about death-chambers, about the sorrows of village
idiots, and about musical critics.   And if, like the
French literary "realists" and "naturalists," his
choice of subjects betrays a leaning to the morbid
and sordid, he never made the mistake, as they did,
of supposing that anything is interesting simply
because it is "life."   Nor did Tolstoy.   Both had
the true artist's ability to select carefully while appearing to pick at random.   "Realism" and
"truth" are not necessarily synonyms for the same
quality in art.   For that matter, realism is not an
affair of quality at all, but of quantity.   All art is a
compromise between phenomena presented to the
senses or to the mind : shapes, colours, emotions,
musical ideas or what not, and certain arbitrary
limits and conventions : five acts, sonata form, a
rectangular canvas, metre, a certain number of instruments.   It is for each artist to decide how near
or how far from nature he is to fix his compromise
—the nearer, the more realistic his work will be;
and artistic truth consists in being true, not to nature
(which is impossible), but to whatever compromise

has been adopted. Mussorgsky, in his unvarying practice, and Tolstoy, theorising at the end of his creative career, gave their votes unhesitatingly in favour of the minimum of stylisation. The less technique was brought into play in converting the raw material of nature into the finished work of art the better.

Naturally, therefore, both detested the worship of technique for its own sake. Mussorgsky thought musicians were worse than other artists in this respect. "Tell me," he asks Stassov, "why, when I listen to the conversation of young artists, painters, or sculptors, I can follow their thoughts and understand their opinions and aims, and I seldom hear them mention technique, save in certain cases of absolute necessity? On the other hand, when I find myself among musicians I rarely hear them utter a living idea; one would think they were still at school; they know nothing of anything but technique and ' shop-talk.' Is the art of music so young that it has to be studied in this puerile way?" Tolstoy, in his downright, bludgeoning style, says : "A man in our time, if only he possesses a certain amount of ability and selects some speciality, may, after learning the methods of counterfeiting used

in his branch of art, turn out unceasingly to the end
of his life works which will pass for art in our
society.   To produce such counterfeits, definite
rules or recipes exist in each branch of art.   So the
talented man, having assimilated them, may produce such works *à froid*, cold-drawn, without feeling."*   When in a later chapter of "What is Art?"
he looked to "the artist of the future, who will be
free from all the perversion of technical improve-
ments concealing the absence of subject-matter, and
who, not being a professional artist, will only produce art when he feels impelled to do so by an irresistible inner impulse," he did not realise that such
an artist had died in Russia seventeen years before.
It would be difficult to imagine music more free
from ready-made (or even self-made) formulas of
expression than Mussorgsky's is.   As Debussy put
it, his music "ressemble à un art de curieux sauvage
qui découvrirait la musique à chaque pas tracé par
son émotion."   Whether Tolstoy was acquainted
with Mussorgsky's work I do not know; possibly he
knew it without recognising it as what he wanted.

---

* In these quotations from Tolstoy's "What is Art?" I have
availed myself of Mr. Aylmer Maude's translation (World's Classics) : the translations from Mussorgsky's letters are my own.

At any rate he dismissed Pushkin's "Boris," on which Mussorgsky based his opera, as "a cold, brain-spun work."

Both Tolstoy and Mussorgsky were obviously realists by artistic instinct. But both were also conscious that stylisation and technical ingenuity, necessary in art devoted to the ideal of beauty, were only an encumbrance to art intended as a "means of conversing with one's fellow-men." They were consciously at war with everything which limits the appeal of art. Art which appealed only to the cultured few seemed to them artificial and even ridiculous. They detested preciousness. Tolstoy devoted heated pages to the destruction of Baudelaire, Verlaine and Mallarmé (such a bull in such a china-shop!); and we find Mussorgsky exercising his sarcasm at the expense of artists "the whole of whose aspirations is comprised in the distilling, one by one, of even little drops" and who "take no interest in the essentials of life."* "People more useful to contemporary art are not to be found, I should think, even in the celestial realm."

---

* This blow seems to have been aimed principally at Rimsky-Korsakov, with whom Mussorgsky was then (1875) completely out of sympathy, and at Tchaïkovsky.

Tolstoy was prepared to reduce to absurdity his theory that art should be universal in appeal, by setting up his favourite type, the "unperverted peasant," as a sounder judge of art than a cultured man "whose taste has been atrophied by his education and life." It is doubtful whether Mussorgsky would have preferred such critics even to those he ridiculed in "The Musician's Peep-Show" and "The Classicist," but he fully shared Tolstoy's admiration for the type. After his death his brother told Stassov, "In his years of childhood and youth as in middle age, my brother Modest always felt a particular sympathy with our peasants; he considered the Russian *muzhik* a *genuine human being*." Perhaps he was over-conscious of the peasant-blood, from his paternal grandmother, in his own veins.

Mussorgsky's and Tolstoy's admiration of the people had yet another consequence. Tolstoy not only desired that art should be comprehensible to the masses; in his novels, above all in "War and Peace," he, so to speak, dramatised mass feeling. He had a theory of necessity and free-will which is summarised by Mr. Aylmer Maude in the introduction to his translation of "War and Peace": "Not only historic life, but all human life, is directed not only by intelligence or will—that is, not by thoughts or wishes that have reached a clearly conscious form —but by something mysterious and strong, the so-called nature of man. The sources of life, both of individuals and of whole peoples, are much profounder and more potent than the conscious choice and conscious reflection which apparently guides people." So, whereas the pessimist braces his will, shuts out compassion and rests all his hopes on the culture of the individual, the optimist comfortably sees salvation in sympathy with the instincts of the masses. The subject of "War and Peace" is the blindly achieved triumph of the Russian people, in spite of their leaders and even in spite of themselves. The real heroes of the book are those— from Kutuzov, the commander-in-chief, to the peasant-soldier, Karataev—who represent the mass-instinct of the Russian people.

Mussorgsky was expressing the same thought rather more vaguely (as becomes a musician) when he said that "the masses present subtle traits, difficult to fathom," and defined the artist's task as the study of these features and the "feeding of mankind" with them. We know how he carried out

that task himself. It has become a commonplace
of criticism to say that the real hero of "Boris
Godunov" is the Russian people. But Mussorgsky had subordinated individuals to masses in
earlier works than "Boris." Stassov tells us that in
"Salammbô" (1863-4), of which Mussorgsky wrote
only the "book" and a few numbers, "according
to the libretto, all these scenes, filled with dramatic
movement in Meyerbeer's style, depicted great
masses of people at moments of emotional excitement; the scenes between the principal characters
were of less importance." Although in the later
"Khovanshchina" more importance is given to individuals, they are important as representatives
rather than for their own sakes. The tragedy lies
not so much in the fall of the Khovanskys and the
destruction of the Old Believers as in the passing
of the older Russia they stand for. Mussorgsky
appears to have progressed from opera in which
masses were employed for their own sake, because
the handling of masses gave him pleasure as an
artist, to opera in which the masses or their representatives were used as visible symbols of what he
conceived to be the profoundest currents of national
feeling.

But after all they are curious people, these artists who are so painfully conscious of what they are doing. They do it so well, so thoroughly—yet so unlike artists. They will have nothing of the labour of technique, yet they labour like ants at the accumulation of correct, matter-of-fact detail. It would be unjust to compare "War and Peace" with Frith's "Derby Day," but in this matter-of-factness lies the secret weakness of both Tolstoy and Mussorgsky as creative artists. It is far more serious in the man whose medium is music than in the man who works in prose. It is (if one may be forgiven such a glimpse of the obvious) in the nature of prose to be prosaic, but prosaic music—recitative, for instance, or "The Market Place at Limoges"—is only half music. No one realised that more clearly than Tolstoy, and one is left with an amused feeling that he might have approved of the more lyrical (that is, the more beautiful) pages of "Boris" and "Khovanshchina" as "simple, clear and powerful music," but would have condemned the inn-scene in "Boris," the baiting of the Simpleton, and songs like "Savishna" and "The Orphan," in which beauty is subordinated to truth, in much the same terms as those he applied to Wagner's "Forest Murmurs"—"absolutely unintelligible musically."

VI—BORODIN AS A SYMPHONIST

WHEN Tolstoy asked and answered the question, "What is Art?" he proved nothing but the impossibility of defining the infinite. We define art and the things that belong to it in terms of ourselves; my definition is little more than a statement of my own limitations. "What is a symphony?" There is no definition (because there is an infinite number of definitions). It may be almost anything, from what the dictionary says to Mahler's "Mir heisst Symphonie mit allen Mitteln der vorhandenen Technik mir eine Welt aufbauen."* We can only fall back on common sense and say we can recognise a symphony when we hear one.

Most people—unless they take the rather severe view of the gentleman who held that Franck's D minor could not really be a symphony because the score included a *cor anglais*—will agree that

---

* "For me a 'symphony' means the building up of a world, using every available means."

Borodin's three works are genuine symphonies. Yet Dvorák, who was not narrowly academic, once remarked to James Huneker that Tchaïkovsky was really a composer of suites—and we understand perfectly well what he meant. Instead of asking, "What is a symphony?" we must ask what is essential to a *good* symphony. What differentiates it beyond dispute from a suite, for instance? Now the answer seems fairly obvious. The material must be worthy of a large fabric (as the second subject of Tchaïkovsky's "Pathétique" first movement is not); the construction must be closely knit, convincing in both its musical logic and its emotional sequence; the arrangement of both material and tonality must be balanced without being mechanical; above all, perhaps, the whole work must be greater than the sum of its separate movements. Perfectly true; yet let us "clear our minds of cant." We say the material must be genuinely symphonic; a man does not make a fresco painting of his pet canary. But how are we to judge it, musical themes being so much less concrete than canaries? A theme in Mozart's "Bastien et Bastienne" is obviously too trivial for symphonic use, while the same theme (apparently) in the "Eroïca" is tremendous. Some-

one may say the difference lies in the subsequent
treatment, but if so I shall beg to disagree.   A succession of rhythmically arranged notes on paper is
not in itself a composer's material.   He thinks of
the notes and feels them in a particular way (as regards texture as well as *tempo* and inflexion).   Beethoven's way of feeling those four bars was entirely
different from Mozart's, therefore his theme is not
the same.   Here is a theme, typical of many of
Borodin's ideas, from the finale of his Second
Symphony :—

Ex. 18

It is first stated by a solo clarinet and appears on
paper to be an ordinary " cantabile contrast " second
subject.   You can think of it as that—and if you do
its subsequent treatment will no doubt fill you with
quite justifiable horror, while a performance under
a conductor who took the same view (and he might
point to the last *dolce* appearance of the tune in self-
defence) would never suggest to you that you were
wrong.   Only if you feel that theme as the fragment of naked savagery it is, do you recognise the

perfect fitness, the inevitability, of Borodin's treatment of it.

That is one form of "cant," the judgment of sound by the appearance on paper of symbols which may mean one thing or some other quite different. There are others—one of them is the superstition, not yet dead, that formal symmetry is more or less a matter of counting bars—but they must pass. To free oneself entirely from cant is hardly possible, but a mind hampered by preconceived ideas on inessential points can scarcely appreciate justly the symphonic work of a composer like Borodin. Not that his symphonies are startlingly unconventional; if they were it would probably simplify matters. It is the apparent almost-usualness which makes the essential difference so liable to be misunderstood.

Let us for a moment recall a few dates and circumstances. Borodin, like Mussorgsky and Rimsky-Korsakov, was not a professional musician. The fact has less bearing on the technical quality of his work than unfriendly critics would have us believe (much that appears naïve and awkward in his work admits of other explanations),* but it does

---

* Tchaïkovsky's statement to Madame von Meck that "his technique is so poor that he cannot write a bar without assistance" can only be described as grotesque.

account for both the smallness of his output and the abnormal time spent over the larger works. The E flat Symphony took five years to complete, the B minor seven, a circumstance which explains the lack of unity of feeling in the earlier work and makes the splendid cohesion of the later one rather remarkable. When he began the E flat Symphony in 1862, at the age of twenty-eight, Borodin had only just met Balakirev. The Symphony was his first big composition and he embarked on it with no experience of orchestration. The Second, the well-known B minor (1869-1876), is roughly contemporaneous with "Prince Igor." The Third, in A minor, is a mere fragment, a *moderato assai* and scherzo completed and orchestrated by Glazunov. Both the E flat and B minor Symphonies were edited by Rimsky-Korsakov after the composer's death, and in view of what we know of his treatment of "Boris" one wonders how broad a view he took of an editor's function in this case also.* Whether

---

* The note on both scores, "Revue par N. Rimsky-Korsakov et A. Glazunov," may have quite a sinister significance. And Glinka's orchestral works are both *revues et corrigées.* Unless we are given the facts, all Russian music of the last century will in future rest under the suspicion of having been more or less written by Rimsky-Korsakov!

Borodin (or even Mussorgsky) would have been as
annoyed with his friend as the theoretical purists
are, is rather doubtful. We must not lose sight of
the fact that interference with each other's work was
a perfectly normal proceeding among the members
of the "mighty handful," and it possibly never occurred to Rimsky-Korsakov that there was any
essential difference between advising one's friends
on the composition of their symphonies and operas
while they were alive and revising their works when
they were dead. To take only one instance : the
opening of the scherzo of the B minor Symphony
was devised by Balakirev, who felt that the key-
contrast (B minor to F major) was too strong. And
Borodin approved, although the reiterated C's on
the horns, coming immediately after the terrific unison B natural with which the first movement closes,
would be extremely effective. One can imagine
what a howl would have gone up from the purists if
the crime had been perpetrated after the composer's
death. The fact that he did approve makes the interpolation none the less unfortunate, for it makes
it more difficult to grasp the (apparently haphazard)
tonal scheme of the whole symphony, based as it is
on a sort of semitone *Rückung* of the type Schubert

invented* and Bruckner worked to death. Borodin originally slipped directly from a long-held unison B natural to eight bars of unison C's, which was clear enough; then, the scherzo being in F, he opened the slow movement (D flat) with a G flat major chord. The movements are detached, but obviously the breaks should be made as short as possible. There is no break at all between slow movement and finale, the D flat-A flat of the final chord of the former being held (enharmonically, as C sharp-G sharp) through the first three bars of the latter—and we are home again in B major. Borodin had previously employed the same unusual juxtaposition of keys† in the E flat Symphony, where first movement and scherzo are in E flat but the slow movement is in D (its middle section sideslipping again to D flat), while the finale returns to the main key. In both works the scherzo precedes the slow movement, as it was evidently to do in the unfinished Third also. The key-scheme is here more

---

* See, for instance, his four-hand Fantasia in F minor, with its sideslip to F sharp minor.

† Rimsky-Korsakov's early symphonic poem, "Sadko," is planned with the key-scheme D flat-D-D flat. He tells us that he chose these particular keys because, with their relative minors, they were "Balakirev's favourite keys"—a fact which probably influenced Borodin as well.

conventional : first movement, A minor (but with
the tonic major firmly established throughout the
last 103 bars); scherzo, D major.

The invention and handling of the material and,
in several cases, the organisation of the individual
movements show the same vigour and individuality
of thought. The First Symphony is not, it must be
admitted, homogeneous; Dvorák might have com-
plained with some justice that it is really a suite.
The scherzo is second-hand Berlioz (though with a
characteristic, folk-songish trio), the finale second-
hand Schumann. The *andante* is picturesque and
Oriental, genuine Borodin, but the rather sac-
charine, harmonically flabby Borodin who contrasts
so extraordinarily with that other Borodin whose
music sounds as if it might have been written by one
of Gogol's Cossack heroes. But the first movement
compensates—as far as one movement can compen-
sate—for the weakness of the others.

First come twenty-eight bars of slow introduction,
indefinite but portentous. Twice we hear a striking
theme :—

Ex. 19

on bassoons and lower strings.   Everything else is
vague and shifting—and then suddenly we break
into the *allegro* in the major key.   But what an
allegro!   Instead of an orthodox exposition we find
we are already plunged into a premature development of Ex. 19—dissected and two of the pieces
thrown at us simultaneously.   Against an extraordinary chord rhythmically repeated for twelve
bars (anticipating "The Planets" by over half a
century) :—

Ex. 20

the drums play continually the second bar of Ex. 19,
while the third bar is tossed to and fro between
violins and violas.   A *sforzando* chord—and the
brass take up bar four :—

Ex. 21

It is not till the twenty-eighth bar of the *allegro*
that the theme is heard in a connected form, though
even here only three bars of it appear. Flying
fragments of the theme are driven contrapuntally
against each other; bar four is worked as a bass,
while bar three (with bar two for a few moments)
is sent flying all over the orchestra. The tremendous rhythmic impetus carries the whole mass
irresistibly forward.

And there we have one of the essential differences
between Russian and German symphonic music.
The forward impulse in a symphony by Beethoven
or Brahms comes from the logic of the music—the
linking up of long-breathed phrases, the unfolding
of an idea, the gradual working toward a new key.
If there is a dominating rhythm, as in the first movement of Beethoven's Seventh, its driving power is
never depended on alone to carry the music along.
With Borodin (and Stravinsky and all the most
typically Russian composers) underlying rhythm is
the only means used to give a sense of progress. All
this ingenious analysis of his theme is a static business; when he goes into another key it is simply for
the sake of variety—he modulates merely as he
changes his orchestration; to use a bass as the ful-

crum of a lever never occurs to him; when he writes
(in Ex. 21) a progression which sounds as if it might
really progress somewhere he uses it only to come
back more emphatically to the chord he has just
left and which he has been hammering home for the
last dozen bars (Ex. 20).

Now this way of writing a symphonic movement
admits of only two explanations; either the composer was hopelessly incompetent or he was looking
at things from an angle altogether different from
ours. To charge with incompetence a composer
capable of the technical ingenuity displayed in this
very movement is, of course, absurd—though it has
taken half a century to convince the musical world
that there was method in Mussorgsky's madness.
Borodin was an amateur, but he was no mere dilettante like Glinka and Dargomïzhsky. Is it too
much then to assume that his ideas on methods of
symphonic construction were as original as, for example, his ideas concerning key-schemes and that
he knew perfectly well what he was doing? (There
are signs of immaturity in this *allegro*—weak chromatic meanderings and so on—but they are invariably trivial and incidental.) What then was he trying to do? Let us look first for a moment at the

second subject.   Here are the essential fragments :—

Ex. 22

Their fairly obvious relationship is made clearer
still when the second violins play (a) with the second
bar in the rhythm of (b).   Taken by themselves
they are not big enough for a symphonic second
subject; but we soon find that they are not to be
taken by themselves.   Before long the key-centre
is shifted farther than it has been at all as yet; what
sounds like an ordinary development begins and
soon we get this sort of thing :—

Ex. 23

(with horns and basses emphasising a pedal E

throughout) which shows that Ex. 22 (b) is simply
a variation of the first bar of Ex. 19.   The development is short, too short for the usual plan, but
it is repeated (in a condensed form and chiefly in
E flat) after the reprise.   There is a big climax,
the peak of the whole movement, with a new variation of the first two bars of Ex. 19 on the full
orchestra :—

Ex. 24

and then an *andantino* epilogue gives us the key to
the whole puzzle :—

Ex. 25

So it was all one then, after all! We have been
shown the two main pieces separately; we have been
teased with all sorts of hints that they were not such
strangers as they seemed; we have been mocked
with something that only *appeared* to be sonata
form. Given the clue, everything is perfectly clear.
Whereas the essence of first movement form as the
great German masters understood it is duality, the
drama arising from the juxtaposition of contrasted
ideas, the essence of Borodin's first movements is
unity. In this First Symphony he obtains it by
that final synthesis after the elaborate analysis of
his material; in the Second by allowing the extremely powerful opening theme (Ex. 1) to dom-
inate the whole movement, so that the lyrical second
subject :—

Ex. 26

appearing but briefly, serves only to throw it into
higher relief and in the development is itself
immediately battered into the shape of the other :—

Ex. 27

In addition, the B minor is more concise than the
E flat and is stamped with a unity of mood which
the other lacks. The *moderato* of the Third, the
A minor, Symphony, is very square and conventional in outline, but Glazunov had to complete a
rough sketch and did so as symmetrically as he
could. Yet here again the unity of mood is striking; the secondary subjects, though unrelated to
the chief theme, continue its mood, modifying rather
than contrasting with it. Such variety as the movement has is obtained by changes of key or colour or
dynamic force.

Such, then, are the ideas Borodin places on his
canvases and his general conception of the symphonic first movement. Broadly speaking, he is
content to use the conventional sonata form plan
for the spacing out of his ideas, but in his hands,
although (perhaps *because*) he uses it for a different
end from that for which it was devised, it ceases to
be a convention and becomes a living organism
again. It is the general outline of sonata form, but
nothing more. The real, as opposed to this apparent, shape of the movement emerges entirely
from the material itself as it works to the foreseen
goal—Ex. 25, with its gathering up of all the

threads, in the First Symphony, the terrible, naked
final statement of the principal theme in the Second,
or the delicately coloured fading of day-dreams in
the Third.

To compare a Borodin symphony with a Brahms,
whether as a whole or in its parts, is like comparing
St. Sophia at Kiev with Cologne Cathedral, or
measuring "Anna Karenina" against "Madame
Bovary." To prolong a dangerous parallel a little
further, Borodin's musical organisms grow and live,
and shape themselves in growing, not unlike novels.
Yet no music is less literary in substance. Borodin
may or may not have had in his mind a gathering of
boyars, with their songs and feasting, in the B minor
Symphony. He said so himself, but the explanation sounds like an afterthought. In any case, it
is hopelessly inadequate. The finale is surely much
more than a banquet of barbaric chieftains, gorge-
ously painted. (What the composer wrote here on
lined paper counts for more than what he is reported to have said to Stassov.) Who could be so
deaf as to hear their songs in that lovely, dreaming
andante, which, if it is anything but pure music, is
summer with its haze of heat, the drowsy summer of
the Caucasus that Tolstoy paints in "The Cos-

sacks"?   We shall be on surer ground if we study
the relationship to "Prince Igor," which was being
written at the same period.   The B minor Symphony sounds like a symphonic version of all that
is best in "Prince Igor"—made a little better.   How
much finer is the *andante* of the Symphony, despite
the harmonic weakness which it shares with most of
Borodin's slow movements, than Vladimir's cavatina, for instance.   As for the scherzo (parts of
which would be perfectly in place if transferred to
the Polovtsian dances), it is unique in orchestral
literature.   So, for that matter, is the entirely different one of the Third Symphony—a *moto per-
petuo* in five-eight time (Ex. 2).   To have created
two such original scherzi, almost two new types of
scherzo, would in itself have been a remarkable feat.
But no composer less derivative than Borodin has
ever lived.

VII — PRINCE IGOR

BORODIN'S attention was first turned to the mediæval epic of Prince Igor, as a possible subject for an opera, by Stassov, who sent him a rough scenario in April, 1869. Acknowledging the receipt of this, the composer wrote to his friend that the subject "pleased him immensely." "Only will it be within my powers? I don't know. 'If you are afraid of wolves—don't go into the forest.' I will try." Accordingly he began the work in May of the same year. Yet at his death in 1887 the score was still unfinished—with some numbers in a fragmentary state, very little orchestrated, the overture not even put on paper (though it had been composed). It was the composer's third experiment in writing for the stage—the fourth if we reckon a parody-pastiche, "The Bohatyrs," largely based on music by Offenbach and others, which had one performance at the Grand Theatre in Moscow in 1867—for he had previously attempted a setting of Leo Mey's "The Tsar's Bride," on which Rimsky-Korsakov was afterwards to base one of his most popular works. And he had collaborated with Mussorgsky, Cui and Rimsky-Korsakov in the abortive "Mlada" of 1872, being responsible for the fourth act of that ill-fated venture.

From the beginning, Borodin realised that the subject of "Igor" was not altogether suitable for a dramatic purpose, but he loved it and, although he abandoned it more than once, always returned to his love. It can hardly be doubted that the B minor Symphony was the result of his despair of ever realising the "Igor" of his dreams. Perhaps in a sense the Symphony *was* the "Igor" of his dreams. Its first movement was written immediately after the first breakdown in the composition of the opera, and the Symphony in turn was interrupted by the commission to set Gedeonov's "Mlada" for the Imperial Theatre in Petersburg.* These three compositions are therefore closely related and there was even a certain amount of interchange of material between them. The "Mlada" music was based to a considerable extent on sketches originally made

---

* Gedeonov, the director of the theatre, was responsible only for the general scenario. The actual librettist was V. A. Krïlov —not to be confused with the author of the famous fables—who had also written the text of "The Bohatyrs."

for "Igor," and, when the "Mlada" project came
to nothing, this material (together, apparently, with
some of the new music written directly for
"Mlada") was restored to the other opera.* Thus
the opening of the Prologue is identical with the
music associated with the priests in "Mlada"; the
"eclipse" music was originally intended to accompany the appearance of the spirits of Prince Yaromir's ancestors; one of the themes in Yaroslavna's
big *arioso* at the beginning of the second scene of
Act I—it reappears in her duet with Igor in the last
act—was the Yaromir motif itself; and part of the
final chorus of "Igor" (that sung by the women's
voices only) was written, or at any rate *used*, to accompany the procession of gods in "Mlada" in the
final scene of the destruction of Radegast's temple
by flood and tempest. Borodin even thought of
using the "flood" music itself in the third act of
"Igor." In the old chronicle, Igor converses with
the river Don as he crosses it in his flight and Borodin had got hold of a tradition that the river over-
flowed its banks to check the pursuit of the Polovtsy.

---

* The other collaborators dealt with their contributions in the
same free and easy way. And it is well known that a number of
passages in "Boris Godunov" were originally composed for
"Salammbô."

However, the composer wisely rejected the idea on further consideration and the music was orchestrated as a separate concert piece by Rimsky-Korsakov after Borodin's death. Incidentally, it was only after "Mlada" had fallen through that Borodin decided to provide "Igor" with a prologue. His original intention had been to write an epilogue, and the splendid "Slava" chorus at the beginning of the work was in the first place designed to end it.

"Slovo o Polku Igoreve"—the Song of the Army of Igor—is one of the oldest of Russian manuscript chronicles. When first printed, early in the nineteenth century,* its genuineness was doubted. It was greeted as the work of some Russian Ossian. But it is now universally accepted as a contemporary account, probably by a professional bard, of an actual historical event. As in the poems of Ossian, the story is told in rhythmic prose. Indeed an interesting parallel might be drawn between Macpherson's forgery (if it was a forgery) and this fragment from Russia's heroic age. "The poem abounds in great lyrical beauties," we are told, "as

---

* By the archæologist, Musin-Pushkin, who discovered the manuscript in the Spaso-Yaroslavsky Monastery in 1795. The manuscript itself was destroyed in the burning of Moscow in 1812, but another copy was discovered in 1864.

well as in original similes and symbols. The tie
between Man and Nature is particularly profound.
Thus Igor is helped in his flight by birds and trees.
Rivers, plains, winds and forests seem to live one
life with men. Certain passages, such as the
laments of Igor's wife, are poignant in their dynamic
simplicity."* Borodin, too, must have been deeply
impressed by them, for his libretto preserves the
original words and they struck out of him some of
the most moving music he ever wrote.

Such was the poem with which Borodin lived for
eighteen years, as Beethoven lived with the "Ode
to Joy" for thirty, and Goethe with the Faust
legend all his life. In order that his "Igor" should
be accurate in every detail, the composer undertook
extensive researches. History, archæology, folk-
music—all were ransacked and every pertinent fragment carefully studied, so that not merely the superficial atmosphere of the time should be reproduced
but its essential spirit made, as far as possible, to
live again. And in Borodin the spirit of that old
barbarism of the vast steppes and their nomadic
warriors did live again. He was naturally adapted
to receive and transmit such impressions; the

---

* Janko Lavrin.

descendant of princes—Caucasian princes—he betrayed both in his personal appearance and in many
pages of even his earliest important composition,
the E flat Symphony, the heroic and the Oriental
elements in his nature.   Yet nothing demonstrates
more clearly the force of the impact on his mind of
the " Song of Igor's Expedition " than the difference between the First Symphony and the Second.
Borodin's musical talent lent itself most readily to
purely lyrical expression; it was only the subject of
" Igor " and the attendant researches that fired the
talent to moments of genius and seemingly armed
it with a new technique of utterance, almost terrible
in its directness.   The epic of Igor led this nineteenth century scientist back to primitive things---
the natural, the physical, the cruel, the healthy.
Almost all his later music glorifies them.   An idea
lived with for eighteen years must necessarily
become part of a man, and if the world of " Prince
Igor " was only a world of escape from the Academy
of Medicine and the lectures on chemistry and the
feminist campaign, it was probably more real to
Borodin than this other more tangible world of
science and sociology.

Borodin captured the spirit of " Igor " so miraculously that the weakness of the dramatic substance in which it is embodied seems at first sight the more deplorable. Igor, Prince of Seversk, sets out to punish a tribe of eastern nomads, is defeated and taken prisoner with his son—and escapes. That is the whole of the essential stuff of the drama, it would seem; the remaining action that pads out the prologue and the four acts of "Prince Igor" appears to be almost extraneous. Igor's brother-in-law stirs up trouble in his absence, but he disappears before the end of the first act; the disorder he causes merely provides a pretext for a stage-picture, just as the Polovtsian dances do at the end of the second act. There is a love-affair in Acts II and III between Igor's son and the daughter of one of the Polovtsian *khans*. It is used to heighten the excitement of Igor's escape, but otherwise the love interest seems to be introduced as pointlessly and arbitrarily as the comic interest, the rather childish clowning of the two gudok-players.* Nor

---

*Buffoons like Eroshka and Skula are stock-figures of classical Russian opera. We find them not only in avowedly comic works like "May Night" and "Christmas Eve" but in epic, fantastic and historical operas—in "Boris" (the drunken monks), in "Snegurochka" (Bobyl and Bobylicka), in "Sadko" (Duda and Sopiel). And Grishka Kuterma in "Kitezh" is just such another—seen tragically. But Eroshka and Skula were the prototypes. They were introduced into "Igor" by Borodin himself

is it an entirely satisfactory explanation to assume that the things we actually see and hear are really employed only to mirror those parts of the story of Igor's own adventures which cannot be shown at first hand on the stage. "Prince Igor" is, in fact, not so much a drama with personal protagonists as a series of scenes from an epic. So little was Borodin himself concerned with the dramatic element in his work that it was found, when he died, that he had never troubled to prepare a scenario, much less a finished libretto, for the second and third acts.

Yet before we finally dismiss "Prince Igor" as undramatic let us be quite clear as to what we mean by "drama" and "dramatic." In common usage the word "dramatic" has been so far degraded as to have become equivalent to "startling"; on a higher plane, we speak of the drama played out by the two principal subjects of a sonata-movement. In any case an element of contrast and clash is connoted and "Prince Igor," therefore, seems to be merely strewn with disconnected fragments of drama. But there is an antithesis which pervades

---

and, alluding to their disproportionate prominence, he jokingly remarked more than once that the opera would be more correctly entitled, not "Prince Igor," but "The Gudok-Players."

the whole work, the antithesis symbolised by the
Russian elements in the music of the Prologue and
Acts I and IV and the Polovtsian in that of Acts II
and III—the clash between Slav and Tartar. Yet
if the subject, of the opera contains very little
material of the type we are accustomed to think of
as the proper stuff of drama, it is, nevertheless, a
subject that not only provides an admirable pretext
for stage-pictures but which can be presented by
such pictures more effectively than by any other
means. And the pictures are in every case of such
a kind that music not merely *carries* them and
heightens their effect but adds a new dimension,
without which they would be incomplete. That fact
alone, it seems to me, amply justifies the making of
an opera on such a subject. Our emotions are
stirred, not by sympathy with any of the characters
(except perhaps Yaroslavna—who, in any case, is
off the stage for two whole acts) or by a conflict of
wills or ideas, but by the combined sensuous appeal
of colour, sound and movement. The cumulative
effect of all these detached scenes is out of all proportion to their effect taken separately. When they
have passed, though passages like the choral dances
and the unaccompanied chorus in Act IV may linger

as high lights in the memory, one is left with a distinct impression of a rounded whole, complete and
single.   The spirit is too strong for the stuff in
which it is embedded.   For a few hours we watch
these pictures of Russia's heroic age, while our re-
ceptive faculties, our imagination and our sensitiveness to impressions are quickened as only music can
quicken them.   The fate of Igor (who, like many
another hero, is merely a lay-figure) scarcely interests us at all, but the re-created world in which he
so signally fails to live abounds in life—and communicates a sense of that life to us.   The real subject of the opera, it cannot be emphasised too
strongly, is not a hero and his adventures but the
spirit of a people and a period.

We must accept "Prince Igor," therefore, not as
a musical drama but as a musical epic, a concert
with action and costumes.   That is to say, we must
be content to allow it to affect us in the same way
that concert-music does.   But obviously the stage-
setting is essential.   An actual concert version of
"Prince Igor" would be as ineffective as a concert
version of "Tannhäuser" or "Figaro."   Let us
look then at the actual musical stuff of "Igor" for
a moment, always keeping in mind the fact that its

function is to increase our sensitiveness to pictures
rather than to underline a drama. But Borodin
never accompanies his stage-pictures, as Wagner
was so fond of doing, with tautological translations
of them into sound. The picture speaks for itself
—*qua* picture; the music, retaining its tremendous
advantage over the other arts of being able to transmit emotion purely, nakedly and directly, simply
gives the emotional content of the picture. Or,
conversely, one might say that the happenings on
the stage illustrate the music. The music is the
subject, the action and the picture the objective
manifestation. The music seldom comments on,
and never analyses, either drama or characters. In
this respect " Prince Igor " is as far removed from
" Boris Godunov " as " Boris " is from " Tristan."

The vocal lines in " Igor " are either frankly
melodic or modelled on Dargomïzhsky's "melodic
recitative." That is : the recitatives are to be *sung*,
are, in fact, really *ariosi*. A direction at one point
in Yaroslavna's long recitative in the fourth act is
highly significant—*avec une grande émotion et
presque déclamé*. Borodin was fully conscious of
the pre-eminently lyrical nature of his opera :
" From the dramatic point of view I have always

been unlike the majority.   Recitative does not enter
into my nature or disposition.   Although according
to some critics I do not handle it altogether badly,
I am far more attracted to melody and cantilena."
And he goes on to mention a quality in which lies a
great part of the secret of "Igor's" effectiveness:
"I am drawn to definite and concrete forms.   In
opera, as in decorative art, details and *minutiæ* are
out of place.   Bold outlines only are necessary; all
should be clear and straightforward and fit for practical performance from the vocal and instrumental
standpoint.   The voices should occupy the first
place, the orchestra the second.   I am no judge of
the way in which I shall succeed, but my opera will
be nearer akin to 'Ruslan' than to 'The Stone
Guest.'"   That was literally a confession of heresy,
for, as we have seen, Dargomïzhsky's "Stone
Guest" was known among the members of the
"Kuchka" as "the Gospel."

So we find in Borodin's score set-numbers like
Vladimir's cavatina and Igor's aria in Act II, as
well as conventional choruses, sometimes frankly
detached from the context, sometimes connected arbitrarily and without continuity of musical thought.
Mingled with stretches of melodic recitative are

purely melodic phrases, even snatches of formal, balanced melody (as in Yaroslavna's arioso, Act I, second tableau). Here one finds the indefinite outlines of lyrical recitative, supported on a shapeless background of chord melting into chord; there the very clear-cut melodic shapes of folk-music. Sometimes an actual folk-melody is employed, as in the unaccompanied chorus of peasants in Act IV—but on this ground one must tread cautiously, for the score contains no indications as to what material is of folk-origin and what is original. Instead of borrowing from existing collections, Borodin carried out folk-song researches on his own account* (the lovely melody of the peasants' chorus was one of his discoveries) and we have no means of determining the precise nature of the relationship of many of the " Prince Igor " melodies to actual folk-material. On the whole it is probably more spiritual than material, for Borodin had obviously absorbed the idiom and, in using it, reproduced the actual shapes of folk-music only subconsciously. This is true more particularly of the " Russian "

* According to Stassov, he also received from friends "some motives from songs of the Turkish races," motives noted by an explorer in Central Asia, and some musical material acquired from actual descendants of the Polovtsy now settled in a certain district in Hungary.

music; in the case of the " Polovtsian," which contrasts so sharply with it, one may venture to probe
with a little more certainty into Borodin's treatment
of his raw material.   But the rather fascinating
little problems to which this examination gives rise
may be more conveniently dealt with later in considering Borodin's employment of the leit-motif.

The use of the leit-motif in " Prince Igor " is
rudimentary—dramatic, for the sake of making
points, rather than systematic as with Wagner.   Yet
it helps to disguise the varying style and uneven
quality of the music, and the interruption of its continuity by the conventional set-numbers, by stamp-
ing it with at least a suggestion of material unity
equivalent to the unquestionable unity (or rather,
perhaps, Slav-Tartar duality) of its general feeling.
Of personal leit-motifs, used on Wagnerian lines in
strict association with a character and never failing
to appear in connection with him, there are only two
—that associated with Ovlur, the Christian Polovtsian who assists Igor to escape, and the striking
theme of falling diminished fifths heard when the
Khan, Konchak, first enters in the second act and
throughout the remainder of Acts II and III.   The
" Ovlur " theme is employed much less frequently

and purely for dramatic emphasis. It is used throughout the scene in which the traitor first approaches Igor with the offer to help him to escape (and some of the solemn Prologue music is heard as the captive Prince's thoughts turn to his people; it calls attention to him as he crosses the stage with *kumïs* for the guards in Act III; and it is used, with some of the other music heard during his previous interview with Igor, in the ensuing scene where he tells the Prince that all is ready for the flight. But here again we are confronted with a doubt which it is difficult to resolve with certainty. Not only is a great deal of the music of this scene between Igor and Ovlur drawn from that of their discussion in Act II, but much of the music of the preceding scene with the guards is also based on material previously used, the quotation of which here can have no dramatic significance. Borodin may have intended by this means to draw the threads of his work a little closer, but we must not forget that he left his opera unfinished and that Glazunov, to whom the completion and orchestration of this third act was entrusted,* may have preferred to make use of

---

* Glazunov also wrote out the overture "nearly according to

Borodin's own themes for the filling up of *lacunæ* rather than to incorporate fresh material of his own in the master's work. This is certainly the case in the Finale of the act, which we know was almost entirely composed by Glazunov. On the other hand the quotations from Igor's big aria in Act II (when he tells Konchak that if he were free he would renew the war and not make peace "till he had drawn water from the Don in his helmet"; when Vladimir, in Act III, is hesitating between love and duty; and during Yaroslavna's lament in Act IV) are dramatically significant and very effective. Then again there is some interesting play of motives in the early scenes where Galitsky is prominent. The music of his brief assurance of fidelity to Igor in the Prologue ironically provides the material for two fairly long passages in the first act, when his

Borodin's plan," having frequently heard the composer play it on the piano, and scored it. The remainder of "Prince Igor," including the Polovtsian March in Act III, was orchestrated by Rimsky-Korsakov. We also owe the music of the beautiful little chorus of Russian prisoners in Act II to Glazunov's memory ; the words and Konchakovna's introductory recitative were added by Rimsky-Korsakov. It is characteristic of Glazunov's modesty that he has destroyed the "legend" that he "wrote out the Overture entirely from memory." Actually, of course, the material all existed in the body of the opera. Glazunov also refuses to "guarantee the precise accuracy" of the chorus of prisoners.

treachery has been fully revealed; a tumultuous
quaver passage is three times associated with him;
and there is a striking "Hail, Prince Galitsky"
motif, first sung by the basses, which is afterwards
developed at considerable length in the final chorus
of the first tableau of Act I ("Let us place him on
the throne"). The last four pages of this scene,
again, pass in review much that has gone before,
rounding it off as a compact musical whole, though
in no way illuminating the dramatic action.

Still more interesting are the themes associated
with the Polovtsy; and in discussing these we are
led back to a subject already touched on, the nature
of Borodin's treatment of the raw material he had
gathered. The Polovtsian, the oriental, element
dominates the music of the second and third acts,
and Act II plunges us at once into the new atmosphere with a striking chorus of Polovtsian girls.
Four typical phrases of its strangely haunting
melody are here quoted separately for convenience
of reference :—

Ex. 28

10

Their relationship to each other is sufficiently obvious. None is a variation of another; all are, as
it were, different aspects of the same idea. It will
be noticed that the features common to these fragments are strongly distinctive and therefore of such
a type that they naturally give a peculiar stamp to
any melody in which they appear. Whether the
whole long extended melody of this chorus* is a
genuine Tartar tune or whether Borodin manufactured it from such fragments as the initial motif of
(a), (b) and (d), the falling triplet of (a), (c) and
(d), and so on, it is impossible to say with certainty.
But it is clearly either genuine raw material or
material in only the first stage of manufacture.
Either Borodin got most of his "Polovtsian"
clichés from this tune or he took this opportunity of
making a synthesis of nearly all the melodic and
rhythmic features he had observed to be characteristic of the folk-music he wished to imitate; and of
the two, the former seems decidedly the more reas-
onable supposition. With the next step, the tracing
of Borodin's "culture" of these germ-themes, we
reach firm ground—and incidentally discover what

* The other melodic shapes are similarly related to these but,
being inessential to the discussion, are not quoted.

gives the music of these two acts its *cachet* of unity.

Of the four fragments of Ex. 28, (d) is by far the most important. We recognise it again first as the generating theme of Konchakovna's cavatina,* "Night, falling quickly":—

Ex. 29

Noch, spu——— skaï_sya sko-reï,

The new feature, the appoggiatura emphasising the triplet, is important and characteristic. The fragment, "I wait for thee":—

Ex. 30

Ya zhdu te-bya.

with the little pendant (to "zhdu tebya"), is also heard in the orchestra in this number, and was again quoted by Rimsky-Korsakov in a pause in the brief recitative for Konchakovna introducing the following chorus of Russian prisoners.

Konchak's big aria later in the act is based, not

---

* The cavatina has a choral accompaniment not by Borodin. The chorus-parts were added gratuitously by Rimsky-Korsakov after the composer's death.

immediately on Ex. 28 (d), but on the variation
Ex. 29 (or rather on the "spuskaïsya" part of it),
with the appoggiatura notes now broadened into an
essential part of the melodic line ("No, no, friend.
No prince, thou art not my prisoner here") :—

Ex. 31

An accompaniment-figure :—

Ex. 32

used later, is more directly derived from Ex. 28
(d). The brief, quick orchestral coda of the aria
preserves the melodic shape of the first three bars of
Ex. 31, but a fresh appoggiatura is inserted before
the triplet. From the new figure thus obtained is
developed the music of Yaroslavna's lament which
opens Act IV :—

Ex. 33

The further transformations of Ex. 31 in the Finale
of Act III are apparently Glazunov's. The adventures of Ex. 28 (b) are less striking, but a variation :—

Ex. 34

plays an important part in the famous dances at the
end of Act II.

Ex. 28 (c) is particularly interesting, for it is
marked by what is perhaps the most personal of all
Borodin's melodic mannerisms, one so peculiar to
him and occurring so frequently in his music that it
almost has the effect of placing his signature to any
melody in which it is found. We find it in the
opening of the B minor Symphony (Ex. 1)—and the
working-out gives it much additional prominence;
in the chief subject of the finale of the Second
String Quartet; and, inverted, in the opening of the
Symphony in E flat (Ex. 19). In " Prince Igor " it
occurs in passage-work, in the melody to which the
curtain rises on the second tableau of Act I, in Igor's
great aria (Act II) in the Polovtsian dances and on
a dozen other pages of the score.

The binding effect of such constantly recurring
motives, in music otherwise diffuse and disconnected, is surprisingly strong, the more so perhaps
because they are comparatively unobtrusive. And
in a slightly different way the triumphal fanfare of
the Polovtsian March, which is heard again and
again throughout the third act, to which the curtain
rises and on which it falls, seems to frame and, if
the idea be not too fanciful, throw into relief the
rest of the music of that act. It also recalls a passage in the B minor Symphony, forcibly drawing
one's attention to the fact that there are material as
well as spiritual links between the two works. The
resemblances between the second subject of the first
movement of the symphony (Ex. 26) and the final
marziale chorus of "Igor" are not less significant
because they are accidental. A motif from one of
the choruses of Act I is used in the finale of the
symphony. And in "On the Steppes of Central
Asia" also (where again the central idea is the musical contrasting of Slav and Tartar) one easily recognises the derivation of the *cor anglais* melody from
Ex. 28 (a) and (d). If the B minor Symphony was
an idealisation of the best of the material gathered
for the composition of "Igor," "On the Steppes of

Central Asia" was clearly made of chips from the same workship. And we know that the trio of the Third Symphony was actually based on material originally intended for the opera (the merchant's account of Igor's defeat, which was originally intended to form part of the finale of Act I).

VIII—RIMSKY-KORSAKOV'S FIRST OPERA

IN November, 1865, at the outset of his career as a composer, Rimsky-Korsakov wrote his first song, a setting of Heine's "Lehn deine Wang' an meine Wang.'" Balakirev, whose influence over the younger man was at that time absolute, approved of the melody but condemned the accompaniment as unpianistic and characteristically wrote a fresh one, with which the song was published. In the following spring, incited by the singing of a certain Madame Zotova, whom he had met at the house of Glinka's sister, Rimsky-Korsakov wrote three more songs, this time with his own accompaniments, and all four were soon after published together as his Opus 2. One of the songs was another Heine setting, "Aus meinen Tränen spriessen" (a poem which also seduced Borodin into unsuccessful competition with Schumann), one the well-known "The Rose enslaves the Nightingale," and the third a setting of the cradle-song in the first act of Leo Mey's drama, "Pskovityanka" ("The Maid of Pskov"). That was Rimsky-Korsakov's first encounter with a work which was to occupy him at intervals for a quarter of a century, of which indeed the last note was not written till 1899, when he inserted in the last act of his opera an additional—or, rather, alternative—aria for Chaliapin as the Tsar.

The idea of turning Mey's play into an opera was born several months later than the song. It originated with Balakirev and Mussorgsky. From the very beginning the first act was seen to offer serious difficulties. Its action takes place fifteen years before the rest of the play and is concerned with quite a different set of characters. It serves only to explain the secret of the heroine's parentage, yet without this clue the drama is hardly a comprehensible whole. The solution adopted by Rimsky-Korsakov and his informal advisory committee, to omit the first act altogether and give the gist of it in a dialogue in the third, was the only possible one. But it never satisfied even the composer himself. "The question of a librettist," he tells us incidentally, "never arose. It was taken for granted that I should have to write the 'book' myself."

For the time being the thought of an opera was

thrust aside by the composition of "Antar." Then in the summer of 1868 came genuine inspiration, provoked by an invitation to visit a musical friend, with whom the Borodins were staying, whose estate was in the Tver Government. The invitation reached the composer in his brother's empty town house and the prospect of a journey into the heart of Russia awoke in him "a sudden, extremely powerful feeling of love for the Russian people, for their history in general and for 'Pskovityanka' in particular." And under the influence of this passionate emotion he improvised at the piano the theme of the chorus with which the people greet Tsar Ivan. During this country holiday he watched the dances of the peasants, and on his return to Petersburg wrote, evidently under the influence of these impressions, the music of the opening scene where the girls are singing and playing in Prince Tokmakov's garden. The tale of the Tsarevna Lada was written at the same time. Then another external event occurred to modify the course of the composition of "Pskovityanka." In the first days of 1869 Dargomïzhsky died and, in accordance with his wishes, his unfinished "Stone Guest" was handed over to Cui to finish and to

Rimsky-Korsakov to orchestrate. The scoring of "The Stone Guest" and the composition of "Pskovityanka" went on side by side, a fact which partially accounts for the exceptionally dramatic tendency of the latter. Both works progressed slowly; Rimsky-Korsakov was still a naval officer, and his duties, though not exacting, took up much time. A heavier hindrance to the work was the composer's astounding ignorance of the technique of composition. He was in the position of a Robinson Crusoe, a workman without tools. On his own confession, he was unable at that time to harmonise a simple chorale properly; he had "only a hazy idea of fugue"; and his "ideas of musical form were very confused." Instinct and a good ear were his only guides; he had an unconscious feeling for good part-writing; and he could distinguish without the least difficulty every note in each chord. But the only chords he knew by name were the major and minor triads and the dominant and diminished sevenths; he had never heard of "six-four" chords. It was the same with his orchestration; like Berlioz he scored colourfully by instinct from the beginning. Just as the Frenchman had written "Les Franc-Juges" without knowing whether it could be

played, the composer of "Sadko" and "Antar"
had no thorough knowledge of the technique even
of the strings! The writing of an opera was a truly
heroic feat for a composer with such equipment,
though Mussorgsky did the whole of his life-work
with very little better. But Rimsky-Korsakov was
not content to play the "inquisitive savage discovering music step by step." He saw how quickly his
creative fantasy was brought to a standstill for want
of fresh methods of treatment. In his own expressive phrase, the acquisition of a technique "freed
his hands." But the delightful spectacle of the
Professor of Free Composition at the Petersburg
Conservatoire conscientiously working figured
basses and harmonising simple melodies was reserved for the year 1874; the whole of "Pskovityanka" in its original form was the work of a complete musical ignoramus. The scoring of "The
Stone Guest" was finished in the summer of 1870*
and its immediate influence was replaced by another.
Various circumstances, principally the illness of the

---

* Many years afterwards Rimsky-Korsakov, dissatisfied with
his treatment of Dargomizhsky's masterpiece, orchestrated it entirely afresh, and at the same time smoothed out, in his usual
editorial manner, the "harmonic crudities of the original." This
second version was completed in 1902.

brother with whom he had been living, led to Rimsky-Korsakov's sharing rooms with Mussorgsky,
and the two men worked at the same writing-table,
one finishing his "Pskovityanka" while the other
was composing and orchestrating additional scenes
(the Polish act and the scene in the forest near
Kromy being the most important) for "Boris
Godunov," in the hope that its new form would
induce the directorate of the Imperial Opera to
reconsider their refusal to produce it. There
were serious interruptions to the composition of
"Pskovityanka"—the death of the composer's
brother in November, with a consequent journey to
Italy to bring home the body, and the composer's
betrothal in December—but the score was finished
by January, 1872.

With "Pskovityanka" began Rimsky-Korsakov's
troubles with the dramatic censorship, troubles
which intermittently attended his career as an operatic composer right up to the banning of "The
Golden Cockerel." The censor objected to the
scene of the "veche," the parliament of the free
citizens of Pskov, which in the sixteenth century was
still a member of the Hanseatic League and practically an independent republic. The Tsarist gov-

ernment would not tolerate the stage representation
of a republican institution, and the perfectly legal
"veche" had to be turned into an assembly of
rebels.   An even more serious difficulty, a ukase of
Nicholas I forbidding the introduction of members
of the Romanov dynasty as characters in opera
(though not in ordinary drama), was circumvented
by backstairs methods,* and Rimsky-Korsakov at
last had the satisfaction of seeing his work produced
in January, 1873, with considerable success.

But his satisfaction was short-lived.   The well-
equipped technician who emerged from the contrapuntal crisis of 1874 was heartily ashamed of the
crudities of his score.   "I was conscious of the
harmonic extravagances, the disconnectedness of
the recitative, the want of sustained melody . . .
and the absence of contrapuntal elements."   He
was dissatisfied also with the scoring—the "sense-
less choice of natural horns and trumpets" (two
horns in F, two in C, and trumpets in C), the ineffective string-writing and the absence of any sonorous
forte.   Balakirev also pressed for the revision of

* Tchaïkovsky was less fortunate with his "Oprichnik" a few
months later. Ivan the Terrible was also to have appeared in
this opera, but the censor insisted on the excision of the part.

"Pskovityanka," on the ground that Rimsky-Korsakov was unlikely to write another opera and that
it was therefore his duty to make the best of his
first-born. Accordingly in 1876 the conscientious
composer set about not a mere revision but an entire
re-writing of the work. He now set Mey's first act
as a prologue, introducing his Op. 2, No. 3, Vera's
cradle-song, and made other additions—among
them, at Balakirev's demand, a chorus of those beg-
ging pilgrims who form such a large proportion of
the floating population of Russian opera. The
work was also entirely re-orchestrated, but once
more, curiously enough, with natural brass "although the harmonies and modulations imperatively
demanded valve instruments." But the second version of "Pskovityanka" pleased nobody, not even
the composer himself. It suffered from excess of
technical ingenuity even more than the first version
had done from lack of it. The additions made the
work too long and destroyed its unity of style, and
Rimsky-Korsakov had to admit that he had
strangled his music in a web of counterpoint. The
Imperial Theatres would not produce the opera in
its new form; so, despairing of seeing it on the stage,
Rimsky-Korsakov again re-scored the new "minia-

ture overture" to the prologue, and the entr'actes, this time with chromatic brass, and issued them as a concert suite "like the music to 'Prince Kholmsky' or 'Egmont.'"

In the spring of 1891 Rimsky-Korsakov heroically began a second complete revision. So far was he from tamely accepting Weber's dictum that "first operas are like first puppies, only fit to be drowned." This time he determined to follow the first version for the most part, only drawing on the second to replace completely unsuccesful passages; the new orchestration was "partly according to Glinka's principles, partly on Wagnerian lines," with triple wood-wind instead of in pairs as before. Among other changes, the overture was transposed from B minor to C minor, completely re-scored, and "the barbaric dissonances at the end replaced by more respectable music." This final version of the opera was finished in 1894, just before the composition of "Christmas Eve," and produced in the following year. The prologue, which had been omitted from the third version, was also brushed up in the spring of 1898 and published as a self-contained one-act opera, "Boyarina Vera Sheloga." Few operas can have had a more eventful history, but in spite of this bewildering succession of re-births we can still accept "Pskovityanka" as Rimsky-Korsakov's first opera. The earlier versions are not available for comparison, but Yastrebtsev, who played Boswell to Rimsky-Korsakov's Johnson, confirms the composer's statement that the final version is for the most part simply a revision of the first. And the internal evidence makes such confirmation almost unnecessary. Not only "Pskovityanka" but the First and Third Symphonies, the so-called "Second Symphony" ("Antar"), the orchestral "Sadko," the "Fantasia on Serbian Themes"—in fact, all Rimsky-Korsakov's important compositions prior to "May Night"—underwent similar revision in later years, so that a critic of the early Rimsky-Korsakov is liable to be tripped up at every step. Fortunately criticism of "Pskovityanka" is simplified by the facts that the music is subordinated to the drama and that the dramatic outline was left practically unchanged.

If anyone wants to see exactly what Dargomïzhsky and the younger Russians of the time were aiming at in opera, without choking himself with dust from the dry bones of "The Stone Guest" or bewildering himself with Mussorgsky's genius in

"Boris," he cannot do better than study "Pskovity-anka." Rimsky-Korsakov was conscientious above all else; he was just the man to write a "model" opera. His own inclinations, like Borodin's, seem to have been towards lyrical opera in Glinka's style, except that his lyrical vein was alloyed with a strongly fantastic element which appears only occasionally in Glinka and not at all in Borodin. Yet he must needs try his hand at dramatic realism in the orthodox Dargomïzhskian manner for which he had no real gift—though, unconvinced on this point, he returned to it in "Mozart and Salieri" and "Vera Sheloga." So in "Pskovityanka" we find the famous "melodic recitative" used almost throughout (though the "melodic" qualification is not unduly emphasised) and an absence of conventional set-numbers, except the interpolated aria for the Tsar in the last act and Olga's arietta in Act II, Scene 1, which was inserted in the second version in place of an *arioso* in the first. On the other hand, a number of passages can easily be detached from the context and performed as self-contained numbers. The folk-song element is well to the fore—real (as the song of the rebels, Olga's pleading "Stay with me, my love" in the first act, and the lovely melody which accompanies the dialogue of the nurses in the opening scene) and imitated (as the song Tucha sings when he first comes striding over the fence into Prince Tokmakov's garden). And the chorus, the voice of the people of Pskov, is the most impressive protagonist in the drama until—an effective point—the appearance of the Tsar himself.

The alternative title of the opera, "Ivan the Terrible," was adopted by Dyaghilev as a concession to the linguistic difficulties of Western audiences. But it is perhaps on the whole more fitting than the original one. It is true the opera is concerned with the love and death of Olga, the Maid of Pskov, but her part in the drama is an almost purely passive one. The central figure is her father, the Tsar. At first it appears as if the real subject of the drama is to be the struggle between the Tsar and the citizens of Pskov, the same subject as in "Boris"—the struggle between a tyrant and the will of the people. But whereas in "Boris" the centre of dramatic gravity remains in this contest (the revelation of Boris's agony being, after all, only incidental), in "Pskovityanka" this issue drops into the background with the love-affair of Olga and Tucha, and

the main drama is seen to be that of the warring elements in Ivan's own soul. Viewed in this light·
"Pskovityanka" appears as one long-drawn dramatic crescendo, of which the full significance is
revealed only at the end. Ivan himself does not
appear till half-way through the second act, more
than half-way through the whole opera, but everything that precedes his entrance is like the gradual
gathering of his shadow. He is first mentioned by
the nurses during the light-hearted songs and games
of the girls in the opening scene; but Vlassevna's
brief account of the sack of Novgorod hardly inter-
rupts the general feeling of merriment. His
shadow grows more distinct in the dialogue between
Tokmakov and Matuta. And in both conversa-
tions his relationship to Olga is dimly hinted at.
Now, when Tokmakov, not daring to tell the truth,
says, "But her father we know not," the Tsar's
theme is heard in the orchestra for the first time—
a curious instance of a potentially dramatic effect
thrown away, for the motif, afterwards so effective,
is at this point not yet clothed with association and
is therefore meaningless to anyone hearing the work
for the first time. The conversation is interrupted

by the ringing of the alarm-bell,* and its tolling—
which continues without interruption throughout the
rest of the scene, the ensuing intermezzo and the
gathering of the people, right up to the great choral
cry to the messenger from Novgorod, "Yes, let him
speak"—creates an atmosphere of tension, the
sense of an overhanging doom, intensified by the
finely conceived choruses of which the rest of the
act consists. Tokmakov tries to soothe the people;
Tucha inflames them. But it is the chorus, the
voice of the people themselves, uttering their fears,
their doubts, their submission or their defiance,
which dominates everything. Nothing could be
more profoundly impressive than the conclusion
when, after the song of the rebels has died away and
the bells are tolling again for the summoning of the
"veche," those left on the stage murmur that "the
end draws near. The Tsar is wrath." In the
broad, falling phrases of the chorus seem to be con-
centrated both the awe of the particular moment and
the essence of that passive, mournful submission to
an invincible destiny which is at once the tragedy
and the salvation of the Russian soul.

The chorus again dominates the whole of the first

---

* Suggested by overtones, as in the "Overture on Russian
Themes" of 1866.

scene of the second act, where the Tsar is immediately expected, and the tension is again drawn to a
gradual climax which reaches its extreme point when
the Tsar rides in and—another most effective point
—the curtain falls immediately.   The shadow has
now become substance; though, paradoxically, the
substance owes all its formidable authority to the
shadow, the dread which the Tsar's name has been
seen to inspire.

Up to this point the composer has been able to
get along very well with purely musical means—
appeals to the people and big, exciting choruses.
Now he has to show Ivan himself and to show him
so that he justifies the general terror so elaborately
painted.   Rimsky-Korsakov really plays his cards
very well.   Having a poor hand in his own natural
gifts, he plays up to his partner, the dramatist, so
well that between them they make trick after trick.
Even the interlude which bridges the gap between
the crowded scene in the market-place and the first
close-up of the Tsar in Tokmakov's house shows
some sense of the theatre.   As a concert piece this
quiet meditation on the naïve themes associated with

Olga would fall rather flat; here, as a point of repose between two dramatic scenes, it not only throws
what follows into higher relief but is extremely
effective in itself.

The scene in Tokmakov's house needs no music
to make it effective.   The character of the half-mad
Tsar reveals itself stroke by stroke : in his quibbling, " To enter or not? . . . I'll enter if the grace
of God Almighty and His blessing rest upon this
house "; in his ironical pretence that he cannot even
sit down without Tokmakov's permission; in his
thanks ao Tokmakov and Matuta, his "two devoted courtiers . . . on the right an angel, on the
left a devil! They're silent . . . yet each one
plots in himself. Well, though I'm but an idiot,
aye, and a miscreant, God's most sinful servant, I'll
judge ye both if God but wills it so."*   Rimsky-
Korsakov's mezzo-recitative is no more than a
vehicle for the words, and the orchestral background entirely woven from the Tsar's motif in imitation and in different registers, is not at all expressive; yet somehow this cold, serenely royal back-

---

* I have followed Mrs. Newmarch's translation of the libretto
throughout.   (Bessel Edition : for which Boosey and Hawkes are
the English agents.)

ground—for it is emphatically background and not
commentary—throws the figure of the Tsar into
striking relief.   Consider, for instance, his outburst
when Tokmakov hails him as "Tsar! Gossudar!"—

Ex. 35

But even the moment when Ivan recognises Olga
as his daughter fails to strike genuinely dramatic
music out of Rimsky-Korsakov; he takes refuge in
convention—soft, slow chords, a quiet harp arpeggio, and then an agitated version of the Tsar's

theme in quick time. The convention is adequate
to the occasion; but one cannot help feeling that
Mussorgsky would have written something that was
more than adequate. Rimsky-Korsakov clearly
did not *feel* such situations and one is very conscious that he is happy to pass on to Olga's simple
lyrical reply and of the relief with which he evades
the point musically by dragging in a folk-songish
girls' chorus as a background to the rest of the conversation. Separation of the musical and dramatic
centres of gravity in this fashion was an ever-present
help in time of trouble to Rimsky-Korsakov.

The third act begins by wandering among ir-
relevancies—the picturesque but quite unnecessary
"Tsar's Hunt and Storm," so obviously imitated
from Berlioz's "Troyens," introduced in the final
version of the opera, the beautiful unison folk-song
chorus of the girls looking for Olga, and the extraordinarily passionless love-duet, a wilderness of
even crotchets in 5/4 time. But when the curtain
rises on the second scene, revealing the Tsar alone
in his tent, the drama reaches its height. We have
seen the growing shadow of Ivan's dreaded coming,
the terror of his reputation; we have seen the man
himself and his behaviour to those about him. And

now finally the whole of his tortured soul is laid bare
to us, like Boris Godunov's, and at last Rimsky-
Korsakov is moved to music of real dramatic power
and psychological subtlety. It is impossible to
believe that Rimsky-Korsakov wrote this scene
without some thought of Boris, whose tragic history,
as we have seen, was being re-shaped during the
composition of " Pskovityanka." And it is something more than a coincidence that Chaliapin became the outstanding interpreter of both parts.
Rimsky-Korsakov's admiration for this "incompar-
able Ivan the Terrible" led him into a curious error
of judgment, the insertion of the aria already mentioned, a piece written in the insipid style of the
weakest pages of "The Tsar's Bride," after the
Tsar's first words, "Well, I have pardoned Pskov,
but the girl still haunts my memory." It is
not only that the brooding phrases of the orchestra in the original version (Ex. 36), seem
to lose their "edge" and character when transferred to the voice; the whole thing is foreign to the
world of dramatic realism in terms of which the
scene was conceived in the first place. Now the
Tsar's thoughts turn to Vera, Olga's mother, and his
declamation is broken while the orchestra seems to

dream as he half whispers to himself, "The past uprises : the wood, the orchard, she herself . . . I saw her, and my heart throbbed past endurance.

Ex. 36.

. . . And now the fruit tastes bitter." Then he recalls his royal mission, as he conceives it : "Aye, but that kingdom's strongest, greatest, most invincible, in which the people know that in one man the power is vested, a single flock gathered around one shepherd." The vision of a holy autocracy reaches its climax :—

Ex. 37

And then comes doubt again: "But will the Lord then grant me strength and wisdom?" He turns the pages of his missal, reading the divine commands "to punish rebels, and make an end of evildoers and sinners; Thou giv'st Thy disciples power to destroy and to crush out scorpions and serpents and to overcome all the forces of the Evil One. . . . " And then, after one of those silences which the stilling of music makes so impressive, the terrible sigh, "Oh, I am sad."

In these pages Rimsky-Korsakov really reaches the highest point of his achievement as a dramatic realist. Nowhere else in the whole range of his work, except perhaps in the music of Grishka Kuterma in "Kitezh," is there anything comparable with this probing of the mysteries of abnormal psychology. It was not his *métier*. And, knowing that, one feels the added exhilaration one always gets from the spectacle of a man doing something unnatural to him and doing it rather well. Ivan's portrait is not yet complete; we have still to see his ungovernable rage against Matuta, to see him playing cat and mouse with the daughter he loves, incapable of kindness without an alloy of cruelty, masking fondness with irony, and finally to see him sobbing over her dead body, commanding her to listen—" 'Tis I, the Tsar . . ."—and frantically imploring the physician, Bomelius, to save her, "my child, my darling." But poignant as is the music which accompanies the final tragedy, it cannot be compared in psychological truth with that of the Tsar's long soliloquy.

Beside this full-length study of the Tsar, the other characters are merely sketched, and his domination of the stage is thus given additional emphasis. But this emphasis is quite unnecessary on the one hand, while on the other it is obvious that the force of his personality is weakened by the lack of a suitable foil. For the most part he is contrasted with Olga, a rather colourless figure; colourless not because she is incompetently drawn, for the charmingly simple, lyrical music associated with her precisely reflects her naïve character, but because she *is* naïve, the first of those innocent, passive heroines who appear in so many of Rimsky--Korsakov's operas. No real daughter of Ivan the Terrible could have been quite as negative as Olga. But she belongs to a type we meet fairly often in Russian literature and which we must therefore assume to be a true portrait of a common type of Russian girlhood, a type which evidently appealed to Rimsky-Korsakov. Tokmakov, too, is negative by nature, and Rimsky-Korsakov contrived to outline his amiable, conciliatory character in such music as the chords which accompany his address to the people of Pskov and the phrase to which he sings, "I am growing old, Matuta," without lapsing into insipidity. On the other hand, Tucha who is positive, the typical rebel, the natural foil to the Tsar (though they never appear on the stage at the same time), is not really alive at all. Or, rather, he begins by being alive when he first comes on the stage with his song about the cuckoo, and gradually becomes more and more wooden. As for Matuta, he is nothing more than a lay-figure from beginning to end—and the mere outline of a lay-figure at that. He seems to have some importance not accounted for in the opera at all.

It is easier to grasp " Pskovityanka" as a dramatic whole than as a musical one. At a first hearing one is inclined to say that it is really typical of Rimsky-Korsakov in nothing but its folk-songish elements and perhaps in the somewhat dry and astringent quality of the harmony. Yet looking at it more closely, one finds in embryo practically all the constituents of the mature Rimsky-Korsakov's musical mentality. The germ of the whole of the fantastic Korsakov is to be found in the accompaniment to Vlassevna's tale of the Tsarevna Lada; for example, where in her description of the dragon Tugarin, she says that "his tail measures twenty-three yards at least":—

Ex. 38

And her short recitative phrases, which so perfectly
match the style of the popular Russian fairy-tales,
are the first example of a very individual type of
declamation one finds in Rimsky-Korsakov's later
"fairy-tale" operas, in "Snegurochka" and above
all in "Tsar Saltan" and "The Golden Cockerel,"
just as Tokmakov's :—

Ex. 39

is premonitive of the peculiar "bilina" declamation
used systematically for the first time in "Sadko."

The composer's sensitiveness to the qualities and
associative powers of different keys, which was only
just beginning to awaken when he wrote the original
version of "Pskovityanka," shows itself in the, possibly accidental, association of Tokmakov with E
flat major.   One notices, too, the progression of
major chords on a bass in descending major thirds,
when Tokmakov cries "Tsar, Gossudar, my hom-
age!" and the descending major scale, with sharpened fourth, first heard when Olga begs Tucha
not to leave her, which recurs like a dark shadow
over their love later in the work.   These points are
not outstanding features of the score, but they are
noteworthy because they are portents.

IX —RIMSKY-KORSAKOV'S GOGOL OPERAS

GOGOL made his literary début in 1831 with a volume of short stories called "Evenings on a Farm near Dikanka." They are tales of village life in his native Ukraine, based for the most part on Little Russian folk-lore, but fantastically and humorously embroidered by the writer's imagination. Historically the "Evenings" are important as the first specimens of finely wrought modern Russian prose. Indeed, Gogol's style in these early stories was almost too rich and ornamental; as one critic puts it, he was "often in danger of drugging himself with the sensuous aspects of words." The "Evenings on a Farm" hardly suggest the Gogol of "The Revizor" and "Dead Souls," but they are masterpieces of their kind—and they provide first-rate material for a certain type of musician.

The first composer to draw on the "Evenings" for operatic material was the now-almost-forgotten Alexander Serov. His choice fell on "Christmas

Eve," and a libretto was prepared for him by Polonsky, a poet whose position in Russian literature is roughly equivalent to Tennyson's in our own. But Serov died in 1871, with the music of "Christmas Eve" hardly begun, and the Imperial Russian Musical Society instituted a competition for the best setting of Polonsky's "book." Rimsky-Korsakov, Napravnik and Nicholas Rubinstein were among the members of the jury and the successful competitor was Tchaïkovsky—Serov's pupil, Solovev being awarded the second prize. Tchaïkovsky's opera, "Vakula the Smith," was produced at St. Petersburg in 1876. But the public took to "Vakula" less kindly than the judges had done, and Tchaïkovsky revised and re-christened the work more than once. After existing for a time as "Oxana's Caprice," it won success at last as "The Little Shoes." In the meantime two members of the "mighty handful" had also begun operas based on stories from the "Evenings on a Farm," and during the late 'seventies we find Mussorgsky and Rimsky-Korsakov working simultaneously at "The Fair of Sorochintsy" and "May Night" respectively. Mussorgsky died with his "Fair" still in a very fragmentary state, but Rimsky-Korsakov's opera was quickly finished—much more quickly than the first version of " Pskovityanka." He had now con-quered the mysteries of counterpoint, after writing a group of works—the String Quartet and Sextet, the Third Symphony, and the second version of " Pskovityanka "—in which it is clear that counter-point had temporarily conquered him. The edit-ing, with Balakirev, of the full scores of Glinka's operas had been his artistic salvation and in his second opera he threw overboard both dramatic realism and technique for technique's sake. Just as " Pskovityanka " is overshadowed by the theories of Dargomïzhsky, " May Night " is illuminated by Glinka's spirit.

Gogol's " Evenings " had had a warm corner in Rimsky-Korsakov's affections from the days of his childhood and " May Night " had always been his favourite tale. Later it acquired an additional sen-timental value, for he and Nadezhda Purgold had read it together on the day of their betrothal in December, 1871, and it was that very sensible and thoroughly musical woman who persuaded him to make an opera of it. But, although musical ideas for the work had been accumulating for some years, it was not until February, 1878, that the composition

was actually begun.   And begun, curiously enough,
with the third act, which Stassov and the composer
himself rightly considered the best part of the work
but which was the only part that displeased the
singers. The score was finished in October of the
same year; the piano version followed later—proof
enough that instrumental colour formed an integral
part of Rimsky-Korsakov's musical thought, even
at this stage when he was still feeling his way as an
orchestrator and writing "in Glinka's transparent
style" for the old classical orchestra, with natural
horns and trumpets. The opera, naturally ded-
icated to the composer's wife, was produced at the
Imperial Theatre, Petersburg, in January, 1880, the
scenery being that used for Tchaïkovsky's unlucky
"Vakula," with December painted into May. Sixteen years later Rimsky-Korsakov again turned to
the "Evenings," his choice this time falling on the
favourite "Christmas Eve," which Tchaïkovsky's
death had just "set free," as he put it. Only the
fear of giving offence to Tchaïkovsky had pre-
vented his setting "Christmas Eve" before. But
he rejected Polonsky's "thoroughly unsatisfactory"
libretto in favour of one of his own composition.

Rimsky-Korsakov was peculiarly well adapted to

interpret Gogol, at least the early Gogol of these tales. He had the same love of the fantastic and the naïvely humorous, and he loved sound for sound's sake very much as Gogol loved words. He followed his author very faithfully, even as regards dialogue, being content simply to put each story on the stage and clothe it with appropriate music, only underlining and filling out (particularly in the later opera) the fantastic parts and references to customs and beliefs derived from the old Slavonic mythology, which since 1875 had interested him so profoundly. That may not be the best way to write a musical drama, but it is not a bad method of turning out a jolly entertainment, and it was certainly the only way of getting Gogol inside an opera-house without taking away everything that makes him Gogol. (And, after all, even Verdi and Boïto knocked a good deal of the Shakespeare out of Shakespeare.)

The subjects of both operas are very similar. In both there are the same young peasants, the same village maidens, the same delightful, simple-minded old rascals of village dignitaries, involved in the same kind of broadly farcical situations, the same solution of the lover's difficulties by comic-

supernatural means, and the same opportunities to
introduce traditional choruses connected with the
season—Whitsuntide in one case, Christmas in the
other.*   Levko, the hero of " May Night," cannot
get his father, the *golova* or headman of the village,
to consent to his marriage with his sweetheart,
Hanna, and, finding that the old man is actually his rival, he avenges himself by egging on
the other young Cossacks to play the wildest
pranks on the *golova*, his sister-in-law and his
friend, the village scribe.   In the third act, Levko,
dreaming by the lakeside, sees the russalkas or
water-nymphs playing in the moonlight, and finds
for them a witch who is troubling them.   In grati-
tude their queen gives him a note which he is to hand
to his father.   At dawn the headman and scribe,
with the watch, find him and, recognising the disguised ringleader of the rioters, are going to seize
him—when he produces the letter.   The scribe recognises the Commissary's writing and reads : " To
the Headman, Eutychius Makogonenko.   We hear

---

* Rimsky-Korsakov, probably rightly, saw in these Christian
festivals little more than modern corruptions of the old rites connected with the vernal equinox and winter solstice. The pantheist
in the nature-loving composer sympathised more with the ancient
than with the modern forms of these ceremonies.

that you, like an old fool, instead of keeping order in the village, have been giving rise to scandal yourself. You are to permit the immediate marriage of your son, Levko Makogonenko, with the girl, Hanna Petritshenkova; likewise to repair the bridges on the post-road. If, on my arrival, I find these orders have not been obeyed, you alone will be held responsible. Commissary and retired Lieutenant, Kosma Derkatsh-Drishpantovsky." The comic-supernatural plays an even more important part in "Christmas Eve." The smith Vakula is in love with a coquettish beauty, Oxana, daughter of an old Cossack, Chub, but she only laughs at him —mockingly promising to marry him, however, if he will give her a pair of shoes like the Tsaritsa's. Now Vakula's mother, Solokha, is a witch whose numerous lovers include the Devil, the village headman, the *dyak* or clerk of the church, and Oxana's father. By ill luck they all choose this Christmas Eve to call on her, and she has to hide them one at a time in empty sacks. Vakula, coming home, carries out the sacks and, finding that chance has thus put the Devil in his power, demands to be taken at once to St. Petersburg. The Devil obeys. Vakula is admitted to the Palace and graciously received by the great Catherine, who, being in an amiable mood, laughingly grants his request for a pair of her shoes, and the smith returns in triumph to Oxana, who is already regretting the supposed loss of her lover.

When a man takes up at fifty a subject so very like one he has treated at thirty-four, comparison of the two works can hardly fail to be illuminating. Beethoven, during the corresponding period of his life, advanced from the " Eroïca " to the " Hammer-klavier " and the " Missa Solennis," Wagner from " Lohengrin " to " Tristan " and " Die Meister-singer." Before " May Night " Rimsky-Korsakov had written only one opera, " Pskovityanka." It is true that only two others, " Snegurochka " and " Mlada," intervened between the two Gogol works, but when he wrote " Christmas Eve " the composer had definitely adopted the theatre as his principal sphere of activity. During the first twenty-five years of his career, from 1865 to 1890, he had written only three operas; during the remaining eighteen years of his life he produced twelve. Moreover, the great orchestral works by which Rimsky-Korsakov is best known, the " Capriccio Espagnol," " Scheherazade," the " Easter Festival " Overture and the Piano Concerto, were all written in the period between "May Night" and "Christmas Eve."

But a mere glance at the two scores is all that is needed to see that Korsakov's style underwent no change at all comparable with Beethoven's or Wagner's. The work of 1894 does not differ materially from that of 1878, either in musical texture or in dramatic treatment. Like most of Rimsky-Korsakov's operas, they accept all the familiar conventions of classical Russian opera; melodic recitative, changing from declamation to definite tunes almost from bar to bar; occasional self-contained numbers, not always very deftly patched into the general fabric; nearly equal division of the interest between voices and orchestra, but with the voices slightly predominating; and so on. But it is obvious that considerable variation of treatment is possible within the limits of this convention. The lyrical element, for instance, with the self-contained "set numbers," may be emphasised, or it may be reduced to a minimum. Borodin definitely inclined to one tendency, Mussorgsky to the other. But Rimsky-Korsakov's practice varied considerably, according to the nature of the subject and to his own experimental inclination at the moment. The fact that the naïvely melodic element is much less important in "Christmas Eve" than in "May Night" is probably due to both causes.

The earlier work is, before everything else, lyrical. A much larger proportion of the score consists of musically independent numbers than does that of "Christmas Eve." The flow of melody is almost uninterrupted, for when the voices declaim the orchestra often picks up the threads. The melody may not always be of the highest value, but it is always undeniably alive. It helps along the most prosaic dialogue (e.g., the trio that opens the second act), provides a lovely background (the Pentecostal song in the first act), or adds an impudent commentary (as in the case of the piccolo solo, accompanied only by a side-drum roll, which makes merry over the village dignitaries as they threaten vengeance on the miscreants who have been playing tricks on them), as well as expressing the emotional content of the love scenes—the weakest parts of the score, as is so often the case in Russian operas—or hinting at the glamour of a summer night in the Ukraine, which Gogol paints so lovingly in his story. It seldom attempts to say very much, but its jolly, unaffected simplicity perfectly matches the subject. Only in the expressive passages where the composer is compelled to cut adrift from the folk-song idiom, fundamentally expressionless in Russia as in most countries, does the melodic inspiration lapse into the really commonplace.* But even when a dramatic situation seems inevitably to demand expressive music, the composer's flair for the picturesque and fantastic often offers him an avenue of escape. The opening of Act III, for instance, where Levko appears in the moonlight by the lakeside, is painted with all the orchestral skill one expects of Rimsky-Korsakov, but the music is more effective in a decorative than in an expressive capacity. The expression of Levko's feelings, intoxicated as he is with the beauty of the night, is beyond the composer's powers—as he soon proves by attempting it. But the situation is retrieved by

---

* The genuine folk-song element in both works is quite considerable. Rimsky-Korsakov borrowed most of his Malo-Russian tunes from A. I. Rubetz's collection of "216 Ukrainian Folk-Songs," and the score of "May Night" contains seven, that of "Christmas Eve" eight, melodies from this source. Thus Levko's first song, the trio and comic march in Act II, several of the choruses and various phrases in the part of the *golova's* sister-in-law in "May Night"—and the "kolyadki," Panas's comic song, Oxana's lament, Chub's duet with Solokha and other bits of melody in "Christmas Eve"—are all taken from this collection of Rubetz's.

the Cossack's naïve song with *pandura* accompaniment and after that, with the appearance of the russalkas, Rimsky-Korsakov is in his element; the scene which follows is perhaps the best part of the whole work. The *khorovod** of the russalkas suggests, particularly in the *poco più animato* sections :—

Ex. 40

the *khorovod* ("Ronde des Princesses") in "The Fire Bird" :—

Ex. 41

---

* This chorus was based on sketches made for the St. John's Eve chorus of girls in Act II of "Mlada"—the collaborative "Mlada" of 1872, of course. When Rimsky-Korsakov returned to the abandoned libretto in 1890 and set the whole of it himself, he privately expressed his regret that he had not preserved the music of this chorus for its original purpose.

Not that there is a very close resemblance as regards the actual notes (though Stravinsky's counterpoint, creeping in drowsy semitones, is also foreshadowed in a later variation of Rimsky-Korsakov's melody), but it is interesting to see how thoroughly the roots of the early Stravinsky had struck into the soil of the preceding generation—just as a descending whole-tone scale for trombones in "May Night" itself, a few bars before the piccolo solo already mentioned, in turn calls up a memory of Glinka's "Ruslan."

"May Night," like "Pskovityanka" but unlike the majority of Rimsky-Korsakov's operas, has a full-length overture based on material used later in the work : some of the russalka music of the third act, Levko's song from the same act, part of the love-duet in Act I, and the finale of the opera. "Christmas Eve," on the other hand, has only a short introduction, "Holy Eve," leading without a break into the first act of the opera. This introduction repays study, however, for a great deal can be learned from it concerning the direction taken by Rimsky-Korsakov's musical thought. After half-a-dozen bars of common chords in a most uncommon progression (on descending thirds—E,

C sharp, A, F sharp, D, B, G—an obviously artificial arrangement of which Rimsky-Korsakov was
remarkably fond) we get :—

Ex. 42

Nothing could be less adventurous harmonically.
The horn solo differs only by a single note from one
in the russalka scene of " May Night."* The wavy
triplet figure had always been one of the composer's
favourite accompaniment devices; he uses it as the

* The fact that in Ex. 42 it is clearly a "telescoped" version
of bars 6-8 throws an interesting light on Korsakov's tendency to
slip into certain melodic grooves.

background to a horn solo in the "May Night" Overture, to go no further afield. In short, there is nothing in the musical substance which distinguishes it from a dozen passages in the earlier work. The difference lies in what one can only call the essence of the music. It is not merely that the "decorative" function of the music is here the only one. Not only genuine lyrical feeling has disappeared but every trace of natural musical fertility with it. No one can deny the originality of such music or its piquancy to the ear, but it is essentially lifeless. As Sir Henry Hadow has put it, "the composer must be the parent of his ideas, not their fabricator," and music like Ex. 42 (and more than one other theme in "Christmas Eve") is unquestionably *made*. It could only have been made by an imaginative mind, it is true, but the imagination brought into play here is not essentially creative; the composer is simply playing with sounds. It is evident that Rimsky-Korsakov's delight in music was always rather naïvely sensuous, a love of sound for sound's sake; at first a love of tunes, with a consequent pleasure in setting them off to the best advantage, later (as in this case) an almost childish delight in the striking juxtaposition of chords and timbres and in such

colour-effects as rushing chromatic scale backgrounds on solo wind—frequently used in "Christmas Eve," as in the great orchestral works of a
year or two earlier, but from which the score of
"May Night" is quite free. The early orchestral
"Sadko" and "Antar" may be adduced as evidence that piquant artificiality played a part in
Rimsky-Korsakov's music from the first, but it was
not until much later that he began to devise melodic
formulæ like that in bars 5-8 of Ex. 42, which (of
course divested of the trills) is used as a vocal
melody in the first act. Here already is foreshadowed the Astrologer's music in the introduction
to "The Golden Cockerel," thirteen years later
still :—

Ex. 43

a piece of mere cold-blooded ingenuity.

The lyrical element is still important in "Christmas Eve," however. The second tableau of Act I

opens with a long aria, sung by Oxana as she admires herself in a mirror, full of arabesques and vocal cadenzas echoing clarinet cadenzas in Korsakov's familiar manner, which could be given without the least alteration as a concert number. But Vakula does his love-making to music even more characterless than Levko's in "A May Night":—

Ex. 44

("*Thou* art both mother and father to me. Thou art dearest of all"; Oxana has been taunting him that his mother is a witch.) It is this falling off in the quality, even more than in the quantity, of the melodic element in "Christmas Eve" which is so significant. The fantastic nature of the story is often better matched with fragmentary motives and pungent chords, set off with frostily glittering orchestration, than with straightforward tunes. The disquieting point is the undistinguished character of the tunes when they do appear. This is particularly noticeable in the ballet music of Act III, the "games and dances of the stars" which occur as an interlude in Vakula's wild ride through the air. The ride itself is painted with Korsakov's usual orchestral skill, though the material on which the skill is exercised—rhythmic figures after the manner of Berlioz's "Ride to the Abyss"*—is hardly interesting enough to bear such extended treatment. As Vakula nears the Palace, a fanfare in polonaise rhythm is woven into the music, and the scene in the Palace itself is accompanied almost throughout by a brilliant polonaise of the conventional kind so often written by Russian composers.

Moreover, while in "May Night" the melodic invention is fresh and original, apart from the folk-song borrowings, in "Christmas Eve," as in all the later works, we find the composer weakly echoing himself in the most obvious way. Thus the second phrase of Oxana's first song, the mirror aria already mentioned :—

---

* It is curious that two or three years before the composition of "Christmas Eve," Rimsky-Korsakov had told Yastrebtsev that he did not consider the "Course à l'abîme" "real music, but rather an extraordinarily brilliant musical *decoration*." I was amused to find that the composer had applied to Berlioz's music the very word which I, not knowing this, had used to define the nature of his own.

Ex. 45

is simply the opening of Snegurochka's first song :—

Ex. 46

in slow *tempo* ! On the other hand, there are numbers in "Christmas Eve"—the "kolyada" choruses,* the humorous duet for Chub and Solokha in Act II, the second *(allegro)* part of the mirror aria, Oxana's lament in the last scene, the epilogue "in memory of Gogol" (most of them directly based on actual folk-melody, it will be noticed)—as fresh and delightful as anything in "May Night" and

---

* A custom very similar to our own carolling, but limited to Christmas Eve. The songs were usually about the birth of Christ, and at the end the singers, young men and girls of the village, would offer good wishes to the members of the household and receive presents of bread, money, etc. Gogol suggests that the word "kolyada" may be derived from an old Slavonic deity, one of the protectors of the sun-god in his battle with the powers of winter. Fanciful etymologists have found its origin in the Latin *kalendæ*. But Rimsky-Korsakov shared Gogol's opinion, for he makes Vakula, during his return from Petersburg, see the aerial procession of the Light Gods, Ovsenya and Kolyada, while the Christmas bells ring out from the village below.

which, as far as the musical texture is concerned, might belong to that score. (It would be difficult to find any pages in "Tristan" that might be transferred to "Lohengrin"!) Indeed, considered as a whole, "Christmas Eve" is perhaps the finer work of the two. If so much the less inspiration went to its making, the making itself is more skilfully done. When he wrote "May Night" Rimsky-Korsakov was wealthier, but by the time he reached "Christmas Eve" he had learned how to get better value for his money.

In "May Night" the themes have their immediate, superficial value only. Leit-motives are used but they could hardly be used less. Some of the music of the russalka scene is heard in the first act when Levko tells his sweetheart the story of the haunted house. (It is curious that in all Rimsky-Korsakov's operas, especially the later ones, the music associated with fantastic and supernatural scenes and characters is not only more highly seasoned harmonically, but more elaborately organised thematically, than that associated with the real and natural elements.) The old headman is associated throughout with two fragments of melody, often combined contrapuntally, to which he relates his never-

ending reminiscence of the time when he was chosen
as guide to the Empress Catherine; and another,
related to one of these, which reminds us of his wooing of Hanna. In the last scene when the scribe
examines the mysterious note, and once or twice
later, a horn dreamily recalls the queen of the russalkas. That is all. The leit-motif is not used
systematically or, except in the last mentioned
instance, with dramatic value or subtlety.

In "Christmas Eve," on the other hand, there are
a number of themes definitely associated throughout
with Chub, with the Devil, with the stars, with the
idea of flight, with witches, and so on. The theme
of Vakula himself :—

Ex. 47

is used with merciless consistency every time he appears, and with little modification or development
(though perhaps the second bar of Ex. 44 is derived
from it). And in addition to motives proper, there
is a good deal of reminiscence of whole passages, a
device which has a certain dramatic value—and a
still greater, perhaps, in knitting together the whole

musical fabric. Towards the end, for instance, when Vakula has brought back the shoes, his love-theme (Ex. 44) steals back on the clarinet* and the smith himself sings the same melody to which Oxana had previously taunted him.

One can even detect a difference in the nature of the humour in which both scores abound. In " May Night " the humour is more natural, a spontaneous bubbling over of high spirits. Unlike so many attempts at musical humour the music is genuinely funny. It would be difficult to listen to the *hopak* or the recitatives of the drunken Kalennik, to the *golova's* absurd wooing or to the ensembles in the second act without smiling, even at a concert performance in a language one did not understand. (Incidentally, the " laughter " in this act is a naturalistic record of the infectious, musical laugh of one of the composer's acquaintances.) Even the whole-tone scale already referred to, underlining the enraged headman's threats of punishment, has an irresistibly comic effect. But in " Christmas Eve " the humour is at once more subtle, more sophisticated and more laboured. The fact that the church

---

* A favourite dramatic device of Rimsky-Korsakov's. He uses it most effectively in "The Tsar's Bride."

clerk sings old liturgical melodies when he is making love to Solokha ought to be funny, Korsakov seems to have felt; but, actually, it is merely ridiculous. And the music which accompanies the absurd scene in Patsyuk's hut is bizarre and fantastic rather than humorous. Only the duet of the two old women in the last scene really recaptures the broad, frank humour of the earlier opera. In his later works, Rimsky-Korsakov's humour tends to take the form of grave and matter-of-fact musical treatment of absurdities, though in "The Golden Cockerel" it is both more obvious and more biting, humorous caricature flavoured with rather sophisticated wit, and in "Tsar Saltan" is tinctured with the delightful, indefinable something which gives that rambling opera its peculiar charm.

Rimsky-Korsakov's gradual transition from a simple, lyrical musical idiom to one in which artificiality, piquancy and technical sophistication predominated may be attributed to one or more of various causes, but it certainly has nothing in common with the normal process of development undergone by creative artists in general. It may have been due to mere pedantic absorption in musical ingenuities as his mastery of technique became more and more sure; to conscious modification conditioned by extra-musical factors, such as the problems of music-drama as an art-form; to actual exhaustion of natural melodic fertility; or to the possibility which cannot be entirely ruled out, that Rimsky-Korsakov never was fertile in the true sense and that his apparent melodic gift was purely imitative. There is evidence in favour of all these views, except the last. And in considering the modification of Rimsky-Korsakov's operatic, apart from that in his musical style, it is well to bear in mind that " Pskovityanka," his first stage-work, is a very self-conscious essay in the problems of musical drama as they presented themselves to the Russian composers of that period. Perhaps as he went on, his intellect and his instinct gave different answers to the same problems. We must remember that Korsakov was always painfully aware of his processes, even musically. No composer more *musically* introspective has ever lived, though he knew the artistic dangers of self-consciousness—" Self-analysis is fatal to creation."

It may be thought that, in comparing these two Gogol operas, I have laid too much emphasis on differences which are astonishingly small, considering the interval which separated them. But the very absence of any more obvious modification of style during fourteen years might surely be taken as evidence that the composer was lacking in the exuberance natural to the creative artist. And it is certainly true that the traces of sterility discernible in "Christmas Eve" are much more apparent in later works. Nor was Korsakov happily unaware of all this; on the contrary it is characteristic that he was far more acutely conscious of it than most of those about him were. Yastrebtsev, who saw a great deal of him during the composition of "Christmas Eve," tells us of his frequent moods of melancholy dissatisfaction and disillusionment. Even when the first two scenes were already finished, Korsakov spoke of the possibility of his not going on with the opera, as it was "not worth while." "You know," he added, "I see clearly that this music is far from being as good as that of 'Snegurochka,' for example, and that my talent is on the wane. And yet I don't find it *difficult* to write." We know from his memoirs that he had just been passing through one of those mental crisis which seem to afflict so many Russian artists in middle age. But how far this crisis was responsible for his despondency or partial sterility or both—or vice versa—it is impossible to do more than guess. They were almost certainly inter-related to some extent, but it would be only too easy to exaggerate the importance of this crisis by overlooking the fatal attractions which experiment and technical dexterity always held for the composer.

X— SNOW MAIDEN

THE gradual hardening and over-intellectualisation of Rimsky-Korsakov's musical tissue did not begin immediately after the composition of "May Night," for his melodic fertility is heard at its freshest in the opera which followed it, "Snegurochka" ("Snow Maiden"). The composer already begins, in the music associated with Tsar Berendey, to toy with finely wrought artificial thematic subtleties, to play that jig-saw game with fragmentary motives of which his later "miniature style" consists. But as a whole the music of "Snegurochka" sounds captivatingly spontaneous, so fresh and delightful that a good case might be made for placing it at the head of all Rimsky-Korsakov's operas. Musically it is in every way finer than "May Night." The composer was now completely master of his craft and completely *himself*. And he was conscious of it. "When I finished 'Snegurochka' I felt that I was a mature musician and that, as an opera-composer, I had firm ground under my feet." Leit-motives are already used far more liberally than in the two earlier operas, though not on Wagnerian lines, for Rimsky-Korsakov as yet knew his Wagner only very superficially. But apart from this material binding together of the music, "Snegurochka" has that unity of spirit which belongs only to living works of art. The transparence of its harmonic and orchestral texture, the flavour of its melodies, are unmistakable. It may not be literally true to say that music from any of Rimsky-Korsakov's other works would at once sound out of place if incorporated in this "spring fairy tale," but "Snegurochka" is such a living, clearly coloured whole, a musical world of its own, that it seems as if any such interpolation would be jarringly noticeable.

When Rimsky-Korsakov first came across Ostrovsky's dramatic poem in 1874* he was not impressed

---

* It had been produced in Moscow the year before, with incidental music (nineteen numbers) by Tchaïkovsky. When Rimsky-Korsakov's opera was brought out in January, 1882, Tchaïkovsky, far away in Rome, wrote to his publisher, Jurgenson, in terms which show how well-grounded was Rimsky-Korsakov's fear of giving offence to the other by following him in setting Gogol's "Christmas Eve": "Is it not equally unpleasant to you to feel that 'our subject' has been taken from us, and that Lel will now sing new music to the old words? It is as though someone had

by it, a fact which he explained to himself in after
years by the reflection that he was then still
too much under the influence of Mussorgsky's ideas
about "naturalism" to be attracted by such an altogether unreal subject. But we must remember that
in 1874 he had not yet begun to interest himself in
the old Slavonic sun-worship which is the philosophical essence of "Snegurochka." It was not
till a year or two later that in making his collection
of folk-songs, the necessity of finding out something about the rites with which many of the songs
were originally connected drove him to the study of
authorities like Afanasev and Sakharov and aroused
in him such an extraordinary interest in Slavonic
mythology that "pictures of the old pagan time and
its spirit rose before my inward eye with the greatest
clearness and attracted me with irresistible power."
From that time onward Rimsky-Korsakov tried to
graft mythological elements on to nearly everything
he touched, whether congruously or not. "May
Night" had offered him very little scope. Beyond

---

forcibly torn away a piece of myself and offered it to the public
in a new and brilliant setting. I could cry with mortification."
But Tchaïkovsky afterwards had the grace to recognise the superiority of his rival's music. In 1887 he notes in his diary that he
has "read through Korsakov's 'Snegurochka,' and was astonished
at his mastery. I envy him and ought to be ashamed of it."

turning Gogol's "souls of the drowned" into russalkas and introducing quasi-ritualistic choruses and
dances, there was nothing much to be done with it.
So when in the February of 1880 he again read Ostrovsky's "Snegurochka," it was probably not so
much the "marvellous poetic beauties" to which his
eyes were now opened, as he thought, as the absolutely congenial nature of the fantastic-mythological
subject which excited in him the wish to make an
opera of it. In 1874 it had meant nothing to him;
now it answered to all his inmost needs as an artist.
And consequently it seemed to him that "there was
no finer material in the world for me than this : there
were no more poetic figures in existence than
Snegurochka, Lel or the Spring Fairy, no better
land than that of the Berendeys with its wonderful
Tsar; there was no religion or philosophy more satisfying than the worship of the sun-god, Yarilo."

And to understand Rimsky-Korsakov properly we
must realise that when he speaks like this he is not
merely using ordinary enthusiastic hyperbole. He
literally means what he says. He longed for absurd, delightful fairy-tale countries like the pre-
historic land of the Berendeys, with its kindly
despot and its gaily painted houses of carved wood,

as Brahms longed for his lost childhood, Franck for
heaven and Wagner for a new earth. In this intellectual rationalist, with his utter disbelief in "everything supernatural, fantastic or visionary," the instinctive longing for the irrational was sometimes
so intense that he could not only as an artist create
Nietzsche's "veil of illusion" but believe in it himself for the time being. The subject of "Snegurochka" awoke in him the dormant pantheist.
Always an ardent nature-lover, his "sun worship"
was a real and intense aspiration, strikingly like that
which Richard Jefferies describes in "The Story of
my Heart."*

Rimsky-Korsakov tells us in his memoirs how he
wrote "Snegurochka" in the hot and thundery summer of 1880, at Stelëvo in the heart of the country,
composing all day and every day—when he was not
looking for mushrooms or helping his wife preserve
fruit from the great garden, shaded with fruit-trees
and "filled with the ceaseless twittering of birds."
"In every gnarled branch or tree-trunk I saw the
Wood Spirit or his dwelling; in the forest of Vol-

---

* "The Story of my Heart" was published in 1883, the year
after the first performance of "Snegurochka." It is curious that
two such different manifestations of the same primitive impulse
in man should have appeared almost simultaneously.

chinets, the magic wood in which Mizgir lost himself; in an isolated hill, Mount Kopïtets, Yarilo's mountain." Publicly, in the "Record of my Life," Rimsky-Korsakov made only this fanciful confession. But the completeness and reality of his abandonment to illusion is shown by his confession to Yastrebtsev that in old trees, the stream, Lake Vrevo, he saw something strange and supernatural. It seemed to him that the animals and birds, trees and flowers, were more conscious than men of the magical and supernatural, that they better understood the language of nature. "You will say that all this was dreadfully nonsensical, and yet it seemed to me that it was so in reality. I believed in it all as ardently as a child, as a dreamer who entirely gives himself up to his dreams, and yet—remarkably enough—the world seemed to me loftier, more comprehensible, and I was, as it were, fused with it."

So powerfully stirred, Rimsky-Korsakov found that the music poured from him easily. Directly he re-read the play, even before he rushed off to Moscow to get Ostrovsky's permission to take liberties with the libretto, ideas came thick and fast— "motives, themes and chord-progressions, while the moods and colours of particular moments became ever more distinct." During the summer at Stelëvo his thoughts flowed so quickly that he was unable to write " Snegurochka " directly in full score, as he had done " May Night," but was obliged to follow the more usual practice and make a piano score. The whole opera was completely sketched out in this way between June 1 and August 12. The scoring, for large orchestra, was done during the following winter, and a year later " Snegurochka " was given for the first time at the Maryinsky Theatre, Petersburg.

It is evident from all this, though the evidence of the music itself is sufficient, that " Snegurochka " was genuinely inspired. Yet it is curious to find how much even of this, probably the most spontaneous of all Rimsky-Korsakov's scores, was borrowed or calculated. The synthetic, rather than spontaneous, nature of the folk-songish melodies with which the score is strewn has already been referred to. In addition there are numerous borrowings of actual folk-songs : e.g., the second part of the choral ballet of the birds; three melodies in the " Butterweek " music of the Prologue appear as Nos. 41, 46 and 47 in Rimsky-Korsakov's own collection, Op. 24, and

14

a fourth, to use the composer's own expression, "sacrilegiously reminds one of a melody in the Russian requiem mass"—here, he considered, restored to something like its original pagan form; the betrothal rites in the first act are introduced by a snatch of a song in praise of bachelorhood (Op. 24, No. 100) played by the clarinet, and the principal melody is a bridal song (Op. 24, No. 78); the opening of the third act, the festival in the Holy Wood—introduction, chorus and Bobïl's song about the beaver —is entirely based on folk-melodies (Op. 24, Nos. 16 and 54, and a dance-theme, a variant of the familiar "Kamarinskaya"); the millet sowing ritual and the antiphonal song to "Grandfather" Lado, the god of Spring and Love, which open "May Night" are repeated in the last act of "Snegurochka," while the people are waiting for the sunrise, but in this case Rimsky-Korsakov has used the two melodies to these words noted by Balakirev.* And then, in addition to lesser borrowings such as the pastoral motives for horn, clarinet and *cor anglais*, associ-

---

* From the Nizhny-Novgorod and Pskov Governments. They appear as Nos. 8 and 9 in Balakirev's "Collection of Forty Russian Folk-Songs." In "May Night" Rimsky-Korsakov kept more closely to a variant from the Saratov Government (No. 48 of his Op. 24.)

ated with the shepherd Lel, there is the call of the
heralds in Act II when they summon the people to
hear the Tsar's judgment, which the composer remembered from his childhood days when each
summer a messenger would come from the Tikhvin
Monastery, and to this melody, so like those of the
old *biliny*, summon the women of the village to help
the monks with their hay-making.   Yet all these
borrowings sound so natural, fall so fittingly into
place, that one accepts them without a murmur.   It
is the same with the bird-calls, "phonographically"
reproduced in Beethoven's manner, not stylised and
idealised in Wagner's—the cock-crow of the oboe
at the very beginning (as it were, Nature's trumpet
call heralding the coming of Spring), the cries of
magpie, cuckoo, bullfinch and the rest.   Rimsky-
Korsakov's musical fantasy takes complete charge
of this "given" material, weaving it into such delightful patterns, harmonising it with such freshness
and clarity, tinting it with such bright, transparent
orchestral colours, that it becomes as definitely *his*
as if it had all sprung originally from his own brain.
Rimsky-Korsakov wrote nothing more deliciously
absurd, more perfectly characteristic, than the
choral ballet of the birds in the Prologue, with its

naïve piping tunes and that "ceaseless twittering" accompaniment straight from the garden at Stelëvo. Incidentally, another "twittering" theme, which appears first in the introduction :—

Ex. 48

and later (in slower *tempo* on a solo horn) becomes one of the motives of the Spring Fairy, fore-shadows a very important motif in "Kitezh." Rimsky-Korsakov in a fragmentary analysis of "Snegurochka," written in 1905 and published posthumously, calls Ex. 48 the theme of "general bird-twittering," the chorus of Nature, while the similar theme in "Kitezh" is identified with Fev-ronya, the pure child of Nature, and is evolved from the music of the murmuring forest.

Rimsky-Korsakov's own melodic invention is never more delightful than in "Snegurochka." The songs of Lel the shepherd singer are particularly beautiful. Rimsky-Korsakov had a special genius for the unaccompanied or barely accompanied song ; his melodic lines are often so complete in them-

selves that to harmonise them is only to write out
what is already fully implied, though he does this
only too frequently. Lel's first song is entirely
without accompaniment. The third, that which follows the tumblers' dance in the festival in the Holy
Wood, accompanied at first only by a drum-roll, is
specially interesting as it is the occasion of one of
the earliest appearances of a melodic pattern (a)
which constantly recurs throughout Rimsky-
Korsakov's later work :—

Ex. 49 *

In this opera we find it also in the accompaniment
to Snegurochka's first song (just after the words " I
live for melody alone ") and in the music of the kiss-
scene in the third act. It appears again in " Sadko "
(Nezhata's " Slava " at the end of the harbour
scene), " The Tsar's Bride " (orchestral prelude to
the sextet), " Tsar Saltan." (the Tsarevna Lebeda's

* I have followed Edward Agate's translation of the libretto
throughout. (Bessel Edition : English agents, Boosey and
Hawkes.)

song at the beginning of the last scene), "The
Golden Cockerel" (Amelfa's music)—to mention
only a few of the passages where it recurs in its
original, unmodified form. Whence did Rimsky-
Korsakov get it? Probably from the familiar
"Sidel Vanya," the chief melody of the *andante
cantabile* of Tchaïkovsky's D major Quartet, for it
is not, like most of the other formulæ which recur
in Rimsky-Korsakov's music, a pattern common to
a number of folk-songs. In addition to these unchanged reappearances it frequently recurs in
slightly modified forms, as, for example, in Fevronya's glorious phrase in "Kitezh" as she
addresses the "strange flowers" springing up about
her :—

Ex. 50

One expects, of course, to be able to trace the derivation of a great many of a composer's themes
from a single germ. The curious point is that
Rimsky-Korsakov, in these later operas, so often re-

peated formulæ with only the slightest modification
or even with none at all. There is remarkably little
evidence in Rimsky-Korsakov of the operation of
that ripening, continually modifying and developing
process one finds going on in the minds of other
composers. His melodic thought slips easily into
old, familiar channels without wearing them into
fresh forms. But Ex. 49 (a) is too important to be
dismissed as something accidentally remembered in
after years. A little monograph might be written
on the function of its first three notes alone in Rimsky-Korsakov's *melos*, and another on the group (b)
in Ex. 49, an unconscious modification of Ex. 48.*
It is no exaggeration to say that the last bar-and-a-
half of Ex. 49 contains the essence of Rimsky-
Korsakov's most characteristic melodic thought.

All this curious arrangement and rearrangement
of (not development of, or growth from) a few elementary melodic patterns, rather suggesting the old
Chinese game of tangrams, must of course have
been quite unconscious. But Rimsky-Korsakov
often plays quite consciously with tiny motives in
the same way. He begins to do it here in the Tsar
Berendey's music, in which we can watch his first

---

* Compare also Ex. 39 in "Pskovityanka."

experiments in this "miniature style." The Tsar's
theme :—

Ex. 51

is dissected into its constituent three-note motives,
which are rearranged :—

Ex. 52

and the new figure thus obtained counterpointed
with a previously heard march-theme (extended
from the first four notes of Ex. 51) :—

Ex. 53

all in the brief march which accompanies the entry
of the Tsar and his courtiers in Act II. But there
is still very little of this artificial mosaic-music in
"Snegurochka." The fantastic element in the
music is prominent only in the snowstorm of the
Prologue and in the scene of the enchanted wood.
Yet it is characteristic of Rimsky-Korsakov that he
was particularly pleased with the chord, made up
of the six notes of the whole-tone scale, which he
devised for the moment when the Wood Spirit
seizes Mizgir from behind.

But in one's memories of the opera these moments
are lost amidst the mass of purely lyrical music : the
Spring Fairy's aria in the Prologue, Snegurochka's
arietta, "Ah ! what woe is mine !" and her charming
"Gathering Berries" song (of which the beautiful
adagio section, recollected in the third act when
Snegurochka finds herself abandoned by Lel, is the
forerunner of such masterpieces as Marfa's great
aria in "The Tsar's Bride" and Fevronya's "praise
of solitude" in "Kitezh"), Lel's songs, the Tsar's
two cavatinas, the love music, the hymn to the Tsar,
and the final chorus in 11/4 time in praise of Yarilo.
The love-music is, as so often in Russian opera, a
little insipid, just as the element of human tragedy

in the story is quite unmatched in the music.   But
there is genuine warmth and passion in the orchestral passage which accompanies the "kiss scene"
and in Snegurochka's ecstatic surrender to Mizgir
in the last act, where part of her chief theme (which
the composer intentionally made "bright, graceful
and playful, but cold in spite of its liveliness") is
transformed into a phrase which perfectly expresses
the warm, human emotion she now feels for the first
time.   If this lyrical current in "Snegurochka"
sometimes runs thin and degenerates into mere pret-
tiness, as in the schoolgirls'-operetta-chorus of
flowers at the beginning of the last act, it also
broadens into passages of marvellous beauty, such
as the scene of the blind *gusli*-players which opens
Act II.   To a few simple chords on piano and harp
(a device borrowed from Glinka for the suggestion
of these old national instruments), the curtain goes
up revealing a hall in the Tsar's palace, fantastically
carved and painted like all the houses of the Berendeys.   The Tsar himself sits on a golden throne,
painting on a pillar, while his blind singers, playing
their *guslis*, sing his praises.   Nothing could be
simpler than the music, a modal melody sung by a
few basses in unison (with a curious two-part refrain)

and accompanied only by the quiet harp and piano
chords :—

Ex. 54

yet the scene is one of the most memorable in all
Rimsky-Korsakov's operas. He often introduced
similar episodes of bards and pilgrims singing to
the accompaniment of national instruments in later
works, but never again achieved anything quite as
gravely beautiful. The modal nature of the melody
(æolian) is characteristic of another tendency of
Rimsky-Korsakov's, to which he allowed full play
in "Snegurochka." He had already introduced
modal folk-melodies in "May Night"; now for the
first time he actually composed in the old modes.
And he wrote in them easily and naturally, reopen-

ing (as he justly claimed) a rich old vein neglected
by all but one or two Western composers—Liszt in
his "Totentanz" (variations on the "Dies Iræ")
for piano and orchestra, and in the middle section
(on the "Pange lingua") of his "Night Procession"
(Episode from Lenau's "Faust"), and Berlioz in his
"Nubian Dance" and his overture to "The Flight
into Egypt." Lel's first song and the hymn of the
Berendeys before the trial in Act II are particularly happy examples of Korsakov's modal writing.
The pentatonic scale is another tonal characteristic
of many Russian folk-melodies (e.g., that which
figures here as Bobil's "beaver" song), which left
its mark on Rimsky-Korsakov's music from the
"Snegurochka" period onward. Some of his most
typical melodies (for instance, that which opens and
closes the Hindu merchant's song in "Sadko") are
pentatonic. On the other hand, the curious clipped
mezzo-recitative phrases of the dialogue between
Kupava and the Tsar :—

Ex. 55

$(\quad = 72)$

55 Kup: Hear me, O mighty Tsar. Tsar: Speak, for I listen. *etc.*

the exact musical equivalent of the style and metre
of Russian fairy-tale poetry, have no prototypes in
popular music. This highly effective type of recitative was the composer's own invention, here introduced only episodically, but very freely employed
in the later fairy-tale operas.

In "Snegurochka" and the coeval "Legend"
("Skazka") for orchestra, based on the prologue to
Pushkin's "Ruslan and Lyudmila," Rimsky-Korsakov definitely emerged as a master orchestrator and
a highly individual one. We cannot study the
scoring of his early compositions, as he afterwards
reorchestrated everything written before "May
Night." We only know, from his own account, that
from the beginning he had an instinctive feeling for
orchestral colour and that even in the 'sixties he was
looked upon as the best orchestrator of the
"Kuchka." Perhaps his early scoring was effective
enough in a rather crude way. As we have seen,
his editorial work on the scores of Glinka's operas
had left him deeply impressed with Glinka's delicate and transparent orchestral texture, and hence
"May Night," the first of his scores which we can
study in its original form, is possibly less individual
than the earlier works. This period of Glinka-

worship probably served to purify his orchestral style as, on his own confession, it did his harmonic and contrapuntal texture. But in "Snegurochka" the composer's inclination for bright, primary colours—and colour for colour's sake—asserted itself (probably we ought to say, reasserted itself). He has called attention himself to the profusion of solo passages for violin, 'cello, flute, oboe and cor anglais and horn, above all for the clarinet, which was at that time a pet instrument of his. And it is these bright, unmixed colours, the musical counterpart of the gaily painted houses of the Berendeys, which give the opera so much of its translucent quality and unique flavour. Rimsky-Korsakov never quite recaptured this delightful naïveté of timbre, for before he wrote his next opera, "Mlada," he had undergone an experience which left indelible marks on his later scores. The "Ring" had been given in St. Petersburg (1888) by a German company under Muck. Wagner's treatment of the orchestra "dumbfounded" him and in his memoirs he naïvely confesses how he and Glazunov attended all the rehearsals and industriously studied and copied the German master's methods. And this was the mature master who, the year before, had produced such marvels of orchestration as "Scheherazade," the "Capriccio Espagnol" and the "Easter" Overture! Humility is a virtue, no doubt, and in the long run Rimsky-Korsakov benefited from this fertilisation of his style by Wagner's. "Mlada" was the only work in which his orchestral writing was really saturated by Wagnerian methods; already in "Christmas Eve," still more in "Sadko," his individuality began to reassert itself, all the richer for the experience. But one cannot help regretting the fatal ease with which Rimsky-Korsakov succumbed to temporary fascinations.

So "Snegurochka," the first fruit of the mature Rimsky-Korsakov as purified by Glinka and still untainted by Wagner, was also the last in the sphere of opera. Important as the naïvely lyrical element remained in his work, it was never again almost the sole one. But it is interesting to see how far Rimsky-Korsakov had progressed in the use of leit-motives in "Snegurochka" while he was still acquainted with Wagner "only a little and very superficially." His claim that he employed them quite differently from Wagner seems to be largely justified. They do not supply the material from which the orchestral part is almost wholly woven; they are still used dramatically, to make points, rather than systematically. But already in "Snegurochka" Korsakov had advanced far beyond "May Night," and the hearing of the "Ring" confirmed his tendency to Wagnerian "logic" so that by the time he wrote "Christmas Eve," as we have seen, he had begun to organise his leit-motif system very thoroughly indeed. As he points out in his memoirs, his leit-motives are often fragments of extended melodies such as that of Snegurochka herself and the Tsar's theme, Ex. 51. The Tsar's first cavatina, for instance, is accompanied by the motif (a) in Ex. 52, treated as an *ostinato* figure on a solo 'cello. And then again Korsakov uses mere chord-progressions or even single unusual chords, like that of the Wood Spirit, "more difficult to distinguish than Wagner's leit-motives, which often remind one of coarse military trumpet-calls."He dwells on this point with characteristic self-satisfaction, oblivious of the uselessness in opera of making points which can only be appreciaated by "a good, trained ear." Rimsky-Korsakov often became so deeply engrossed in the purely intellectual aspects (one is often tempted to say, the mere "paper" aspect) of music, that he quite lost sight of the true function of devices like the leit-motif. He forgot that a curious chord is likely to interest even a trained musician more for its own than for the action's sake, that it communicates no feeling and evokes no memory —except of its own previous appearance.

In the already mentioned analysis of "Snegurochka," Rimsky-Korsakov distinguished between the true leit-motives in the work and those themes and complete melodies which recur, partly or as wholes, as reminiscences for the sake of dramatic effect. The same distinction may be applied to the motives of all his later operas. But in all of them there is a great deal of important material which does not recur at all, which serves its purpose episodically and is then thrown aside; Rimsky-Korsakov never went quite as far as Wagner in weaving his musical fabric entirely from leit-motives, except perhaps in the unimportant "Kashcheï the Immortal." Nor, curiously enough, are Rimsky-Korsakov's theme-reminiscences always dramatic in purpose; sometimes their function is purely formal. In "May Night" the composer had already broken away from "dramatic truth" enough to give symmetrical *musical* shape to separate numbers. Beginning with "Snegurochka" he now attempted to

give a distinct, architectural pattern to bigger
stretches of music (scenes like the "Butterweek"
episode, that of the blind *gusli*-players and the
games in the Holy Wood), a tendency which he
pushed to its extreme limit in parts of "'Sadko" and
"Kitezh." In accordance with the same desire to
formalise, he also organised the key-schemes of his
operas with as much care as if they had been symphonic works. "Snegurochka" and all the later
operas were laid out in accordance with a carefully
prepared modulation plan, a plan not arbitrary but
conditioned by two factors, the composer's peculiarly acute sense of key-colour and this need for
architectural cohesion and symmetry. Rimsky-
Korsakov's feeling for the "absolute" quality and
colour of each key had begun to awaken as early as
1867, but "Snegurochka" was the first composition
in which it played a predominant part in determining the choice of keys for each part of the work.
Thus the idea of Spring is connected throughout the
opera with A major, "the key of youth, gladness,
Spring and dawn," as he calls it in the "Record of
my Musical Life." D flat is associated with warmth
and love, as in the Spring Fairy's aria in the Prologue, the song in which Lel tells the Tsar that his

gift of song comes from the Sun-God ("In my words and in my songs brightly burn his glowing rays"), the kiss scene, and the love-duet for Snegurochka and Mizgir. D major is the colour of bright daylight; A minor suggested to Rimsky-Korsakov "the glow of sunset reflected on a white, cold, snow-covered winter landscape"; and so on. Rimsky-Korsakov did not, of course, allow himself to be rigidly bound by these associations. There are plenty of passages in "Snegurochka" and the later operas where this rather tormenting obsession of his seems to have left him in peace. But it would be quite true to say that he associated certain keys with particular moods and emotions as consciously and consistently as he did leit-motives with characters.

"Snegurochka" must be given an important place in Rimsky-Korsakov's life-work for another, a non-musical, reason. "Pskovityanka" is pure, realistic drama. "May Night" is a humorous-fantastic tale told for its own sake, with mythological trimmings of no special significance. But with "Snegurochka" begins Rimsky-Korsakov's dabbling with that symbolism one discerns dimly in "Sadko," more clearly in "Kitezh," and which, turned bitter, gives "The Golden Cockerel" its subtle flavour of irony. Rimsky-Korsakov read into this "Spring fairy-tale" a deeper significance than Ostrovsky perhaps intended, possibly more than he himself had seen in it at first. Years afterwards when he sat down, in 1905, to analyse this favourite work, he divided its characters into three categories: the purely mythical incarnations of natural forces, like Snegurochka's parents Spring and Frost; the ordinary mortals, like Kupava and Mizgir; and the three half-real, half-mythical characters—Snegurochka herself, the wise old Tsar Berendey, and the shepherd singer Lel. And it was this last group that particularly interested him, especially Lel. The Tsar is the perfect "paternal" ruler. He personifies the social life of a legendary golden age when men were happier because they were closer to Nature, when kings were also priests and the gods still real and visible.* As Rimsky-Korsakov points out, the Tsar is "ever old" as Lel is "ever young." They represent things which are ageless and timeless. The significance of Snegurochka herself, Spring outside like her mother, Winter within like her father, is not so clearly defined. She seems to

---

* At the very end of the opera Yarilo is seen on the summit of his sacred hill—a youth robed in white, bearing in his hands a human head and a sheaf of corn.

be merely a figure in a pretty fairy-tale, one more of those fairy beings, common to folk-lore the world over, whose gratified longing for human things leads to their destruction. But Lel is highly significant. He is the ideal type of folk-artist, a forerunner of Sadko. Like Sadko, he personifies music itself and its miracle-working power. (And like Sadko, too, he is rather heartless and irresponsible.) He gets his music, his power, immediately from the sun, from nature, and it is difficult to avoid the conjecture that the composer saw something of himself in the legendary figures of Lel and Sadko. There is, however, no trace of subjective expression in Lel's music (or in Sadko's).

And there is no trace of meaning, and little of definite emotion, in the music of the opera as a whole. The composer's possible self-identification with Lel and the deeper meaning we know he read into the poem are not expressed musically, only observed with Korsakov's characteristic detachment. It is impossible to agree with Russian critics like Lapshin, who sees in this "pantheistic Hymn to Nature and glowing apotheosis of love" a "worthy companion-piece to 'Tristan'" and who draws a parallel between Snegurochka's final "And yet I faint! With ecstasy or pain?" and Isolde's "Liebestod"! Rimsky-Korsakov's music is never more than that of a delightful fairy-tale. But it is so charming and, in its way, so perfect that one can understand the composer's "conviction" (in 1892, with "Sadko" not yet written) "that 'Snegurochka' is my best work," even if one cannot endorse his amusing, and characteristically complacent, reflection that it was "not only that but perhaps, on the whole, the best of all contemporary operas."

XI — SADKO

THE story of Sadko, the poor minstrel who
became rich through the love of the Sea
King's daughter, which occurs in the eleventh century "Novgorod cycle" of *biliny* or epic legends,
had attracted Rimsky-Korsakov as early as 1867,
when he wrote a short symphonic poem on the subject.* The idea of turning it into an opera had
occurred to him in the 1880's but nothing definite
came of it till the summer of 1894, when the music-
ologist Findeisen sent him the outline of a libretto.
Rimsky-Korsakov was not altogether satisfied with
Findeisen's plan and finally decided again to be his
own librettist, drawing on the story of "The King
of the Sea," from Afanasev's "Russian Fairy
Tales," the "Kniga Golubinaya" or "Dove Book,"
and other sources for his text and for various incidents not found in the original Sadko legend.
Stassov had a hand in the planning of this as of so

---

* His Opus 5. It was revised in 1891.

many other Russian operas and it was on his suggestion that Rimsky-Korsakov inserted the first scene, that of the banquet in the council-room at Novgorod. The composer had already decided to utilise the material of his early symphonic poem again in the opera.

As usual Rimsky-Korsakov spent the summer of 1894 in the country, on the estate of Vechasha by the shores of Lake Pezno, "an enchanting spot of earth" of which he gives a delightful picture in his memoirs. He was working hard at "Christmas Eve," but he could not get "Sadko" out of his head and various ideas—the melody of Sadko's aria in the fifth scene and the first of the songs of the *gusli*-player, Nezhata, among others occurred to him at this period. He takes an almost Pepysian pleasure in recalling precisely where these thoughts visited him—"on the long bathing-stage built out into the lake. It led out through high thick rushes; on one side one saw the fine old willows of the garden, on the other stretched Lake Pezno."

The completion of "Christmas Eve" and the difficulties attending its production, with other matters, thrust "Sadko" into the background, and although Rimsky-Korsakov was full of ideas, and the libretto of the work as originally planned was practically finished, only the first scene was completed when the composer returned to Vechasha in 1895. This summer was entirely devoted to "Sadko." The first, second, fourth, fifth, sixth and seventh tableaux were written, and the first and second actually scored, when the composer made a curious addition to his plan by deciding to introduce Sadko's faithful wife, Lyubava, who was mentioned but did not appear in the original version. This interpolation, which necessitated the writing of the third tableau as we now have it, as well as additions to the fourth and seventh tableaux, seems to have been suggested by V. I. Belsky, a man of varied intellectual gifts—jurist, scientist and mathematician—who was afterwards to be the librettist of "Tsar Saltan," "Kitezh" and "The Golden Cockerel." Rimsky-Korsakov had met Belsky the previous winter in St. Petersburg and found in him not only the possessor of common interests in Russian antiquity and Russian folk-music, but also an enthusiastic admirer of his own compositions and those of the so-called "new Russian school" in general. Belsky was spending this summer on an estate only about six miles from Vechasha, and the

two men passed much time together. Belsky suggested various additions to the plan of "Sadko,"
with the result that, as the composer afterwards admitted, the work became too long. At first Rimsky-
Korsakov could not make up his mind to any altera-
tions in his scheme. Not until the opera in its original form was practically finished did a curious
circumstance turn the scale. The composer tells us
that he felt a vague wish to write something in the
key of F minor which he had long neglected and
which did not appear in "Sadko." It was this
"vague wish" which "irresistibly" impelled him to
compose Lyubava's lament in that key. The aria
satisfied him and he at once asked Belsky to write
the text of the remainder of the third tableau. (The
text of Lyubava's song is by Rimsky-Korsakov himself.) The completion of the work was thus de-
layed and Rimsky-Korsakov records how, towards
the end of the winter, he was overcome by fatigue
and disgust for work, a feeling he then experienced
for the first time but which afterwards recurred regularly just before the completion of every big composition. He relates an incident which shows the
extent of his mental fatigue. After finishing the
scoring of the sixth tableau he was overcome with

dismay at the thought of the labour which still lay before him, of orchestrating the last scene. It was only the finding of the score, as he was turning over his papers, that reminded him that this was already finished.

Rimsky-Korsakov considered that "Sadko" marked the end of the middle period of his career as an opera composer. It was a work of which he was particularly proud. He grouped it with "Mlada" and "Christmas Eve," speaking of these two operas as "large-scale studies for 'Sadko,'" and, though a candid and surprisingly objective critic of his own work, he dwelt with much satisfaction on many passages of "Sadko." The "Gold! Gold!" scene of the fourth tableau, indeed the whole of the harbour scene, pleased him especially, and he considered the lullaby which Volkhova sings to the sleeping Sadko at the beginning of the last tableau, and the music of her disappearance, the best pages of fantastic music he had written. Yet, strangely enough (though the composer does not remark on the fact), some of the music which he himself considered the best in this splendid mature work —Sadko's descent to the submarine kingdom, the general dance which concludes the wedding revels, and the prelude to the last tableau—is actually taken from the symphonic poem of 1867. And as regards this early orchestral piece, Rimsky-Korsakov many years afterwards not only admitted that his music was derivative, but frankly avowed the precise sources which fed his musical fantasy in writing it. The passage so marvellously painting the swell of the calm sea, the profound breathing of the infinite ocean desert, which opens and closes the poem (in the opera it serves as the prelude to the first scene and its theme permeates the whole work as a sea-motif) was harmonically modelled on Liszt's "Ce qu'on entend sur la montagne," and the storm was suggested by Liszt's "Mephisto Waltz" and Balakirev's not yet finished "Tamara." The music of the Sea King's festival "is harmonically, even perhaps melodically, a little reminiscent of my favourite among Balakirev's songs, 'The Goldfish,' and of the introduction to the 'Russalka's' recitative in Dargomïzhsky's opera of the same name." Sadko's descent was likewise a reminiscence of the carrying-off of Lyudmila in Glinka's "Ruslan," except that Glinka's descending whole-tone scale was replaced by another artificial scale, consisting of alternate tones and semitones. Rimsky-Korsakov became strangely enamoured of this scale, using it again in the third movement of "Antar" and in various later works. It plays a very important part in the operatic version of "Sadko," being employed, in both ascending and descending forms, either as a simple scale or as the basis of a chord-progression in the second tableau (in which the Sea Princess and her sisters first appear to Sadko), during the intermezzo between the fifth and sixth tableaux (Sadko's descent), in the submarine ballet, at the climax of the storm, at the point where the curtain rises on the last tableau and Sadko and the Princess are seen in the meadow by Lake Ilmen, and again in the accompaniment to the Princess's lullaby.

There are, naturally, few traces of Liszt in the operatic "Sadko," though Glinka and Balakirev so thoroughly permeated Rimsky-Korsakov's musical personality that one occasionally detects the shadow of one or the other in the background of even such a mature work as this. And there are occasional reminiscences of Wagner. Most of these coincidences of musical thought (they are no more), the swan-motif in the second tableau, the incessant violin-figure of the "Tannhäuser" overture in the accompaniment to the Venetian merchant's song, and the rest, are unimportant. But it is curious to notice how, on their first appearance, Volkhova's sisters are much more nearly related to the Rhine-maidens, or even to the nymphs of the Venusberg, than to Rimsky-Korsakov's own russalkas in his " May Night " of eighteen years earlier. When the Sea Princess's sisters come out of the water to Sadko in the second tableau, the music plainly announces that Sadko is Siegfried approaching his end and that Lake Ilmen has somehow become the Rhine :—

Ex. 56 *

But in fairness it must be admitted that, in spite of

---

* A passage which Rimsky-Korsakov seems to have recollected when he wrote the accompaniment to Gryaznoy's confession in "The Tsar's Bride."

these resemblances and of the fairly elaborate system of leit-motives, "Sadko" is in no sense a Wagnerian opera. It is not only Rimsky-Korsakov's
best opera (in the sense that it contains much of his
best music in each of his different styles and that the
musical level is more consistently high throughout),
but his most individual—that in which he is most
completely and exuberantly himself and most profoundly Russian. He may have been exaggerating
when he claimed that in "Sadko" he had written
music "the true character of which could only be
appreciated by an audience Russian to the core,"
but it is certainly true that "Sadko" is Russian in
every fibre. Although a picture, not a searching
analysis, it is a marvellous evocation of the spirit of
a people. The spirit is idealised, no doubt; Novgorod never could have been like this fairy-tale city
even in its prime, in the half-historical, half-legendary time of the old epic songs when Christianity
began to mingle with the old pagan beliefs and for a
time lived with them, side by side—never, as Rimsky-Korsakov believed, quite conquering them.
The darker streaks in the national character are sup-
pressed in "Sadko." Just as the hero's fortune is
what the artist's fortune *should* always be, the

Russia of "Sadko" is an ideal Russia, the land of
the Berendeys brought forward in time, made a
little more real, commercialised—and not quite so
well governed.

Something has already been said of the episodic,
undramatic nature of Russian opera at its best, and
"Sadko" is an outstanding example, comparable in
this respect with "Boris" and "Prince Igor." In
none of his earlier works, except perhaps "Mlada,"
had Rimsky-Korsakov quite so frankly thrust the
dramatic element into the background. Even in
"Mlada" there is drama in intention, only, as he
admitted, "the description of old customs and the
fantastic element come too prominently to the fore."
But "Sadko" is deliberately styled "opera-
bilina"* and the composer carefully emphasises the
fact that it is no drama, but a series of scenes from
an epic put on the stage and set to music. The
story is little more than a pretext for brilliant stage-
pictures and for music—above all for music, which
Rimsky-Korsakov had by this time begun to consider definitely the most important constituent of

---

* The *bïliny* are epic legends, popular in origin, dealing with
Vladimir the Great and other half-legendary heroes, handed down
orally (by singing) among the peasants for many generations.

opera. How far he had drifted from the dramatic realism of Dargomïzhsky, Mussorgsky and his own "Pskovityanka" (and how radically his views differed from Wagner's) may be seen from his prefatory notes to the score of "Sadko": "I am convinced that an opera libretto should be considered and judged only as an integral part of the music. Apart from the music it serves only as a filling-out of the bare action; it is certainly not an independent literary work. I have not hesitated to take liberties with the poetic metre wherever the music demanded them. In opera the poetic rhythm must be subordinated to the musical, not vice versa." So far had he travelled from "the note as the direct expression of the word"! And just as the poetic metre is made subservient to that of the music, the stage action is to a certain extent moulded to a musical form. Rimsky-Korsakov's tendency to purely musical architecture in the build of opera-scenes, noticeable as early as "Snegurochka," is brought to its highest development in the fourth tableau of "Sadko," the harbour scene with its ever-changing mass of people—merchants, pilgrims, buffoons, soothsayers and elders. When he speaks of "the clear and broadly laid out symphonic form (some-

what in the manner of a rondo)" of this scene, up
to the point where the hero enters, the composer is
using quite accurate terms—although we must accept with caution his use of the word "symphonic."
Rimsky-Korsakov's symphonic construction was
always sectional rather than organic (think of
"Scheherazade," for instance), and his music is
never symphonic in the sense that Wagner's is. It
is symphonic in outline but not in growth and
texture.

"Sadko" is, in a sense, an affair of superimposed
planes, one background behind another. But the
backgrounds are so brilliantly painted that perspective is destroyed and the significance of the individual figures in the foreground diminished to van-
ishing point. And yet this very defect, as it
apparently is, deepens the work's charm, underlining its resemblance to some archaic tapestry come
to life. Furthest in the background is the sea, its
confused murmur painted in a musical pattern, half-
realistic, half quaintly stylised, like the stiff waves
in some archaic painting or on an old chart, yet fresh
and full of savour. For a sailor-composer Rimsky-Korsakov was not prolific of seascapes (and he
was quite content to use the "wave" motif of

"Scheherazade" again in "Tsar Saltan") but the
sea prelude to "Sadko," written, as we must remember, soon after his long cruise in the "Almaz," is a
study direct from the life. And the sea music does
more than paint a mood. (In fact there can be no
question of the prelude's preparing the hearer's
mind as the prelude to "Rheingold" does, for the
curtain does not go up on a sea scene.) The sea is
the ground-tone of the whole opera, and its motif
recurs like a motto-theme throughout the work,
being thundered out in a triumphant *fortissimo* at
the very end.

When the curtain rises on the first tableau,* the
hall of the feasting merchants, we come to the
second background—the people of Novgorod. For
the first time since "Pskovityanka," Rimsky-Korsakov now makes the chorus (and individuals, like
Nezhata, who are representative types rather than
characters) a chief protagonist. There are finely
constructed crowd-scenes of popular life in most of
Rimsky-Korsakov's operas; in fact, the harbour

---

* The seven tableaux of the opera may be divided into three or
five acts. In the first case tableaux one and two constitute the
first act; three and four, the second; and five, six and seven, the
third. Or the first, fourth and seventh tableaux may be treated
as separate acts, the second and third, and fifth and sixth, tableaux being grouped together.

scene in " Sadko " is essentially only an elaboration
of the market-scene which opens the second act of
" Mlada "; but in none of his other operas has the
chorus anything like such a predominant rôle
throughout the work. It is true the people are only
superficially and idealistically painted, even in the
kaleidoscopically brilliant fourth tableau, not
studied in Mussorgsky's manner. Yet their rôle is
no less important in " Sadko " than in " Boris."

In the first scene two very different types are
sharply contrasted—the proud, boastful merchants
and the buffoons who have to amuse them, the two
extremities of the social scale. Each is characterised by folkish music, the dance-tunes of the buffoons being specially typical of Rimsky-Korsakov's
essays in this genre, and at the end of the scene the
merchants' chorus is combined with the dance music.
All this provides the most important element of the
scene, though the relatively unimportant solo parts
of Nezhata and Sadko himself are more interesting
to the student of Rimsky-Korsakov's music. The
song of Nezhata, the young gusli-player (the part is
written for a contralto), which comes as an interlude
between the over-long opening chorus and the striking chorus in $11/4$ time (all for male voices only),

introduces the element of the old epic legends, in the atmosphere of which "Sadko" is steeped from beginning to end. He sings the *bïlina* of the Kiev hero, Volkh Vseslavich, to a monotonous sing-song, half melody, half recitative, of the kind to which these old tales were sung or recited by many generations of Russian peasant bards. Some of these *bïlina* melodies, taken down by Mussorgsky from the singing of Ryabinin, one of the last of these bards, are given by Rimsky-Korsakov in his "Hundred Russian Folk-Songs," and the melody of one of them, the song of Volga and Mikula, is sung by the two monks in the last scene of "Boris." But in "Sadko" Rimsky-Korsakov uses the style of this peculiar *bïlina*-recitative very extensively. It is this—"drawn," as the composer puts it, "like a scarlet thread through the whole opera"—which does so much to give "Sadko" its unique flavour. Sadko's own recitatives, all in this style, are specially noteworthy; for instance, the phrase :—

Ex. 57

57   Kaby   by - la   u menya   zolo - ta kazna   *etc*

to which he begins to tell the Novgorod merchants

what he would do if he were as rich in gold as they, a phrase which, in one form or another, assumes almost the importance of a leit-motif in the course of the work. The incessantly repeated phrase of the blind pilgrims in the fourth tableau :—

Ex. 58

is not imitated, but a genuine fragment of *bïlina* song to which the legend of the holy " Dove Book " was recited.* The falling third cadences of both Ex. 57 and Ex. 58 are specially characteristic. Such melodic patterns woven again and again into the score subtly impregnate it with their archaic flavour.

All the real scenes of " Sadko," which are as usual differentiated from the fantastic ones by their harmonic simplicity and the diatonic nature of their melodies, are similarly dominated by the chorus and have the same epic character—with one exception. The third tableau, much of it a monologue for Sadko's wife, Lyubava Busslaevna, was not a very

---

* See No. 4 of the Filippov collection of forty folk-songs, harmonised by Rimsky-Korsakov. Another song connected with the "Golubinaya Kniga" is given in his Op. 24.

happy afterthought. The "F minor aria" itself is
no masterpiece and the whole scene, with the later
episodes in which Lyubava makes her appearance,
seems to belong to the world of "The Tsar's Bride"
rather than that of "Sadko." Those of its phrases
which have the authentic ring of Rimsky-Korsakov
at his best are all more or less exact reminiscences.
The emphatic cadence of the unison orchestral passage which opens the scene is directly taken from
Lel's first song in "Snegurochka." And Lyubava's
joyous phrase, "Here he comes, my husband, my
darling" :—

Ex. 59

(♩=132) Allegro

To i - det, to i - det muzhe-nek, mil na - de - zha moï'l

is simply a (clearly unconscious) rearrangement of
the melodic elements in the song which in the preceding scene Sadko has sung for Volkhova's sisters
to dance to ("Sound, sound, my gusli," etc., Ex. 60).
The patterns of 49 (a) and (b) provide the substance
of both tunes,* yet Ex. 59 seems to be an immediate
recollection of Ex. 60, without there being any dramatic or other reason to lead one to suppose that the

* The trumpet-theme which serves as a "Novgorod"-motif is
also based on Ex. 49 (b), or rather on the form Ex. 48.

Ex. 60

composer made it so consciously and intentionally.
And it is equally doubtful whether Rimsky-Korsakov was consciously quoting Ex. 60 (a) in Volkhova's lullaby in the last scene. The connection
between the song of Soloveï Budmirovich in the
fourth tableau and the chorus of sailors in the fifth
provides a similar problem. If these similarities
were confined to a single work one would naturally
accept them as intentional (and rather subtle) devices to give it unity. Recurring in one opera after
another, they seem only to betoken poverty of invention, inability to do much more than ring the
changes on a few highly original ideas and on
others, like Ex. 49 (a), directly borrowed from folk-
song.

But the tendency to succumb to the tyranny of an
idea, and to repeat it unmercifully with little varia-

tion, is perhaps a Russian characteristic allied with
that other tendency to think in circles about a point,
rather than in a straight line, which we have already
noticed. Tolstoy hammers home his theory of history, of the "great men" subordinated to the will of
the masses, in much the same way in "War and
Peace." It is certainly one of Rimsky-Korsakov's
most characteristic mental traits, for he constantly
repeats not only themes and characters but even
scenes and dramatic situations in later works, with
only slight modifications. It is impossible to see
and hear the second tableau of "Sadko," for instance—Sadko wandering on the shore of Lake
Ilmen in the summer night, singing to his *gusli* accompaniment, and the appearance of Volkhova and
her sisters—without thinking of Levko and the russalkas in "May Night." As Van der Pals says,
"The second tableau of 'Sadko' appears in both
action and music to be a later and riper companion-
piece to the russalka scene in 'May Night.'"* But
when he goes on to say that all the harmonic, colour-
istic and romantic elements which only appear in
germ form in the earlier work, here come to full
flower, it is less easy to agree with him. The

---

* "N. A. Rimsky-Korssakow: Opernschaffen."

"Sadko" scene is far more elaborate, the handling more skilful, but it is questionable whether the essence of the music shows any greater maturity, any sign that the composer's musical thought, as opposed to his mere technical skill, had advanced at all in the course of seventeen years.

The music of the fantastic scenes, this one by the lakeside and the more elaborate sequence centring about the sixth tableau, the scene in the Sea King's realm, is written in two styles—graceful, lyrical (predominantly vocal) love-music and brilliant highly chromatic, orchestral tone-painting (or, rather, pattern drawing) of the kind Rimsky-Korsakov made peculiarly his own. The artificiality noticeable in "Christmas Eve" reaches a more advanced stage of development in "Sadko." Rimsky-Korsakov was probably right when he said he had never written anything better of its kind; the orchestration is particularly gorgeous. But the actual substance of the music, the framework on which the colour has to be laid, consists of brittle nothings, diatonic commonplaces disguised by the sharpening or flattening of one degree of the scale (usually by sharpening the fifth). It is a curious paradox that this fantastic music of Rimsky-Kor-

sakov's is actually the most coldly calculated. Like
his scale of alternate tones and semitones it is, in
conception, purely paper music, springing from no
natural impulse to create, expressing nothing, com-
municating no emotion—only tickling the ear with
its pungency and unusualness. Nor do these artificial fragments of theme act in the composer's mind
like the irritant inserted in the pearl-oyster's shell,
serving as the nucleus about which the play of his
musical imagination can create genuinely living
music. Take this theme, from the procession of
the sea monsters in the sixth tableau :—

Ex. 61

derived from an earlier choral phrase of the sea
nymphs and set against the characteristic tone-semi-
tone scale background. It is nothing as it stands,
a mere pretext for orchestral colour, but in the
minds of some composers it would have generated a
natural continuation—and the music would have
sprung to life. But Rimsky-Korsakov is content

simply to repeat the two bars without alteration and then exactly to repeat all four a fourth higher.

The artificiality of the music can be justified here; its cold sensuousness and glittering emptiness match the world of unreal beings in which Sadko finds himself. Yet the purely intellectual spinning of music in this way, the laying of one little self-contained block of sound against another, the mechanical sense of progress obtained by systematic modulation through cycles of keys, rising or falling regularly in major or minor thirds, the failure of the music to generate a vital impulse from its own nature—all this is frequently characteristic of Rimsky-Korsakov's music even when he is not deliberately aiming at unreality and insubstantiality. (It is very noticeable in the early " Serbian Fantasia.") The non-musician is seduced by the brilliant colours and his ear intrigued by the curious melodic intervals and the pungency of the continual succession of augmented and diminished triads. And the musician, who might be expected to detect the emptiness of all this, is too dazzled by the play of the composer's mind in the manipulation of themes and the contrivance of harmonic subtleties to notice it. It *is* marvellous, this music; no other composer has ever produced anything quite like it. *Mathematical imagination*, if one can speak of such a quality, is the only term which describes the nature of Korsakov's musical thought in these pages of " Sadko " and similar ones in other works. It is a sort of chess in terms of sound, and communicates hardly any more æsthetic emotion. The more genuine physical excitement of the storm must impress every hearer, though it can hardly be compared with that of Borodin's Polovtsian dances, for instance. Yet this storm is merely an amplification of the corresponding section of the early symphonic poem, a fact not without significance (though it would be unwise to attach too much importance to it.)

Against the background of such a pageant of sound, coldly brilliant and racily alive by turns, but painted throughout in the brightest colours, the figures of Volkhova and Sadko himself, to say nothing of the mournful Lyubava and the incidental minor characters, are dwarfed to insignificance. In spite of the beauty of the love-music, some of the best Rimsky-Korsakov ever wrote, and the sensitive charm of such music as that in which Sadko tells the assembled merchants how, if he were rich enough, he would buy one-and-thirty fair ships,

freight them with all the wares of Novgorod and
sail through all the seas of the world for trade and
adventure—in spite of all the delightful music
centring about his person, Sadko remains less a
character than a symbol.   He symbolises, of course,
the power of art.   Like Levko and Lel he is able,
by the magic of his music, to gain admission to the
supernatural world (or, rather, to a world in which
the powers of nature, taking human form as in the
old myths, are accessible to normal intercourse).
And not only admission to it, but a certain power
over it.   This world of illusion, where he mingles
with the forces of nature almost like one of themselves, is as real for him and for every artist as the
human world of everyday life.   He is equally at
home in either, and though his immersion in dreams
sometimes makes him cold and heartless in his
human relationships, he is able to enrich the world
of men by the magic gold he wins from the supernatural world.   This theme constantly recurs in one
form or another in Rimsky-Korsakov's work.   Fevronya in "Kitezh" is just such another intermediary
between man and nature, except that her power is
that of love, not of art.   If Sadko seems to be a
reincarnation of Lel, Volkhova likewise recalls

Snegurochka, another daughter of a nature-power. She even shares the Snow Maiden's fate—by melting! The composer himself pointed out the similarity of both to the queen of the russalkas in "May Night" and to the shade of the Princess Mlada (who is dead before the opera begins and only appears as a spirit), "visionary female figures who sing and vanish." But Rimsky-Korsakov's symbolism is never very thoroughly worked out, even in "Kitezh' where it is most obvious. In "Sadko" it merely provides a little intellectual ballast to a fairy-tale epic which is perfectly comprehensible without it.

XII — THE TSAR'S BRIDE

"THE first act of 'The Tsar's Bride' contains several unfortunately dry passages perhaps, but after the opening scene of the second act, which is written with a practised hand, the interest of the action increases, and in the fourth act the moving lyrical drama attains a high degree of tension. 'The Tsar's Bride' is exceptionally grateful from the singer's point of view. The scoring and working-out of the accompaniment are effective and not without interest, although the voice parts always predominate and the orchestra employed is only the normal one. . . ." The critic who thus impartially sums up the merits and defects of Rimsky-Korsakov's "Tsarskaya Nevesta," allowing a fairly ample balance in the composer's favour, goes on to reveal his identity and his freedom from false modesty in the following sentences. " The composition of the ensemble pieces, the quartet in the second act and the sextet in the third, particularly interested me as it was a new kind of task. In my opinion operatic ensembles with such polished and independent part-writing have not been composed since Glinka's time." Indeed it was just this desire to try his hand at extended arias and concerted vocal numbers in the old Italian style, "not merely the accidental, more or less fleeting concatenations of voice parts imposed by the modern conception of 'dramatic truth,' according to which two or three characters must never be allowed to sing at the same time," it was this dilettantish spirit of experiment which seems to have finally prompted Rimsky-Korsakov to make an operatic setting of Mey's play. The possibility of turning to account this typically operatic tragedy of passion, jealousy and potions, which Borodin had considered and rejected years before, had occurred to him at least as early as 1891, but it was not until 1898, immediately after the completion of the short "Vera Sheloga" (the reconstructed prologue to "Pskovityanka," also by Mey), that the composition was actually begun. I. F. Tyumenev was entrusted with the task of altering and adding to the original text so as to afford the necessary opportunities for arias and concerted numbers, and the work was composed very rapidly, and partly orchestrated, in the course of the summer.

Rimsky-Korsakov's reversion to a more conventional operatic style than he had as yet written in, after the composition of such a finished masterpiece as "Sadko," can be explained but remains no less difficult to understand. He seems to have been discouraged by his own success, to have felt that in the purely national vein, in epic-fantastic opera, he would never be able to surpass "Sadko." And so in the six or seven years before he returned to it in "Kitezh" we find him experimenting in all directions, though with conspicuous lack of success. In the one act "Mozart and Salieri" (1897) he goes right back to "The Stone Guest" and dramatic truth. "Vera Sheloga" (spring of 1898) is naturally an attempt to recapture the style of "Pskovityanka"—Dargomïzhsky tinctured with lyricism. "The Tsar's Bride" is a hybrid, the old operatic convention of the first half of the nineteenth century decked out with Wagnerian leit-motives and Dargomïzhskian "melodic recitative" and mildly flavoured here and there with the Russian folk-idiom. In 1899 Rimsky-Korsakov returned in "Tsar Saltan" to purely national, fantastic opera, but emphasising the humorous rather than the epic elements and paying more attention to fineness of detail than to breadth. Then came "Servilia" (1900) and "Pan Voevoda" (1903), which may be described as Wagner-and-water, and "Kashcheï the Immortal" (1901), another hybrid in which Wagner is crossed with the "miniature style" of "Tsar Saltan" and the later "Golden Cockerel." Van der Pals, one of Rimsky-Korsakov's apologists, has put forward the specious defence that this wandering in the wilderness was "a necessary intermediate stage in the composer's artistic and spiritual development. To reach his goal, to be able to express the future mission of his people" (in plain English, to write "Kitezh"), "it was necessary for Rimsky-Korsakov to tear his imagination from macrocosmic views and ideas of periods long past and, at any rate for a time, to busy himself with the microcosmic, with the artistic analysis of individual soul-life." There are certainly signs that these experiments in more genuinely dramatic music bore fruit in "Kitezh" but unfortunately the quantity of seed is out of all proportion to the crop. We shall be on safer ground if we assume that Rimsky-Korsakov, with characteristic intellectual restlessness, was amusing himself by trying his strength in new directions, as he actually confesses to doing in "The Tsar's Bride."

The composer tells us in his memoirs that when, after the completion of "Sadko," he composed four songs to poems by Alexey Tolstoy—the first he had written for a long period, he found that the melodies came to him quite otherwise than before. Whereas in his earlier songs the melodies had occurred to him as quasi-instrumental ideas, often conditioned by the harmonic basis which he had conceived first, they now took a purely vocal form. He realised that this was "the only way to write genuine vocal music" and the immediate consequences were a number of settings of A. Tolstoy, Maykov and Pushkin, and "Mozart and Salieri." "The Tsar's Bride" was the first large-scale work in which Rimsky-Korsakov could employ his new vocal style. And at the same time he had in his mind an extraordinary idea, reported by Yastrebtsev, of the possibility of "reconciling Wagner with Glinka, or rather even Wagner with Bellini." It is hardly to be wondered that "The Tsar's Bride," though the best of Rimsky-Korsakov's experimental operas and the only one which ever attained popularity, is something less than a masterpiece.

It is clear that Rimsky-Korsakov, in spite of the candour with which he judged his own music, was often unable to distinguish between intention and achievement. He admitted the "dry passages" in the first act of "The Tsar's Bride," probably because he found the composition of them rather heavy going, but he evidently mistook fluency for inspiration. Usually self-conscious and over-intellectual in the process of composition, he now wrote in a more normal way perhaps for the first time since "Snegurochka." The stream of music flowed so easily that he never noticed how thin it was. "The Tsar's Bride" was at the same time an experiment and a relaxation, some parts of it "written with a practised hand," others by a hand practising new and amusing tricks. Unfortunately, the composer being in a hurry, the practised hand wrote too easily and the practising one avoided difficulties. The subject was there ready-made, a fully developed drama like "Pskovityanka," not a fairy-tale or a village incident waiting for music to cover its bare bones with flesh and blood. On this smooth track Rimsky-Korsakov's mind appears to have moved so easily and rapidly that large stretches of "The Tsar's Bride" are to all intents and purposes *im-*

provised music. "Snegurochka" was also composed very rapidly, it is true, but in that case Korsakov had accumulated a large reservoir of ideas, inspirations of his own and borrowings from the treasury of folk-music, before he began the actual composition.

"The Tsar's Bride" contains only one folk-song, the favourite "Slava" tune which is employed as the motif of Ivan the Terrible, and the former purist in the treatment of folk-melodies so completely forgot his principles that he allowed himself to torture it into duple time in the prelude to Act III :—

Ex. 62

At the end of Act III, when Malyuta announces the Tsar's intention of marrying Marfa, the "Slava" theme is combined with the "Ivan the Terrible"

motif from "Pskovityanka" (Ex. 35). But this
freedom of the score from self-conscious nationalism, in conjunction with the more or less improvised
nature of so much of the music, gives the work a
peculiar interest from a critical point of view. It
affords a unique opportunity of testing the quality
of Rimsky-Korsakov's natural musical thought, of
watching the stream of his musical consciousness at
the average moment. When a composer's writing
outpaces the intellectual processes of revision and
elaboration we can observe the mysterious spurts
and floods, which we call "inspiration," in this
stream of thought and the blocks and stoppages
when the composer simply carries on with the aid
of familiar technical processes, as well as the normal
quality of the current, much more clearly than we
can see them in work made with an infinity of pains.
In this instance, it gives us a chance to discover to
what extent the folk-song element had really
become absorbed into Rimsky-Korsakov's musical
mentality, conscious imitation apart.

The folk-songish passages in "The Tsar's
Bride" are for the most part limited to self-con-
tained numbers: the choral "Song of the Hop,"
Lyubasha's unaccompanied solo, Sobakin's song

behind the scenes in the second act, the chorus of
Oprichniki at the end of the same act, Domna
Saburova's song of the falcon and the swan. And,
with the exception of Lyubasha's lovely song in the
æolian mode :—

Ex. 63

they are all rather flavourless. In one or two other
little snatches of tune—the orchestral phrase which
heralds the "Hop" chorus, the short *allegro* passage in the middle of Marfa's aria, the orchestral
introduction to the sextet—there is more of the genuine tang of folk-music. The characteristics of
Rimsky-Korsakov's melodic thought are still present in even the most insipid passages of "The
Tsar's Bride," but so mingled with platitudes and
emasculated by banal rhythmic transformations that
they are hardly recognisable. There is an example
of this in the opening of Lïkov's aria, "Storm
clouds flying away," inserted in the third act after
the first performance at the request of the singer,

Sekar-Rozhansky, because his part was "so poor
from the musical point of view":—

Ex. 64

It begins with the familiar first three notes of Ex.
49 (a), as the first phrase of Ex. 63 ends with them.
But how different the effect is here in another
rhythm and context. Nothing could be more commonplace. Ex. 64 sounds like a feeble echo of
Vakula's insipid love-making in the second scene of
"Christmas Eve" (Ex. 44). The original folk-
songish pattern has lost every trace of its parentage.
On the other hand Lyubasha's lament, unaccompanied throughout, will bear comparison with any of
Rimsky-Korsakov's other essays in this genre. It
contains no new musical elements, but the old ones
are so transmuted that one does not feel the composer is merely serving up a re-hash of familiar
ingredients, as he only too often does.

The chief melody of Marfa's big aria in the
second act, the finest thing in the opera, also belongs
to a familiar type in Rimsky-Korsakov's music and

stands out as one of the finest examples of the type :—

Ex. 65

Adagio (♩=44)
dolce

Kak te-per glya-zhu na ze - le-nyi sad, Gde s mi-

lym druzhkom my rezvili - sya,

(She sees " as if it were now, the green garden where with dear friends we used to play.") It is one of Rimsky-Korsakov's most spontaneous inspirations, long-breathed, each curve flowering naturally and inevitably into the next. Ernest Newman was hardly exaggerating when he called it "one of the purest and profoundest expressions of purely melodic ecstasy in the whole of music." There are few more poignant moments in Russian opera than that when in the last act this melody steals back on the clarinet as the background to the unhappy girl's delirium. But the beauty of these one or two outstanding passages only serves to emphasise the insipidity of the music as a whole.

And "The Tsar's Bride" is hardly stronger dramatically than it is lyrically. It is significant that the most gripping effect in the work is produced by

means of pure musical beauty. Rimsky-Korsakov
can make nothing very remarkable of the dying
girl's hallucinations *directly*, as a genuinely dramatic composer would do. He moves us by the
contrast between what we see on the stage and the
happy past of which the orchestra reminds us—and
by the ideal loveliness of the melody itself.   The
composer opens his first act quite promisingly from
a dramatic point of view.   Gryaznoy is discovered
alone, brooding, and the opening phrase, his leit-
motif :—

Ex. 66

admirably suggests both the man and his mood.
(Incidentally, nothing could demonstrate more
clearly the way in which Korsakov's mind tended to
work in fixed melodic grooves than the almost-identity of the motif (a) with part of Ex. 65, where there
can be no question of intentional resemblance.)
The musical development of the whole of this first
scene from Gryaznoy's motif—both melody and
accompaniment of his aria, as well as the orchestral

commentary on his recitative monologue—is ingenious, if a little "dry" as the composer confessed.
Though the scene is not dramatically gripping, it
strikes the right note. One feels that genuine
drama may develop at any moment. But it never
does. With the entry of Lïkov and the absurd vil-
lain Bomelius (whom we have already met in the
last scene of " Pskovityanka "), and the fugal chorus
of the Oprichniki, the first act lapses into old-
fashioned, conventional opera—and not very good
conventional opera at that. The aeroplane has
taxied very well, but instead of rising it has stopped
dead. After that we get nothing more than isolated
dramatic moments; and the most striking of these,
the scene in the third act where Ivan the Terrible
makes his only oppearance on the stage throughout
the opera, owes little to the music. The effect of
the unseen Tsar overshadowing the visible actors is
used to a different end in " The Tsar's Bride " but
no less impressively than in " Pskovityanka." His
regal motif keeps him musically in one's mind and
this single silent appearance gives his shadow a
cogency it would lack otherwise.

But there is no blinking the fact that Rimsky-
Korsakov, although during the last decade and a

half of his life he adopted the career of opera-manu-
facturer as definitely and exclusively as any Bellini
or Rossini or Verdi, was not a true dramatic composer at all. The musical expression of emotion of
any kind was not his *forte* and to find music for the
crude clash of feeling, the broad sweep of emotion,
demanded by the theatre was altogether beyond
him, except at a few inspired moments. Nor had
he as part of his ordinary equipment anything like
Mussorgsky's subtle psychological insight. Here
again the few happy exceptions in ' Pskovityanka "
and "Kitezh" only emphasise the rule. Given a
fairy-tale or village legend, Rimsky-Korsakov
could dwell at length on every incident, expanding
its essence with lyrical or picturesque music, over-
laying it with inessential but wholly delightful
detail, and building up a perfectly satisfying, self-
contained dream-world of his own. In this half or
wholly fantastic type of opera, so peculiarly Russian, he could be himself throughout, or almost
throughout. However badly he managed the love-
making, it was soon over and the adventures began
again. But in " The Tsar's Bride," and other later
works, he had hardly any opportunity to be himself.
Given a fully developed drama, an infinitely better

subject from the point of view of the normal operatic composer, he had neither the ability to identify himself with the different characters nor even the instinct for writing the kind of music which really intensifies a stage situation. Marfa is the only character in the play who is really portrayed in the music associated with her. And she is less a character than a type, one more of Rimsky-Korsakov's naïve, submissive heroines and quite indistinguishable from, say, Olga in "Pskovityanka." It is significant that the parts of "The Tsar's Bride" where Rimsky-Korsakov is most himself are purely lyrical ones where the action is at a standstill, passages like the "Slava" and "Hop" choruses, Lyubasha's song, and the bridal song in the third act, inessential to the action and which naturally hold it up. But the greater part of the play, being true drama—very theatrical drama, neither gave Rimsky-Korsakov opportunities to write the sort of music natural to him nor naturally suggested *any* kind of music to him. And so for long stretches he was, apparently unconsciously, impaled on the horns of the Voltairean dilemma, "the necessity of saying something and the perplexity of having nothing to say."

XIII — KITEZH

STUDY and enjoyment of Rimsky-Korsakov's last opera but one are somewhat hampered by the feeling that too much has been claimed for it. "Kitezh" is one of the composer's most characteristic scores. It contains some of his best music. If he had not written "Snegurochka" and one had forgotten "Sadko," one might more readily agree that "Kitezh" is Korsakov's finest opera. But to speak of it as "the Russian 'Parsifal,'" as some critics have done, is to invite a comparison it will hardly bear—and to draw attention to one or two superficial points of resemblance in some of the musical ideas. The two works really have nothing in common except their general Christian tendency. The relationship of the natural Christian individual (Fevronya and Parsifal) to the orthodox Christian community (the people of Kitezh and the Knights of the Grail) is quite different in the two operas. The sentimental, typically Wagnerian idea of re-

demption through another has no place in "Kitezh."
Grishka Kuterma is not redeemed by or through
Fevronya; she can only show him how to save
himself.

From a non-musical point of view "Kitezh" is
unquestionably the profoundest of Rimsky-Korsakov's operas, a fitting crown to a life-work.   In it
the composer finds an unexpected, yet apparently
from his own point of view satisfying, resolution of
his spiritual discord.   He shows us a reconciliation
of his pantheism, his love of nature and natural
forces, his healthy "yea-saying" to life, with something very like orthodox Christianity.   The maiden
Fevronya evidently embodies the power of universal love. When Prince Vsevolod finds her in the
first scene, she is surrounded by birds, with a young
bear at her feet, and is examining the wounds of an
elk.   She loves all living things, fears and hates
nothing.   Yet this universal love is a sort of innocent paganism, rooted in intense joy of living, in
keenest and purest delight of the senses.   She re-
joices in light and warmth, the colours of the flowers
and the thousand mysterious voices of the forest,
"not knowing in which the day is brighter or the
sun warmer, in dreams or in life."   When she

speaks of dreams and mysterious voices, Vsevolod, educated in the orthodox faith, is disquieted, and tells her that the wise men of Kitezh teach differently, that dreams are illusions. "One must seek the truth." When he asks her if she goes to pray in the churches, she answers simply, "No. Is not God everywhere?" and in a mystical ecstasy goes on to sing—significantly to a melody of the Russian church—her confession of faith : the forest itself is a church, and day and night there goes up from it a hymn of praise, all the voices of the beasts and birds continually glorifying their Maker. And finally she seems to place beside God, *zemlya matushka*, the Earth Mother. Vsevolod again thoughtfully contrasts her belief with the teaching he has been accustomed to hear, that one can only gain Heaven by turning one's back on earthly joys, and he feels that she is right. In a third song Fevronya, after reaffirming her faith in universal love and forgiveness, goes on to prophesy the coming of a millennium which shall be simply an endless spring idyll, a naïve and delightful conception of an earthly paradise full of flowers and birds.

So far everything is quite comprehensible, but at this point the young Prince dispels the trans-

cendental atmosphere by ecstatically proposing
marriage in the conventional operatic way. The
motivation of the rest of the opera is never quite
clear. Perhaps we may put it that the artistic vitality of the work was too much for its ethical content.
Fevronya goes out into the world, showing the same
patience, love and forgiveness in the face of every
trial. It is apparently through her prayers that the
city of Kitezh is made invisible and saved from the
Tartars. Yet when at the end of her ordeal her
prophecy comes true (the poetic symbol of her
death) and an unnatural spring returns to the earth,
lighted candles appear on the trees and the forest
birds find words, it is her dead lover, the son of
orthodoxy, who appears, giving her bread and telling her that whosoever eats it shall have everlasting
joy (not "everlasting life"), and who leads her to
the Invisible City. The dialogue in the last scene
between the Maiden and the old Prince Yury suggests that Rimsky-Korsakov was thinking not so
much of an orthodox heaven beyond the clouds as
of the earth in some future age, transfigured by
human love and compassion, a world peopled with
Dostoevskian Myshkins. "Dreams have become
realities. What before was only thought is here

alive," says the old Prince, and Fevronya is told
that she is worthy to live in the transfigured Kitezh
because of three gifts she has brought to God : her
dove-like gentleness, her loving kindness and her
compassionate tears.

Fevronya is clearly Rimsky-Korsakov's ideal
Christian, who understands the truths hidden from
the wisest of the orthodox teachers. The orthodox
community is saved through her prayers. But the
composer can hardly have meant by his conclusion
that, in turn, the intervention of the orthodox was
necessary for *her* salvation. Perhaps he was
merely stating his belief that orthodox and un-
orthodox alike are travelling to the same goal.
Fevronya seems to embody the fusion of everything
good in the old nature-worship with the purest
essence of Christianity, but Rimsky-Korsakov has
merely shown her as reconciled with orthodoxy—
without showing *how*. He could claim that he was
under no obligation to do so, being an artist, not a
religious teacher. But "Kitezh," though it may be
"first and foremost a *musical* work," as the composer says in his preface to the score, is obviously
intended to have a significance other than a purely
artistic one. And the very fact that this inner sig-

nificance is unclear, mystical and illogical, points to a radical change in Rimsky-Korsakov's thought at this period of his life.

It is unfortunate, though perhaps not without significance, that the composer's memoirs, so full of details concerning the planning and composition of the earlier operas, give only the barest records of the writing of "Kitezh" and not a word concerning the ideas at the back of it. Apparently Rimsky-Korsakov first thought of combining the two legends of "The Invisible City of Kitezh" and of "St. Fevronya of Murom" in a single opera soon after the finishing touches had been put to "The Tsar's Bride."* He notes that in the winter of 1898-9, while he and Belsky were preparing the scenario of "The Legend of Tsar Saltan," they discussed this as well as other possible operatic subjects : Byron's "Heaven and Earth," which he kept in mind till the end of his life, and the "Nausicaa" episode from the "Odyssey," to which in 1901 he wrote a choral prologue, published separately as "A Page of Homer," Op. 60. "Tsar Saltan" was followed by two of Rimsky-Korsakov's

---

* Yastrebtsev says he had discussed the suitability of the Kitezh legend as the subject of a symphonic poem as early as 1892.

weakest operas, "Servilia" and "Pan Voevoda,"
and the short "Kashcheï the Immortal," interesting
for its advanced harmony and as the high-water
mark of Wagner's influence on Rimsky-Korsakov,
but of no great musical value. But all this time the
idea of "Kitezh" was maturing in the composer's
mind. In the spring of 1903, before "Pan Voevoda" was finished, he began to make sketches for
the first act of the "Legend." Belsky prepared the
libretto in the summer of that year, discussing even
the most insignificant details with the composer. By
the end of the summer Korsakov had composed the
first act and both tableaux of the fourth; on his return to Petersburg for the winter, he sketched out
the second act and the first tableau of the third.
The score of "Kitezh" was finished during the
summer of 1904 at Vechasha. That is all the composer is disposed to tell us about a work which appears to be the result of some spiritual crisis and
which, if the claims of its admirers are not greatly
exaggerated, must have been written in a white-heat
of inspiration. Rimsky-Korsakov has told us about
the almost clairvoyant condition in which he composed "Snegurochka" and, in considerable detail,
of his rather less intense excitement during the

writing of "Sadko," but he dismisses "Kitezh" as
if it were of no more importance than "Servilia" or
"Pan Voevoda." It is true the whole of the latter
part of the memoirs is somewhat scant of detail, as
if the writer were weary of his self-imposed task
and could bring no interest to the retailing of the
events of only a year or two before. Yet none of
the other operas is passed over as curtly as
"Kitezh."

From a purely musical point of view "Kitezh" is
at the same time a step backward and a summing-
up. After "Sadko" Rimsky-Korsakov, as we have
seen, had for a time abandoned the folkish-fantastic
style of which he was a complete master for a more
conventionally dramatic type in which he was reduced to the level of an unversed apprentice. Un-
decided in musical method, wavering between predominantly *sung* opera, as in "The Tsar's Bride,"
and almost pure Wagnerian declamation, as in
"Kashcheï," he had also been trying to cure his
music of its Russian accent, its principal charm,
for the sake of "freedom of style." Neither "Servilia" nor "Pan Voevoda" has anything like the
dramatic power of the last scene of "The Tsar's
Bride," and the stream of lyrical inspiration runs

through them even thinner. Of the seven operas
written between "Sadko" and "Kitezh" only
"Tsar Saltan" is written consistently in the national
idiom. In "Saltan" the striving for drama and
psychological subtlety is temporarily relaxed; the
composer is content once more merely to tell a Russian fairy-tale; and in consequence "Saltan" is
musically a sheer delight. But it was not till he
wrote "Kitezh" that Rimsky-Korsakov regained
the level of "Sadko."

"Kitezh" is composed in the contrasted styles of
which Rimsky-Korsakov was so fond, the harmonically piquant but essentially artificial music usually
associated with the fantastic and supernatural elements being replaced by barbaric pseudo-Tartar
music of a very similar nature. The folk-songish
music of the "Russian" scenes differs in no respect
from that in the earlier operas. Indeed the score
contains hardly any fresh elements. Even the
melodies borrowed or imitated from the music of the
Russian church have precursors in "Sadko" (the
appearance of St. Nicholas), "Tsar Saltan" (chorus
at the end of Act II), and "Christmas Eve." Nor
can it be said that the experiments of the dramatic
operas bore much fruit in "Kitezh." There is a

certain advance in the expressive power of the vocal
music, it is true; and the treatment of Grishka
Kuterma, his impudence, the torment of his spirit
and his growing madness, makes this drunken vaga-
bond one of the most striking and psychologically
convincing characters in the whole range of Rimsky-
Korsakov's operas. Yet Grishka cuts a more ordinary figure when compared with the characters of
Mussorgsky's world. After all, his portrait (though
more elaborate) is no more cleverly drawn than that
of the terrible Tsar in Korsakov's own " Pskovityanka." The mere fact that he is alive at all, a
human being with a battered human soul, not a mere
type or character in a fairy-tale, throws him into
relief against the background of unreal and half-
real creatures who people so much of Korsakov's
dramatic work. He is a symbol, but something
more substantial as well. And the same may be
said of Fevronya herself. Though she conforms
superficially to Rimsky-Korsakov's favourite type
of passive heroine, whose only characteristics are
patience and forgiveness, she is far more positive
and definite than any of the Olgas and Marfas and
Militrissas of the earlier operas. One little trait
after another gives her sharper definition and deeper

individuality, till near the end when, having taken
the bread of everlasting joy, she throws the crumbs
to the birds and she and her lover set out hand in
hand on their journey to the Invisible City to the
sound of twitterings and cuckoo-calls, she stands out
as one of the most memorable figures in the whole
of operatic literature. Vsevolod is a poor thing to
mate with her. He is the conventional tenor hero
to the life—or, rather, in the lack of it. When Fedor
Poyarok brings to Great Kitezh the false report that
it is Fevronya who has betrayed the city, her lover,
though he seems to believe the story without question, only remarks *poco agitato*, "What? What,
she? O God, be merciful!"—and leaves it at that!
His father, the old Prince Yury, is the personifica-
tion of priesthood, and the simple music associated
with him is deeply impressive. But the other characters are of little account. Bedyay and Bouroun-
day, the Tartar chiefs, belong to the slightly comic
world of Fafner and Fasolt; it is impossible to
believe that they are the terrible figures they are intended to be. They will not bear comparison in
any respect with Borodin's Konchak.

But "Kitezh" is, even more than most operas,
"first and foremost a musical work." Its characters

live and its religious message has meaning only in
so far as they are enveloped and expressed in living
music.   Fevronya, in particular, is a purely musical
character.   That is to say, she is not a woman completely drawn and then set to music as Isolde or
Brünnhilde is.   She is like Mozart's heroines in
that all, or at any rate the most important part, of
what we know of her, is told us only by her music.
Her music develops from a few simple germs and
the rest of the work is formed about it as about a
nucleus.

Like " Sadko," " Kitezh " opens with a piece of
nature-painting, a vague murmur centring for the
most part about a single chord :—

Ex. 67

In " Sadko " it is the confused murmur of the sea,
here that of the forest, which sets the pervading
mood of the greater part of the work and recurs from
time to time throughout it.   But instead of breaking
off, like the prelude to " Sadko," these *Waldweben,*

so like Wagner's as regards the means employed
and so unlike in the end attained, lead directly into
the first scene and are heard as a background
throughout the greater part of Act I.   More definite
themes are evolved from the vague rustle of the
violins, like chaos itself taking shape.   Above the
divided string tremolo the oboe begins to sing a
long-drawn melody expanded from Ex. 67 (a):—

Ex. 68

of which the last two bars are the chief motif of
Fevronya herself, so that she is, so to speak, musically identified with the voice of Nature.   The essential similarity of this motif to Ex. 48 in
" Snegurochka" has already been pointed out.
Bird-calls are heard, also recalling " Snegurochka ";
more naturalistic, less idealised than the voice of
Wagner's "forest bird."   And then comes a warm,
broad melody in D flat, a "glorification of solitude,"
as Korsakov called his prelude :—

Ex. 69

When the curtain goes up Fevronya sings Ex. 68,
oboe and flute echoing her. Already her musical
portrait is beginning to take shape. There is something indescribably moving about the simplicity of
Ex. 68. And just as this theme, a variation of
the ever-recurring Rimsky-Korsakovian idea, Ex.
49 (b), suggests the passive side of Fevronya's
nature, her humility and gentleness and naïveté, the
melody of "glorification," Ex. 69, which she now
sings in C major, expresses the active side, her warm
love for all living things and her dreamy exaltation.
Musically it is a not unworthy counterpart to
Marfa's great aria in "The Tsar's Bride," though it
has not the same sweep and finality. The scene
with the birds and animals is developed almost entirely from the separate motives of Ex. 68, interwoven with naïve bird-calls and rhythmic figures associated with the bear and elk. When Fevronya
tells the bear that when he is older he will be tamed
and taught to dance, the clarinet plays a snatch of
melody almost note for note the same as the chief
theme of the well-known "Tumblers' Dance" in
"Snegurochka."

On the appearance of Vsevolod the texture of the
music weakens. The love-music, almost passion-

less—as ever with Rimsky-Korsakov, is less banal
than that which he usually wrote for situations of
this kind. Its idyllic purity strikes no note false to
the general feeling of the scene. Yet the temperature of the musical inspiration has dropped perceptibly. The music is still derived from Ex. 68, but
in its new 6/8 guise it has lost its virtue and drifted
dangerously near the commonplace. Only the re-
currence of the earlier music leads us back from the
world of opera to the world of legend. Gradually
fresh themes begin to be associated with the original
ones. When Fevronya sings to the Prince of the
wonder of the flowers and the mysterious voices of
the forest, a new melody delicately outlined by flute
and harp is heard over the murmuring semiquavers.
And when she tells him that the forest is the vast
temple of a divine mystery, a hymn-like melody
emerges from Ex. 68 in imitation :—

Ex. 70

and is taken up by Fevronya in a broad, tranquil

alla breve. As she sings with ever-increasing ecstasy
of the future world transfigured by universal love,
other themes later associated with the Paradise
Birds, Sirin and Alkonost, are heard above the
rustle of the forest till at the end this vague, continuous undertone takes definite shape (as if a long-
held discord had been resolved at last) in a passage
which suggests the ringing of innumerable little
bells :—

Ex. 71 (a) and (b)

This " carillon of eternal bliss " takes several shapes
besides the two quoted here, but its last four notes
always remind the `hearer of its connection with
Fevronya and the murmuring forest.

Later, after Vsevolod's disappearance, the arrival
of Poyarok and his men with their lusty folk-song

takes one back to Rimsky-Korsakov's earlier operas. At the very end of the act, when they reply to Fevronya's enquiry as to the Prince's identity, a new theme flames out on the trumpets at the word " Kitezh," reminding one of the fanfare-theme associated with the city of Ledenets in " Tsar Saltan."

The second act of " Kitezh " opens with a crowd-scene, a feature of Rimsky-Korsakov's operas almost as inevitable and conventional as the ballet in the operas of pre-Wagnerian days. The scene in Little Kitezh is constructed in the usual way from material of familiar types. The bear-leader's repeated cry to his " Mikhaylushka " and the old *gusli*-player's song are both of the *bïlina*-melody class and the various dance-themes are distractingly like dozens of similar tunes in Rimsky-Korsakov's earlier works. The only fresh feature is the baiting of Grishka Kuterma, who thus makes his first appearance on the scene; his theme, alone of those from which this self-contained interlude is built up, is of importance in the musical architecture of the opera as a whole. It is not till Fevronya appears that the symphonic web begins to develop afresh, first with a motif in 5/8 time to which in the first act

Fevronya has greeted Vsevolod, now in the orchestra and quickly used in counterpoint with Ex. 69.
Then in the scene between Grishka and Fevronya
we hear still further metamorphoses of Ex. 68 :—

Ex. 72 (a) and (b)

the first when she tells him not to sin, the other when
she speaks of the humility proper to a maiden.

The irruption of the Tartars introduces a fresh
group of themes : first, a motif of the conventional
"barbaric and threatening" type which, having no

Ex. 73

real musical vitality of its own, is easily twisted into
any number of shapes, equally meaningless, without
violence to its nature. Then, more directly associated with the two chiefs, the old Tartar song, "On
the river Darya" (Ex. 73), links this last but one of
Rimsky-Korsakov's great works with his first, for
the *andante* of his First Symphony is based on this
very tune.* A third Tartar theme, sung by the two
chiefs in thirds :—

Ex. 74

is actually another version of the same song,† though

---

* This was the "Russian theme" which he tells us was sent
him by Balakirev and on which he wrote the *andante* while his
ship, the "Almaz," was lying in the Thames during the winter
of 1861-2. "I composed it without a piano," he says. "We
hadn't one on the vessel; perhaps once or twice I played through
what I had written in some river-side beer-shop." The history
of music records few incongruities more pleasant than this—the
first performance of parts of the first Russian symphony on the
piano of a Thames-side public house. The melody was evidently
a favourite of Rimsky-Korsakov's, for he made a choral setting of
it in 1876.

† Both songs, with yet a third melody to the same words, are
given in Rimsky-Korsakov's "Hundred Russian Folk-Songs."
All three were taken down by Balakirev from the singing of
P. Yakushkin.

Van der Pals* curiously enough takes it for " a variation or, more correctly, a distortion of the carillon theme " (that is, of Ex. 71b), an example of the pitfalls which beset the path of the too ingenious analyst.

The phrase to which Fevronya sings her prayer, " Lord, make invisible the town of Kitezh," which plays such an important part in the next act, might also be considered a variation of the carillon motif, though they really have nothing more in common than the fact that both are based on the same formula as the bell-theme in " Parsifal." The whole of the first tableau of the third act, the midnight scene in Great Kitezh itself, belongs to the same mental world.   Here Rimsky-Korsakov does really seem to be breaking fresh ground. The music, above all in the long monologue of the old Prince Yury, has a mystic depth—attained by the simplest means—quite without parallel in any of his other works.   Only in the continually recurring " Kitezh " fanfare, the folk-songish flavour of the choral greeting to Poyarok and the vivid tone-painting which accompanies the youth's first narration can we recognise the characteristic Rimsky-Korsakov.

---

* " N. A. Rimsky-Korssakow ; Opernschaffen."

The beautiful long-drawn melody of the youth's second narration ("Woe, woe to the city of Kitezh! The crosses are gone from the domes of the churches"):—

Ex. 75

reminds one (in feeling, not melodically) of the unaccompanied chorus of peasants in " Prince Igor." The cadential pattern (a) is noticeable in several themes in "Kitezh"—the men's chorus at the end of Act I, the leit-motif of Poyarok, and others; it may have been unconsciously derived from the end of Ex. 68. Here in Act III it recurs in the finely conceived chorus of Vsevolod and the Kitezh warriors as they go out to battle, irresistibly reminding one of the similar scene of Tucha and his followers in "Pskovityanka." Their song fades away into the music of the transformation scene, a wonderful piece of sensuous sound dominated by the theme of Fevronya's prayer and (as the bells begin to ring of their own accord) the carillon of endless bliss.

The interlude leading to the second tableau of this act, "The Battle of Kerzhenets," is sometimes performed as a separate concert-piece, though the playing off of the chorus of the Kitezh warriors against the various Tartar themes and Korsakov's stereotyped "ride" figure (as used in "Christmas Eve," for instance) is not very interesting. Like the other big orchestral interlude in "Kitezh," the "Journey to the Invisible City" in the last act, it reveals all Korsakov's typical weaknesses as a symphonic writer, in particular his inability to build except by the primitive method of laying blocks of sound end to end.

The second tableau takes us back to Fevronya and Grishka, from the epic to the psychological. These two have already confronted each other, but now for the first time they are alone together. The juxtaposition throws an ever more and more piercing light on the character of each. Grishka's mind is already beginning to give way. The sound of the bells of the city he has betrayed rings ceaselessly in his ears. (And now we do really hear a "distortion" of the carillon theme.) Gradually his poor, tormented soul is stripped naked before Fevronya, as he cries out in terror and begs her to free him,

now wheedling and cringing, now telling her defi-
antly that life has nothing more to offer her, since
he has spread the report that it is she who is the
traitor. Then softening before her infinite compassion he pours out the whole of his misery, his
grievance against fate and society and himself, half
in truth, half in the endeavour to move her to release
him through pity, while Fevronya with each reply
seems to grow in spiritual stature. The end of the
scene, as the first rays of dawn show the reflection
of the Invisible City in the waters of the lake, brings
the emotional tension to a climax. The real bell-
sounds, with the fanfare-motif, alternate with their
distortion in Grishka's maddened mind; and his
wild laughter as he rushes off, dragging Fevronya
with him, is not easily forgotten. Yet even this terrible piece of soul-painting is surpassed in the forest
scene of the last act. Up till now we have been
witnessing a tragedy, very horrible but of a kind
which music can hardly intensify. Unlike Fevronya, Grishka is altogether complete without
music. The music adds nothing to his portrait. It
matches it but, if the truth must be told, only intermittently helps to deepen its effect. But now
Grishka tells Fevronya to pray if she wants to—only

"not to *Him*, but to the Earth"—and there is a curiously moving quality in the music of the prayer which this crazed wreck of humanity mutters after her, his mind gradually wandering, till he breaks off and cries out in terror, thinking he sees the Devil himself. The wild music of his dance, as he sings and whistles to appease his tormentor, will bear comparison with Mussorgsky's essays in the macabre— even with Boris's hallucination. Rimsky-Korsakov himself wrote nothing else quite like it, for it is no mere grotesque pattern of sounds. It communicates an authentic shudder of horror. From this point till the end of the tableau Rimsky-Korsakov's musical imagination continued working at full pressure. The hysterical flood of sound as Grishka rushes off, leaving Fevronya to her fate, dies down to the quiet murmur of the forest. And then Fevronya sings a gravely beautiful little lullaby to her tired heart, while harp, glockenspiel and celesta decorate the strangely, disturbingly sweet music of the miraculous transformation with twinkling little points of sound-light. The last motif of Ex. 68 undergoes one final transformation growing out into a magnificent, long-breathed phrase, over mounting violin figures :—

Ex. 76

expressing the exaltation of the girl's soul as it gradually frees itself from the limitations of mortality. The voice of Alkonost tells her of the approach of death, no longer fearful, and just before the appearance of Vsevolod comes a deeply moving passage where the motif to which in the first act she has sung the praise of Mother Earth grows into that of the "glorification of solitude." Now she sings them to welcome "sweet Death, dear guest, my long desired one":—

Ex. 77

Prikho-di, moya sme-rë - tushka, gost - yushka mo-ya zhe-lannaya,

As in Act I, the coming of the Prince perceptibly lowers the imaginative temperature of the music until the scene of the mystic giving of bread. Vsevolod's phrase, "Whoso eats of our bread":—

Ex. 78

(heard already in the third act when Fevronya tells Grishka of the great mystery of God) assumes great importance in the last scene, though it is less impressive in the grandiose form in which it appears there than in this simple one which so perfectly expresses the nature of the most solemn of Christian rites. The final scene in the Invisible City is a marvellous piece of musical fresco painting; not flawless, for not all the material is of equal value and there is a great deal of the usual symmetrical repetition, though the formal, highly stylised character of the whole scene supplies a motive for this other than the customary "purely musical" one. Yet, even in these, perhaps the loftiest pages he ever wrote, Rimsky-Korsakov's creative fire failed to generate enough heat to fuse mere structure into living organism, or rather to fuse all the little separate eight-bar or sixteen-bar organisms into one big one. To say that is not to deny the sustained imagination and all-through impulse which alone could have made such a satisfying synthesis of so many thematic elements : the bells, the fanfare, folk-song and church-melody, the motives of Fevronya and the murmuring forest, and the voices of the mysterious Paradise birds. But music of the level of "Kitezh" can be judged only by the highest standards, and, applying these, it is easy to see that it lacks that spontaneity as a whole of which there is plenty of evidence in the parts, above all in Fevronya's questions and the replies of the other soloists.

We know that Rimsky-Korsakov was a religious
sceptic, though as he confessed he had, as an artist,
an extraordinary predilection for depicting religious
ceremonies. He said of his " Easter Overture "
that to understand it "one must have attended a
Russian Easter mass in a cathedral, among the
closely packed masses of people, during the simultaneous celebration of the mass by numerous priests
and deacons." But there was something of the
priest about Rimsky-Korsakov himself. One has
only to look at his photograph to see that he needed
nothing but the dress to turn him in appearance into
a typical Orthodox *mitropolit*. It is obvious that
" Kitezh " was not conceived objectively as a mere
external representation of a belief to which the composer was indifferent or in which he was interested
only as an artistic subject. The " Easter Overture " may be such, a purely artistic recollection of
mass-excitement and the physical joy of sharing it.
But " Kitezh " is so clearly something more than
that, that it is impossible not to speculate as to its
significance in connection with the composer's own
spiritual development. Was the idea of " Kitezh "
simply a triumph of instinct over reason? Was
Rimsky-Korsakov actually becoming reconciled

with orthodox beliefs as he grew older? Or did he
and Belsky really think, as it appears, that they had
found the essence of Christianity in nature itself?
No one can say. The "Legend" is too unclear in
thought. But, after all, art is more important than
the artist. His personal problems, fascinating as
they may be, are of only incidental importance.

XIV — THE GOLDEN COCKEREL

RIMSKY-KORSAKOV'S perverse refusal to round off his career by dying after the composition of "Kitezh" appears to have aroused a slight sense of grievance in more than one critic. "Kitezh" would have been such an appropriate final message to the world that the humour and irony of "The Golden Cockerel" seem to have struck critics as an unpleasant discord sounded after a perfect cadence, almost as a sort of death-bed joke. Yet the "Cockerel" was in no wise the work of a dying man, or even of a very old one; the composer was only sixty-three. It is true the attacks of *angina pectoris* compelled Korsakov to take life easily, but his health became really serious only in December, 1907, after the completion of the "Cockerel" and just six months before his death. The curious point is that after "Kitezh" Rimsky-Korsakov did actually wonder whether the time had not come for him to give up composing. The last page of his autobiography, finished in 1906, is over-shadowed by the old fear of becoming a " singer who has lost his voice." And although he was still thinking of further operas and he and Belsky went on discussing plans, Pushkin's " Golden Cockerel " was not one of them. He still kept harking back to the subject of Byron's " Heaven and Earth " (a fact which suggests that the religious trend of his thought in " Kitezh " was no mere episode) and toying with that of the Volga pirate, Stenka Razin, the hero of a symphonic poem by Glazunov. But ideas would not come and, very much as Tchaïkovsky decided that he was played out just before writing " Casse-Noisette," Rimsky-Korsakov seems for a time to have made up his mind that there was nothing left for him but to close his account with the past by re-storing some of the cuts in his edition of " Boris," orchestrating a few songs—his own and Mussorg-sky's, touching up " Kashcheï " and the short orches-tral " Dubinushka," and working at his great book on orchestration. The decision to compose " The Golden Cockerel " was made quite suddenly in Sep-tember or October, 1906, but when it was taken Korsakov threw himself whole-heartedly into the task and worked at full pressure until it was finished.

It is only natural to compare "The Golden Cockerel" with the "Tsar Saltan" of eight years before. Both are based by Belsky on tales by Pushkin. In each the central figure is a naïve, absurd tsar. Both are composed in Rimsky-Korsakov's so-called "miniature style." But there the parallel ends. Not only is the musical texture of the two operas different, mainly diatonic in "Saltan," predominantly chromatic in the "Cockerel," but the whole point of view is different. In "Saltan" one feels that the composer has identified himself with the childish, dream-like world of the fairy-tale. In none of his fantastic operas does he accept the ridiculous and extraordinary more gravely and matter-of-factly. Much of the charm of the thing is due to this apparent ingenuousness of a narrator who seems to believe every word of the extravagancies he is reciting. But in "The Golden Cockerel" the composer often appears to be standing outside the ridiculous drama and on a more sophisticated plane of thought from which he *sees* that it is ridiculous. In "Saltan" the music is one with the story throughout; in the "Cockerel" it frequently comments on it. The naïve humour of "Saltan" is still present in "The Golden Cockerel" but mingled with it is a

strong flavouring of biting, and slightly bitter, wit.
When Rimsky-Korsakov wrote music for Saltan he
had had one or two brushes with a paternal autocracy, it is true, but they had not been serious. He
had suffered nothing worse than the compulsory substitution, on the demand of the censor, of a vague
male "highness" for the Empress in "Christmas
Eve." But in the interval before he wrote music
for Dodon (in 1905, to be exact), there had been an
almost-revolution in which the composer had openly
sympathised with the wrong side. He had been involved in a warfare of manifestoes and student-
demonstrations and had been dismissed from his
professorship at the Conservatoire. So when he
came to draw Dodon he did so in a less kindly spirit.
Autocracy, recognising the caricature, took its re-
venge by preventing the performance of "The
Golden Cockerel" during the composer's lifetime
and so hastening his death, it is said, by the
annoyance.

Different as "The Golden Cockerel" is from
"Kitezh," the two works have this in common—that
both hint at some mysterious, hidden meaning which
no one has yet managed to elucidate quite satisfactorily. Delightful as "The Golden Cockerel" is

as pure nonsense, the prologue with the Astrologer's hint at a moral (together with Rimsky-Korsakov's predilection for symbolism) sets one hunting for a deeper significance in the story. But it is evident from Belsky's preface to the libretto that even he, and presumably Rimsky-Korsakov himself, had failed to see what Pushkin really meant by it. He invents a mythical origin for the story,* which explains nothing, and says that it "draws a lesson from the unhappy consequences of human passions and weaknesses." But beyond the rather obvious lesson that old men are likely to get into trouble if they run after young women, there is not very much to be learned from the opera. In Dodon Pushkin may have been satirising not only autocracy but that typically Russian variety of laziness which, from the hero of Goncharov's famous novel, has become known as "Oblomovism." But the Cockerel itself, which at first seems so obviously the symbol of *something*, cannot be made, except by the most tortuous ingenuity, to symbolise *anything*. When the Astrologer comes forward at the end and tells the

---

* It seems to be based, he says, on some fabulous attempt of a powerful magician (the Astrologer) to carry off the Queen of the Air (the Queen of Shemakhan) by the aid of a mortal king (Dodon). The attempt failed and the magician consoled himself by inventing the story of the king's ingratitude.

audience that he and the Tsaritsa, who have appeared to be fantastic beings creating confusion in
a more or less real world, are actually the only realities and that all the rest is illusion, he only makes
the puzzle more bewildering than ever. So one is
obliged to conclude, not very satisfactorily, that
after all, Queen, Cockerel and Astrologer are simply
an elaborate mystification, that there is no moral
deeper than the obvious ones, and that the satire is
equally superficial, merely adding spice to an ordinary fairy-tale. But it is not unlikely that Rimsky-
Korsakov was attracted to the subject in the first
place by this suggestion of a deeper meaning, and it
is certainly true that he and Belsky (who, as usual,
consulted him with regard to every detail) under-
lined the satirical element and added a touch of
malice not in the original.

Musically "The Golden Cockerel" cannot be
compared with "Sadko" or "Kitezh" on the one
hand, and it owes nothing to "The Tsar's Bride"
and the other "vocal" and "dramatic" operas on
the other. In the highly chromatic harmonic texture of so many of its pages, its predominantly orchestral nature and the almost unbroken continuity
of the music, it resembles "Kashcheï the Immortal,"

Rimsky-Korsakov's nearest approach to pure Wagnerian music-drama, while in other respects, in the style of the recitatives and the dry, humorous characterisation by short-winded folk-songish leitmotives, it is closer to "Tsar Saltan." Stylistically, then, "The Golden Cockerel" lies midway between the two earlier "miniature" operas, both of which it surpasses in achievement. As in the big fantastic operas, a simple, diatonic idiom is contrasted with a more complicated, chromatic one. But whereas in "Sadko," for instance, the two styles are kept more or less separate, one or the other definitely predominating in any scene, in the "Cockerel" they are closely interwoven and the chromatic idiom instead of being the secondary, contrasting element in the music is now the chief one. Though much of the melodic material is diatonic it is enveloped in a web of highly spiced harmony. The purely diatonic style is reserved for one or two unimportant characters, the Tsar's sons and his housekeeper, Amelfa, and for brief episodes like the delightful music which lulls the Tsar to sleep in the first act. The Tsar's own themes, like the foolish old man himself, are continually entangled in the magic chromatic net of the Queen of Shemakhan. The Astrologer's music, continually see-sawing between distant keys (see Ex. 43), is as insubstantial as the sinister figure himself.

In this sort of musical characterisation, Rimsky-Korsakov was a master. Almost incapable of painting a full-length musical portrait, he was peculiarly adept in the musical labelling of characters. Even in his earliest operas we find him striving by no means unsuccessfully to give each character a distinct musical speech. In "Sadko" the hero, who hardly exists at all as a human being seen in the round, is to a certain extent characterised by his distinctive type of recitative. His music tells us nothing about him. It is far from being musical portraiture, as Ivan's music is in "Pskovityanka." Yet it distinguishes him far more satisfactorily than the mere *etiquette* of a leit-motif would do. As a matter of fact, Rimsky-Korsakov's personal leit-motives in most of his operas are not conspicuously successful. Themes as expressive as Fevronya's are exceptional with him; they are usually only more or less striking tags. But the musical characterisation in "The Golden Cockerel" is brilliantly successful. Again there is no question of genuine portraiture, though the fact that the music is associated with persons with sharply defined characteristics instead of with negative, shadowy beings like Snegurochka and Sadko gives it substance and validity. But the leit-motives are extraordinarily apt. Consider these themes associated with the foolish, pompous old Tsar :—

Ex. 79

with the perpetually bad-tempered *voevoda* Polkan :—

Ex. 80

and with the fussy old housekeeper, Amelfa :—

Ex. 81

(this last one practically identical with that of the

Novgorod merchants in "Mlada"). Not only are
they effective as mere labels but their development
is so consistent and so complete, very little of the
score being independent of leit-motives, that from
beginning to end every character is sharply defined
in the music. Again, take the arabesque pattern,
perhaps the most important theme in the whole
score, associated with the seductive Tsaritsa :—

Ex. 82

Could the coldly sensual, demoniac nature of the
woman, her mystery and her insubstantiality, be
more strikingly suggested musically? And unlike
so many of Korsakov's fantastic themes, it sounds
spontaneously created, not consciously invented, in
spite of the ease with which it can be made to progress infinitely by minor thirds (a circumstance exploited to the full in the long clarinet cadenza in
the prologue) and of the fact that it sounds equally
well upside down, as the composer obligingly demonstrates immediately after this cadenza :—

Ex. 83

The almost-identity of the first four notes of Ex. 82
with an important motif in the Astrologer's greeting
to the Tsar, and to which he first sings of "my
Golden Cockerel," may be intended to hint at the
mysterious connection between him, the bird and the
Tsaritsa. (Though the song about the Cockerel
can hardly have been meant to recall the Hindu
merchant in " Sadko " !)

It is easy to see how the extraordinary flexibility
of Ex. 82 made it perfect material for Rimsky-Korsakov's peculiarly constituted mind to work on. It
can be subjected to almost innumerable metamorphoses without losing its identity or its expressive
power, and it lends itself to an infinite play of harmonic and contrapuntal ingenuity—as in this delightful passage at the end of the Tsaritsa's tale of
her magic island :—

Ex. 84

And the same is almost equally true of the themes of the Tsar and the Cockerel. Nothing could be more characteristic of Rimsky-Korsakov than the trumpet-fanfares behind the scenes, which follow the Cockerel's alarms in Act I :—

Ex. 85

where the composer's thought-process is the precise equivalent of the substitution of $(x + y)^2$ for $x^2 + 2xy + y^2$ in an equation.

Indeed, "The Golden Cockerel" is perhaps the most elaborately fabricated of all Rimsky-Korsakov's scores. Whatever doubts one feels as to the spontaneity of his inspiration (and as usual the ideas that appear most spontaneous are also the weakest) and the natural vitality of a great deal of the music, there can be no denying the composer's unsurpassed intellectual brilliance in his last composition. Rimsky-Korsakov was always essentially a miniaturist, perhaps—partly by instinct, partly owing to his limitations. Freed from the necessity of filling a huge canvas like the submarine scene of "Sadko," writing for a quickly moving comedy of individuals instead of a static, impersonal epic, the composer could here file away to his heart's content. He does not entirely neglect purely musical symmetry of architecture—in the council of war in the first act, in the sleep episode with the Cockerel's two alarms, in the opening of Act II, and other places, where he takes advantage of the formalised nature of the fairy-tale. But he abandons the attempt to write symphonically—there being no inducement—with happy results. He can lay his finely wrought musical filigree carefully on the incidents of the story, knowing that the story alone will be sufficient to bind it together and give it shape. In some respects he almost seems to have returned to Dargomïzhsky, with his detailed underlining of the action and sharp characterisation of each actor. Indeed, but for the nature of the recitative, slightly stylised to suggest the grotesque nature of the characters, and the predominance of the orchestra (two very important "buts," of course), "The Golden Cockerel" is written more or less according to Dargomïzhskian principles. The "vocal" style is abandoned as completely as the pseudo-symphonic, for even the melodies of the Tsaritsa's songs—her "Hymn to the Sun," for instance—are really instrumental in nature. Actually, of course, Rimsky-Korsakov had not returned to Dargomïzhsky at all. He arrived at the style of "The Golden Cockerel" by way of Wagner and his own previous experiments.

The interesting point is that, cold detached commentary as it is, a great deal of the orchestral fabric of "The Golden Cockerel" seems to have developed far more spontaneously than, for example, the fantastic pages of "Sadko" or the barbaric Tartar music of "Kitezh." There are numerous lapses; nothing could be more obviously artificial than the music of the Astrologer, the beginning of the second act, and dozens of shorter passages. But many of the ramifications of the Tsaritsa's theme sound like the natural unfolding of musical thought, controlled only to a normal extent by the composer's conscious mind. Even in some passages where the composer's quasi-mathematical intelligence is definitely in charge (as in the wedding march in the third act) the mosaic patterns are inlaid with such skilful ease that their artificiality is almost perfectly concealed. If the themes do not come to life and move of their own accord, the puppets are controlled so naturally that one almost takes them for actors of flesh and blood. For this reason, although it is lacking in the lyrical beauty of the best of the earlier operas, "The Golden Cockerel" must be given a high place in Rimsky-Korsakov's work.

Of beauty in the deeper sense of the word there is none in "The Golden Cockerel." Naturally the subject allows no scope for it. The most charming pages of the score are provided by the drowsy sleep music in Act I, particularly delightful when the drowsy melody steals back on the 'cellos, while the wood-wind delicately outline the Cockerel's motives of reassurance and warning (both transmuted here to a lulling accompaniment) :—

Ex. 86

But even this brief interlude, recalled at the end of the opera when the people think regretfully of the tranquil reign of this best of rulers, will hardly bear comparison with the best pages of "Snegurochka" or "Sadko" or "Kitezh." The other definitely lyrical parts of the "Cockerel" are undistinguished, though never insipid. The spirit of folk-song impregnates the straightforward, humorous music connected with Amelfa and the fatuous princes, and actual folk-melody steps in with the welcoming chorus that follows the wedding march in Act III, one last borrowing from the treasure-hoard of popular art which the composer himself had collected.*

The songs and dances in the second act are typi-

---

* The melody is No. 59 of his "Hundred Russian Folk Songs."

cal of Rimsky-Korsakov's oriental music, a side of
his work which, owing to the popularity of "Scheherazade" and trifles like the Hindu song in
"Sadko" and the Tsaritsa's greeting to the sun in
the "Cockerel," is commonly supposed to be more
important than it is. Actually these, with a few
songs, "Antar," and the Cleopatra episode in
"Mlada" (only too clearly echoed at the beginning
of the seduction scene in the "Cockerel"), represent
the whole of it, a very small, though attractive, proportion of his total output.   As Calvocoressi has put
it, the oriental tendency of Russian composers has
always been "an instinct rather than an attitude,"
but Rimsky-Korsakov's orientalism is rather superficial even in the two symphonic suites.   He never
achieved anything like the voluptuous warmth of
Balakirev's "Islamey" and "Tamara," though
these were evidently his models.   (He approaches
it most nearly in "Antar," perhaps.)   Nor did he
actually invent many themes of an oriental type.
The melodies are either closely derived from Glinka
or Balakirev (the solo violin theme of Scheherazade
herself, for instance, from a melody (see Ex. 87)
in "Tamara"), or are actual eastern tunes—three
of the Arabian melodies in "Antar," the Persian

Ex. 87

dance in "Mlada," and others. And the composer
treats these oriental and quasi-oriental themes with
the same favourite harmonic formulas that he uses
for the Russian folk-themes. In short, Rimsky-
Korsakov's orientalism though more natural and
more nearly authentic than that of any Western composer, is little more than a convention. Balakirev's
and Borodin's quasi-eastern music is also conven-
tionalised, of course, but with them the oriental influence went deeper. One has only to compare the
hard, symmetrical, highly stylised arabesque patterns of the "Cockerel" with the profusion of
ornament in the opening of "Tamara" or the natural efflorescence of the 'cello melody in the *andante*
of Borodin's First Symphony, as it goes on, to hear
the difference. What with Rimsky-Korsakov was
something to be applied externally was in the cases
of the other two composers a natural mental trait.
But to condemn Korsakov's orientalism on that account would only be pedantic. These facts concern

the critic only in so far as they help to distinguish the composers' characteristics.

After all, if Rimsky-Korsakov's orientalism gives one the impression that it is merely external, so do many of the other and more important elements of his music. They seem not to have sprung from something deep and vital in the composer, irrepressibly finding an outlet, but to have been observed by him, absorbed and coloured (but seldom wholly transmuted) by the play of an imagination at once precise and fantastic, a musical imagination literally unique in quality. The music which seems to have poured from him with natural *élan* is sometimes very beautiful and individual, but far more often weak and insipid, especially in his later works. Not infrequently the two elements are incongruously juxtaposed as in the Tsaritsa's " Hymn to the Sun," where the banality of the melody is scarcely disguised by the exotic trimmings. It may have been consciousness of the external nature of so much of his work which prompted that curious remark about art being "essentially an enchanting and intoxicating lie." It is difficult to imagine Chopin or Schubert, to say nothing of Bach or Beethoven or Mozart, coming to that conclusion even in a moment of depression. One can understand a man doubting the value of his own work in such a moment, or bitterly resenting the smallness of the reward or recognition it had brought him, but not his giving way to the thought that art itself is futile and false. Art may be only a veil of illusion drawn over the face of reality, but the illusion has very little value if it is not convincing. The great creative artists of all ages have all had this in common, that they have believed intensely in their work, in the importance and reality of art. The intensity of their belief communicates their conviction to us. Rimsky-Korsakov's fatal weakness is his self-consciousness. He sets out to create illusion, knowing all the time that it *is* only illusion. We frequently cannot believe in his music, simply because he frequently does not believe in it himself. The artist may be sceptical about anything in the world, but not about his art. Rimsky-Korsakov is a priest celebrating the rites of a religion in which he has no faith—or, at least, not the deep and burning conviction which is true faith. He enjoys doing it. He does live wholeheartedly in the ritual; it is immensely important to him. And so he makes the ceremonial itself very impressive. Quite often he works himself up to the point of temporarily convincing himself that there really is a deeper truth behind it. But the sceptic in him always triumphs over the believer. So it is, after all, more fitting that this tragedy of an over-sophisticated man should close with the question-mark of "The Golden Cockerel" rather than with the affirmation of "Kitezh."

The tragedy was a real one, for Korsakov was not always content merely to enjoy his marvellous command of the resources of music and the exercise of his inexhaustible imagination in manipulating them. He *needed* to believe. His serious breakdown of health in 1892-3 seems to have been the result of a profound inward dissatisfaction, contrasting curiously with the self-satisfaction of so many pages of his memoirs. Does not this interlude, which had echoes in later years, when the composer's "love for music cooled entirely" and he restlessly devoured systems of philosophy and æsthetics, suggest that the composer suffered from a sense of something indefinable lacking in himself, from that "melancholy of impotence" which Nietzsche imagined he saw in Brahms, very much as Snegurochka was tormented by her lack of human warmth? His case is one of the most curious in the history of music.

XV —BALAKIREV: A FLAWED GENIUS

BALAKIREV is one of the great enigmas of
music. His shadow lies over the whole of
the "classical" period of Russian music. During
the dozen or so years following Glinka's death he
was, next to the Rubinstein brothers, the most prominent figure in the world of Russian music, without exception the most vital. Yet all through this
period, in spite of his generally acknowledged creative gifts and his position as leader and mentor of
a group of composers, he actually wrote comparatively little. Then after a quarter of a century or
more of almost complete silence, came another
period of nine or ten quiet, but comparatively fruit-
ful, years. Balakirev was born before Queen Vic-
toria came to the throne of England and died only
four years before the outbreak of the Great War.
He had known Glinka personally, yet before he died
Stravinsky had written "The Fire Bird," a ballet
on the subject he had considered from an operatic

point of view far back in the 'sixties. He had bullied Rimsky-Korsakov and Tchaïkovsky and Borodin and Mussorgsky, interfered in the composi- · tion of their works, helped them, exasperated them and outlived them all. Without Balakirev the Kuchkisti would all have been different and lesser men; they might even have failed to become composers at all. Even Tchaïkovsky was under a heavy debt to him. Yet his own position as a composer is strangely equivocal. He was so obviously "the strongest personality of his circle," as Tchaïkovsky told Madame von Meck, that one feels he ought to have been the greatest of all Russian musicians, instead of the brilliant failure he is generally considered.

It is easy to see why Balakirev lost the position of social leadership in the musical world which was naturally his. He seemed to be marked out by destiny as a sort of Russian Liszt; for there is an obvious similarity between the two men, even as composers. But Balakirev lacked one of Liszt's assets and one of his useful weaknesses, his unfailing charm of manner and his tendency (whether due to polite hypocrisy or genuine kindness of heart it is difficult to say) to scatter indiscriminate praise.

Where Liszt would have praised and flattered, Balakirev condemned and bullied. He was masterful and violent (if one may speak of intellectual violence), a musical Peter the Great or Ivan the Terrible, and it is easy to understand why his despotic personality repelled the sensitive Tchaïkovsky, the dry and precise Rimsky-Korsakov and even the amiable Borodin, apart altogether from his habit of criticising their compositions with brutal frankness. "Balakirev is living here," writes the twenty-nine-year-old Tchaïkovsky to his brother in 1869, "and I must confess that his society weighs on me. He is a very good fellow . . . but—I don't know why—I can never feel absolutely at home with him. I particularly dislike the narrowness of his taste and the acerbity of his tone." Rimsky-Korsakov records similar feelings; indeed many pages of his memoirs are unpleasantly flavoured with resentment against the man he had once idolised, a resentment only partly justified by his belief that Balakirev had caused him to waste years of his life in following wrong paths.

Full of a sort of demoniac enthusiasm himself, Balakirev was never happy unless he was infecting other people with his ideas, inciting them to do

things and worrying them to do them differently.
He seems to have put a great deal of the best of his
creative self into other men and their works. He
largely frittered his genius away in improvisations
which he never bothered to write down, and wasted
vital energy in non-creative work, concert-direction
and other activities for which he was not really
suited. It was only after his spiritual *volte-face*,
in his retirement from active musical life and
between the intervals of religious absorption, that
he began to produce (and write down his earlier pro-
ductions) steadily and industriously. The tragedy
is that it was then almost too late.

So we find that Balakirev's compositions belong
to two periods. The first consists of those of the
late 'fifties and early 'sixties, works of immature
genius like the Russian, Czech and Spanish Overtures, the "King Lear" music, "Russia" and the
best of his songs. The period definitely closes with
"Islamey" in 1868, though "Tamara," conceived
long before, appeared as a dazzling afterthought
early in the 'eighties. The second period opens in
1898 with the appearance of the First Symphony
(begun far back in 1866), and includes another Symphony, a Piano Concerto, a Piano Sonata, and a

Cantata written for the dedication of the Glinka Memorial in St. Petersburg in 1906—works of a lonely old man living, probably, on memories of the brilliant days of forty years earlier. In Balakirev's music, therefore, we have the dawn and sunset of genius with little of its full day.

The invention of themes was not one of Balakirev's strongest points. It is curious that of all his earlier orchestral works only the "King Lear" music is based on original ideas. The others are founded on folk-songs—Russian, Spanish or Czech. All three themes of "Islamey" are borrowed from Caucasian and Armenian sources. The theme of the first *allegro* of "Tamara" is an oriental melody which he and Rimsky-Korsakov heard in the barracks of the Imperial Escort. When he does invent them, Balakirev's own themes, though very individual, are not always of the finest quality. The chief subject of the first movement of the C major Symphony, which undergoes such extraordinary adventures in the course of the movement, is as unpromising as a theme well could be. The clarinet melody of the *andante* of the same symphony is beautiful, but not to be compared with that of the slow movement of Borodin's B minor Symphony, for example. And yet it would be absurd to say that Balakirev was unfertile or uninventive. It was only, apparently, that his creative imagination needed a given starting-point. He had genuine creative fire but he was often obliged to borrow fuel to start it. But the extraordinary conflagrations he was able to produce from remarkably little fuel provide ample evidence of his inventiveness. The symphonic poem, "Russia," and the piano fantasia, "Islamey," two works which superficially appear to have nothing in common, both show in the clearest possible light the nature of Balakirev's genius. Something has already been said of "Russia" in discussing Balakirev's treatment of folk-songs. "Islamey," very much more than the mere virtuoso-piece it appears to be, shows even more clearly the special quality of Balakirev's creative power, though that power is not easy to define in words. Principally, it consists of ability to build round the thematic nucleus a wealth of sound, materially derived from it but essentially the stuff of the composer's glowing imagination. In some respects this reminds one of Rimsky-Korsakov. But Balakirev has that warmth and exuberance in reality which Rimsky-Korsakov only seems to have. Whereas

Rimsky-Korsakov's sensuousness is almost always cold and well under control, Balakirev's is warm, passionate and insufficiently restrained; comparison of "Scheherazade" with "Tamara" shows the difference most graphically. Balakirev is what Goethe used to call *dämonisch*, exuberantly following his every impulse without check. In this, the intensity with which he lives in the present moment, he reminds one of Tchaïkovsky, except that Tchaïkovsky's intensity of feeling is definitely emotional and expressive, while Balakirev's is purely musical, a keen savouring of melody, harmony, rhythm and timbre. Just as some epileptics are said to have unnatural brilliance and clarity of vision in the moments before a fit, Balakirev often seems to have "seen" his musical material with almost morbid intensity.

Having handed on to Tchaïkovsky in a letter an idea "which had just accurred to him involuntarily" for the other's "Romeo and Juliet" Overture, he continues: "If I were going to write the overture I should take fire from this germ and I should brood over it, or rather bury it in the depths of my mind—and then something vital would come of it." That is interesting and significant. But unlike the great German masters who have done wonders with unpromising material, Balakirev seems less to discover and exploit the hidden possibilities of his themes, than to see in them pretexts for unloosing the flood of his own imaginings. And his exuberance is not checked by technical limitations. His musical speech is easy and assured. The brilliance of his scoring is hardly surpassed even by Rimsky-Korsakov, and in his exploitation of the resources of piano colour he ranks not far below Chopin and Liszt and Debussy. "Islamey," with all its hideous difficulties, is splendidly pianistic. For all its lavishness, there is no squandering. Every note tells. The piece is, admittedly, a *tour de force*, but there is nothing in it that is not musically essential, no display for the sake of display.

These great natural gifts were crippled not by technical incompetence but by external circumstances and defects inherent to the composer's mental constitution. The history of the prolonged composition of "Tamara" is enlightening. According to Rimsky-Korsakov a "considerable part" of it had already been "improvised together" in 1866-7, and often played by the composer to him and other members of their circle. In October, 1869, Bala-

kirev himself writes to Tchaïkovsky that his last
letter "made me feel so jolly that I went for a walk
on the Nevsky Prospect, hopped and skipped, and
even composed something for my 'Tamara.'" A
little later Rimsky-Korsakov reports the complete
abandonment of Balakirev's creative activities
(specially referring to the interruption in the composition of "Tamara") owing to pressure of other
work. Then came Balakirev's first period of complete withdrawal from the musical world, the period
when as Tchaïkovsky put it he "suddenly became
pious, and spent all his time in church, fasting and
prostrating himself before relics—and nothing
else." But at the very period (1878) when Tchaïkovsky was writing in these terms to Madame von
Meck, Balakirev returned to his old musical life
and again took up "Tamara." Even then the work
progressed very slowly and this not exceptionally
long symphonic poem was not finished till 1882,
fifteen years after a "considerable part" of it had
been invented (though apparently not written down).

In view of this mental and spiritual restlessness
of Balakirev's, this inability for one reason and
another to concentrate on creative work, his reproach
to Tchaïkovsky for the latter's "inactivity due to

lack of concentration" seems almost humorous. But interruptions of this kind are not enough in themselves to account for the delay in the completion of "Tamara," especially when one considers how little ground there is for Rimsky-Korsakov's complaint of its fragmentariness. As a matter of fact, neither "Tamara" nor the C major Symphony bears obvious traces of its protracted birth. Part of the explanation probably lies in Balakirev's peculiar method of composition, the planning in advance of a definite whole and then the "brooding," improvising method of filling in the separate parts. His account to Tchaïkovsky, in the letter already quoted from, of his process in the composition of his "King Lear" Overture is an invaluable revelation: "Having first read the play, I was inspired with the wish to compose an overture . . . and not yet having any materials, I fired my imagination with a general outline. I planned an introduction, *Maestoso*, and then something mystical (Kent's prediction). The introduction dies away and a stormy, passionate *allegro* begins. This is Lear himself, the discrowned, but still mighty, lion. The characteristic themes of Regan and Goneril serve as episodes, and finally the second subject of the calm and tender Cordelia. Then the middle section (storm, Lear and the Fool on the heath), with the repetition of the *allegro*: Regan and Goneril finally crush their father, and the overture dies away softly (Lear over Cordelia's corpse); Kent's prediction—now fulfilled—is heard again, and then comes the grave and quiet death. I must explain that, at first, I had no musical ideas, but these soon came and fell into place within the framework I had devised.''* Possibly the process of actual creation took no longer with Balakirev than with other composers. But he would then carry the more or less complete work in his mind for years, playing it over to his friends, "burying it in the depths of his mind," and letting it slowly ripen. Balakirev's characteristically Russian inertia and a peculiar reluctance to put things in a definite form on paper, reminding one of Borodin's hesitation with "Prince Igor," also played a part. This lassitude seems to have been of a different nature from ordinary dislike of the physical drudgery of writing out a composition, such as we know was felt by Mozart and Wagner, just as the

---

* Ravel has confessed to a somewhat similar plan of action in writing his sonata for violin and piano, though in his case purely musical considerations—form, style, and general character of the material—took the place of Balakirev's literary outline.

gradual natural maturing of ideas lying in the composer's brain differs from Beethoven's careful filing and polishing of themes. Perhaps it is this ripening process which is responsible for the over-richness of works like "Tamara," the lack of chiaroscuro, of background shades and low lights. Every part is almost equally rich in flavour, but at the same time one feels that the composer has lived with his most brilliant inspirations so long that he has grown a little tired of them. If "Tamara" betrays its long-drawn fœtation it is not in the unevenness of quality and lack of structural cohesion alleged by Rimsky-Korsakov but in the general over-ripeness of its texture.

The case of the First Symphony in C major is even more remarkable than that of "Tamara" for, according to Rimsky-Korsakov, at least a third of the first movement was in score and sketches had been made for the scherzo and finale as early as 1866, though the finished score bears the date "April 23rd, 1898." Yet it is almost impossible to say what was written by the Balakirev of twenty-nine and what by the Balakirev of sixty-one, and the other late works give one surprisingly little help in this respect. The fiery "Scherzo alla Cosacca" and the brilliant finale of the Second Symphony (1908) have all the heroic exuberance of the compositions of nearly half a century earlier.* Balakirev, unlike Rimsky-Korsakov, had not advanced with the times; his latest music still belonged harmonically to the middle of the nineteenth century. And yet he was in no sense repeating himself. Nearly all his themes are stamped with the impress of his vivid musical personality, yet there are none of those hardly disguised resuscitations which irritate one in Rimsky-Korsakov's music. The first movement of the C major Symphony differs from the rest of his work only in its more pronounced intellectual character. It is first and foremost a piece of musical thinking. Like Borodin's E flat Symphony it begins with a slow passage which, far from being a mere introduction, is a vitally important statement of material. The apparently insignificant opening bars :—

---

* Some of the material, at least, of this scherzo was actually originally intended for the First Symphony.

contain the germs (a) and (b) of practically the whole
of the first movement, a movement so ingeniously
spun that almost a bar by bar analysis is necessary
to unravel it. This may have been one of the
reasons why Balakirev abandoned the symphony for
so many years. He probably lost himself in an intellectual labyrinth. The problems to be solved
here were not of the kind that could be cleared up
by "brooding." And so when he came back to
them in later years, he dealt with them rather cava-
lierly, riding rough-shod over difficulties. There is
very little left of conventional sonata-form, but a
definite design emerges from the musical argument
—and the urgent sweep of the movement carries
conviction. The composer plunges boldly ahead,
pushing over the dry patches by force of intellect,
heedless of the banality of some of the (very unimportant) subsidiary material, much as in the last
movement he relentlessly drives his not very well
matched themes side by side in rough counterpoint

Ex. 88a, after a bad unison beginning to the *allegro vivo*, soon surprisingly comes to life and effectively dominates the whole movement.   Ex. 88b becomes by turns argumentative and heroic :—

Ex. 89

and later undergoes still more striking metamorphoses.   There is nothing consciously self-expressive about the music and yet in this unswerving logic (a sort of doctrinaire logic-without-commonsense),

developing what is essentially only a single idea
with such pertinacity, yet with such natural exuberance, taking very little notice of side-issues but full
of curious little twists and pivotings of thought (like
the " enharmonic puns "), it is surely not too imaginative to see the brilliant, narrowly dogmatic, argumentative Balakirev who oppressed Tchaïkovsky
and irritated Rimsky-Korsakov.

After a restless, enigmatic scherzo comes a rather
luscious *andante* in D flat.* None of Balakirev's
idiosyncrasies is more noticeable than this perpetual
tendency to gravitate to the keys of D and D flat
and their relative minors, and to contrast them as if
they were closely related—a trait which, as we have
seen, made an impression on Borodin.   Balakirev's
affection for these keys left its marks on the other
members of the " Kuchka."   In his own case it
almost amounted to a mania, for the greater part of
practically everything he wrote is in D, D flat, B
minor or B flat minor.†   Even in this Symphony,
nominally in C major, the last tremendous clinching

---

* Judging from a remark of Yastrebtsev's, this movement was
originally intended for a *Third* Symphony!   It is characteristic
of Balakirev that he should be planning a Third Symphony before
even the First was put on paper.

† " Balakirev really likes no keys but D flat major and B
minor," Rimsky-Korsakov once remarked to Yastrebtsev.

restatement of Ex. 88a, thundered out *fortissimo* in semibreves just before the end of the first movement, is in B flat minor and the final C major trumpetings hardly restore the tonal balance. And so the slow movement is in D flat (reached ingeniously through the tonic major close of the A minor scherzo) and the second subject of the finale in D; and one is consequently less surprised than one ought to be on finding that the first movement of the Second Symphony, otherwise conventional enough in design, has drifted within forty bars of the opening from D minor to D flat major. The mannerism is not only rather exasperating in itself but does a great deal to give a false impression of the want of variety in Balakirev's music.

It is this lack of balance, this inability to resist an artistic temptation, which more than anything else prevents Balakirev from taking a place in the front rank of symphonic composers. There are other weaknesses, admittedly. The *andante* of the First Symphony, beautiful as it is, has not symphonic breadth and dignity. And the corresponding movement, the *romanza*, of the Second is one of Balakirev's weakest creations, little more than an orchestral "song without words." (In fact one

22

of its themes seems to have been devised purely with an eye to its use in the finale.)   The chief theme of the polonaise of the Second :—

Ex. 90

strikes one at first as more suitable for the finale of a suite than of a symphony.   But the nervous energy of the melodic rhythm grows on one.   Its peculiarities are seen to be essential, not merely decorative as they appear at first.   There is just enough suggestion of the second subject of the first movement to show that they belong to the same family, and by the time the folk-song theme appears on the *cor anglais* :—

Ex. 91

one accepts the symphonic nature of the movement without question.

But when all Balakirev's limitations as a symphonic composer are admitted, it is difficult to understand why these two fine works are neglected as they are. But conductors, like most prominent musical executants, are notoriously unwilling to play works which are neither established classics nor contemporary novelties, and an overlooked composer like Balakirev stands a poor chance of recognition except as the result of persistent propaganda by a devoted champion. (An isolated performance now and again is of little use.) Yet his symphonies

could hardly fail to be welcomed in a world which
has not yet grown tired of Tchaïkovsky's and still
listens with a certain amount of pleasure even to
Schumann's. The fact that they must have
sounded a little old-fashioned when they appeared
would not weigh with modern audiences. They are
old-fashioned now only in the sense that they bear
the marks of a period, as all music does. The circumstance that the period is that of the composer's
youth instead of that of his old age is only accidental, the result of his curiously interrupted career.

But Balakirev, though living in the past during
these concluding years of his life, was not content
tamely to accept old conventions. The first movement of the C major Symphony is not the work of
a radical-turned-conservative, and the B flat minor
Piano Sonata shows the composer experimenting
just as eagerly with new forms as he had done forty
years before. Indeed the design of its *andantino*
first movement is more adventurous than that of
anything else he wrote. It is, in effect, a reconciliation of fugue with sonata-form—or at least with its
broad outline of statement, development and re-
capitulation. And it is followed by a mazurka,
charming but so long that it upsets the balance of

the sonata as a whole,* and a curious, enigmatic *larghetto* "intermezzo," the theme of which reappears in the fiery finale. Yet for all this looseness of build the sonata is a real sonata; very free, but by no means the mere concatenation of separate pieces it superficially appears to be. Nor is there any sign of decreasing physical and inventive vigour in such themes as this one which plays an important part in the finale :—

Ex. 92

It is true that the later compositions lack the exotic glamour of "Islamey" and "Tamara," the

---

* Actually the mazurka was written first, as a separate piece, and the other movements were, so to speak, composed round it.

sheer wizardry which in those works conjures up such splendid fabrics of sound from the slightest basic material. Except the scherzo of the Second Symphony they have not the epic hardness and terseness, the bold, clear-cut outline of "Russia." But in compensation they have greater breadth and more sustained power. It seems that continuous creative activity, like that of a normal composer, spread over that tragic blank of more than twenty years—blank but for the completion of "Tamara," that is—could hardly have failed to produce a series of masterpieces of the first rank.

But Balakirev was abnormal in almost every respect. He and Rimsky-Korsakov present two of the most baffling enigmas which confront the student of musical psychology, though their cases are entirely different. Whereas Rimsky-Korsakov seems to have composed with the cool precision of a mathematician, Balakirev threw out music very much as a volcano throws out lava, sometimes erupting at terrific heat, sometimes lying quiet, apparently extinct but actually storing up power for a fresh outburst. The superficial resemblances between Balakirev and Rimsky-Korsakov are entirely due to the latter's unconscious borrowings and conscious imitations, often frankly admitted in his memoirs. Borodin was almost equally indebted to Balakirev, but in his case there were real affinities with his mentor in his strong vein of lyricism (both were delightful song-composers), his "heroic" tendency and his power of large-scale construction. But there the parallel ends. The easy-going, level-headed scientist and man of the world, composing little and spasmodically as he did, achieved more than the fiery mystic who devoted, or could have devoted, his whole life to music. Balakirev remains an isolated phenomenon, the more remarkable the more one studies him—and most remarkable of all in his failure to gain the peaks that seem so easily within his reach.

XVI—TCHAIKOVSKY REVALUED

TO offer the English reader a valuation of Tchaïkovsky is rather like laying down the law about the value of an $a + b$ in which the a is the only quantity known to everybody, and b, considerably larger, is simply whatever the writer likes to say it is. Most composers are known by only a portion of their music, but in nearly every case we can say with some certainty that the proportion of their work unknown except to the specialists is poor stuff, not worth knowing, or at any rate (as in the case of many of the Bach church cantatas and the lesser known Mozart symphonies) shows us nothing of its creator that we cannot see better in the things we know. No one but a specialist need worry about Wagner's juvenilia. One might even go through life in complete ignorance of all Beethoven's violin sonatas, important as they are, without getting at all a false idea of Beethoven's music as a whole. But with Tchaïkovsky it is quite different. Judged by bulk, he was quite as much a stage-composer as a symphonist. (And I am not sure that we ought not to regard the " Pathétique " as a dramatic work with the stage-element omitted !) He wrote ten operas, to say nothing of ballets and incidental music, and of these the great majority of English music-lovers know nothing but one or two numbers from " Eugene Onegin " and perhaps " The Battle of Poltava " from " Mazeppa." After all, most of us know only three, or perhaps four, of his six symphonies; probably the first of his three string quartets and the first of his three piano concertos. The unfamiliar works are not merely an extension of the Tchaïkovsky we know only too well; many of them show quite another side of his musical nature. The earlier operas, particularly " Vakula the Smith," and the first two symphonies show a more intimate sympathy with folk-music than do any of the later works where the folk-tunes have the effect of flies in amber. Nor is the " Casse Noisette " Suite really typical of Tchaïkovsky's lighter, lyrical vein; it consists of too much icing and too little cake to be a fair specimen. Except Handel, during the long period when he was remembered in this country by hardly anything but his oratorios, no composer of such importance has been seen so one-sidedly as Tchaïkovsky.

I do not suggest that the Tchaïkovsky everyone knows is not the best Tchaïkovsky, though the "Pathétique" certainly seems to be the product of over-ripe genius rather than of genius in maturity. I should rather regard the Fourth Symphony as, in many respects, the peak of Tchaïkovsky's musical achievement, the two later ones as psychological (or pathological) studies. In them the composer is no longer quite his natural musical self—only the abnormal Tchaïkovsky happens to be more interesting than the normal, healthy one. To avoid quibbling about purely musical quality and the interest of musical neurosis, let us put it that it is this later Tchaïkovsky which embodies most of what makes his contribution to music so individual and which ensures its lasting interest. But to base one's conception of his output as a whole on these last over-strained compositions is to see his work in totally wrong perspective, even to give a false colour to one's judgment of such hackneyed products of Tchaïkovsky's earlier days as the B flat minor Concerto and the "Romeo and Juliet" Overture. To restore the balance, to get Tchaïkovsky in proper focus, one must always keep in the back of one's mind recollection of that vast quantity of not very distinguished but always natural and unforced lyrical music which is as definitely the essential Tchaïkovsky as the "Figaro" Overture is the essential Mozart. "But how," someone may ask, "is it possible to judge the B flat minor Concerto from a 'false' standpoint? Does one not judge it by itself, by its own qualities?" In this way, I think : that we tend to read into passages like the opening of the Concerto, which are really only a naïve revelling in sensuous sound-effects, a highly strung emotional significance which really does not belong to them at all. You will get a far more accurate idea of the B flat minor Concerto if you think of it as the work of a naïve and lyrical musician, with a strong leaning toward ballet music, rather than of the man whose vein of morbidity finally reduced his genius to an infinite capacity for feeling pain.

That element of "ballet music," of luscious melody and piquant rhythm and flavour, is at the heart of all Tchaïkovsky's work. How did it get there? Undoubtedly from early impressions. which planted in him a lifelong love of Italian opera and the tuneful music of such composers as Bizet,

Grieg and Délibes. His Mozart worship put a finer temper on his mind; but it is significant that he admired rather than loved Beethoven and that, of the *Kuchkisti*, he was more repelled by Mussorgsky's uncompromising realism than by the melodious insipidity of Cui. The creative faculty naturally produces from whatever seed is thrown into it, however its products may differ in appearance from the "parent." In Tchaïkovsky's case the most important seeds were the operas of Mozart—and Donizetti and Bellini; from them developed the fibres which form by far the greater part of the texture of Tchaïkovsky's musical thought. These fibres, which for convenience' sake I have followed S. I. Taneev in calling the "ballet music" element, are easy to trace through the symphonies; easier still in Tchaïkovsky's other works. They are particularly obvious in the scherzo and parts of the first movement of the First Symphony, in the two middle movements of the Second, throughout almost the whole of the Third. It is something more than a coincidence that the pizzicato scherzo of the Fourth was written shortly after Tchaïkovsky had made the acquaintance of the score of "Sylvia." When a little later he heard "Sylvia" for the first time on an orchestra he was moved to write that "nothing during the last few years has delighted me like 'Carmen' and this ballet of Délibes."* And it is significant that he cites "Sylvia" as an example of good music written for the ballet when he defends this Fourth Symphony against Taneev's complaint that "in every movement there are phrases which sound like ballet music." The very wording of the composer's reply shows (if it is anything more than an expression of annoyance) how completely he misunderstood the nature of the criticism. Does Taneev consider any lively dance melody as ballet music? If so, what has he to say of dozens of pages in Beethoven's symphonies? Or does he mean that parts of the symphony are "in the style of Minkus, Gerber or Pugni?" Tchaïkovsky quite failed to see *what* it was in his music that made Taneev's "inner eye involuntarily see the *prima ballerina*." Are not the *andante* melody of the first movement of the "Pathétique" and the whole of the slow movement of the Fifth Symphony simply "ballet music" strained to an emotional expressiveness foreign to its nature?

---

* Even before this (August, 1876) he had confided to his brother his conviction that "the ballet 'Sylvia' is a thousand times finer than 'Götterdämmerung'"!

The impression of something-less-than-greatness that we get from Tchaïkovsky's biggest and most tragic works may be largely due to the fact that he had not at his command a musical speech adequate to express what he wanted to say. But it is also caused by his morbid egotism, his inability to be universal. Sharing Hardy's view of a Destiny not merely blind and indifferent, but actively hostile to man and his happiness, he had nothing of Hardy's detachment and antiseptic irony. We must allow the truth of the charge of morbidity invariably brought against Tchaïkovsky but—and it is a very important "but"—it is true of only a very small proportion of his music, though deservedly the best known portion.

The other criticisms, equally familiar, are aimed more directly at Tchaïkovsky's artistic reputation, for morbidity is no great crime and may even have a value of its own in art. He is vulgar. His ideas and his musical architecture are not genuinely "symphonic." And, in addition, he has played the part of shuttlecock in a game of battledore between critics who have warmly debated his "Russianness" —not an obviously vital point, though an interesting one. These are the reasons why Tchaïkovsky is

looked at askance by the *soi-disant* intelligentsia.
Let us re-consider them as objectively as possible.

What is vulgarity? Frankness of utterance, obviousness, naturalness, lack of restraint and fastidi-
ousness? All these we must admit to be Tchaïkovskian characteristics. He is often noisy and
blatant . . . But let us in fairness remember that
the composer himself recognised in the Fifth Symphony, the worst case, "something repellent—
patchiness, insincerity and 'manufacturedness.'"
The blatancy of the last movement of the Fifth is
certainly a sign of hysteria, just as certainly as the
vulgarity of some of his earlier work, the opening
of the B flat minor Concerto, for instance, is a token
of exuberant vitality. After all, it is better to have
too much life than too little. Tchaïkovsky's current
of thought seems rather anæmic at times, particularly in that great "unknown quantity," but it always
flows naturally, is never in any need of pumping.
However banal his ideas, they seldom seem manufactured—even in the Fifth Symphony itself. The
magnetic power of the "Pathétique," the unique
fascination it exercises on the semi-musical, is
largely due to the intensity of its life. However
vulgar and sentimental some of it may be, there is

not a bar in it which is not musically alive. There
are few symphonies of which it can be said that they
do not contain a bar of padding, a bar which was
not *felt* by the composer; but the "Pathétique" is
one. In this respect it is the best of all Tchaïkovsky's symphonies. He was painfully conscious of
his limitations as a musical architect and confessed
to Madame von Meck in 1878, "I have always suffered from my inability to round and polish the
form of my works. Only after strenuous labour
have I at last succeeded in making the form of my
compositions correspond, more or less, with their
content. In earlier days I was too careless and
gave too little attention to the critical re-examina-
tion of my sketches. Consequently my *seams* always showed, and there was no organic union
between the separate episodes. . . . But the *form*
of my works will never be *exemplary*, for the essential qualities of my musical nature can be improved,
but not completely altered"—a most just criticism
of his own weakness. And ten years later he repeats the statement to the Grand Duke Constantine
in almost the same words: "There is frequently
padding in my works; to an experienced eye the
stitches show in my seams, but I can't help it."

That is why Tchaïkovsky is not a really great symphonist. He lives too intensely in the parts of a work; the symphonic mind must be capable of conceiving a whole. Inability to conceive a great composition in this way is not, of course, a specifically Russian weakness; it is not even common to all Russian composers. But a tendency to think episodically instead of synoptically *is* a peculiar characteristic of Russian creative minds, of novelists, dramatists and composers alike. The present moment seems to be felt by a Russian artist with such intensity that he forgets the past and takes no heed of the future. That is why the " Pathétique," though it contains no dead matter, is not a great symphony. It does not, like Tchaïkovsky's earlier symphonies, achieve artificial shapeliness through padding and vain repetitions, but it remains a collection of episodes. (I am thinking particularly of the first movement, but the same remarks apply with even more force to the symphony considered as a whole.) They have grown together, are not patched together; yet they never form one whole, they are important only for their own sakes.

So Tchaïkovsky *is* essentially Russian in at least one respect, then? His Russianness seems so obvious to most people, yet it has been vigorously denied by some who ought to know. When Tchaï-kovsky's music first burst upon Western Europe he was universally hailed as the typical Slav. Then came a reaction when people, first of all in France, then in Britain, were assured that Tchaïkovsky's music was not truly Russian in spirit, a statement which had its origin in three reasons : that it was partly true, that Cui, of the rival camp in Russia, had said so in his book, " La Musique en Russie," and that experts have a natural weakness for con-tradicting generally accepted opinions. We must remember that the 'sixties and 'seventies in Russia, the " period of reform " after the emancipation of the serfs, when Tchaïkovsky and his brilliant con-temporaries were shaping themselves, was a period of reaction from the romantic Byronism of Pushkin and Lermontov. The Slavophile party, who be-lieved that Russia could develop best along her own lines, not by copying Western ways of thought, were playing with the idea that the way of salvation lay in following the unconscious will of " the people," and their intellectuals, Tolstoy and poets like Nekrassov and Nikitin, were indulging in a sort of *muzhik*-worship of which Mussorgsky's " Boris " was one of the chief artistic products. Even their opponents, the progressive "Westernizers," had no patience with the old sentimental romanticism; their attitude toward it is clearly expressed by the hero of Turgenev's "Fathers and Sons." Tchaïkovsky, therefore, definitely belonging by his sympathies to this past age, cuts an isolated figure among his contemporaries. He owed his original popularity in his own country to the admiration of the numerous people of ordinary intelligence and not too fastidious taste who cared nothing for intellectual fashions; to the same class, in fact, equally innocent of artistic snobbery and artistic discernment, who still think very highly of him in England. But for that popularity he had to pay by the undeserved abuse of the progressive intellectuals, just as he had to pay for his alleged Western sympathies by the abuse of the Slavophiles. Far too much, however, has been made of these contemporary criticisms by later French and English writers. We to-day ought to be able to see that, although Tchaïkovsky was a romantic and an individualist in an age which admired realism and "the people," he was at heart, if not superficially, as Russian as the narrowest of nationalists. The question of his attitude to folk-music has already been touched on. He borrowed freely from the treasure-house of popular music, much more freely than many people are aware, but his own music never acquired the accent of folksong. So we must admit that if he thought in Russian he did not naturally express himself in Russian. But then how could he have done? The folk-idiom could hardly have been forced into the expression of passionate feeling. As for actual folk-melodies, they could only be a mask for an individualist, and as Tchaïkovsky's utterance grew more intensely personal he cared to use the mask less and less.

Tchaïkovsky's music is the counterpart of Pushkin's reflected Byronism and of Turgenev's polished prose and rather Western sentiment and outlook. It was no mere coincidence that Pushkin's masterpiece inspired his most thoroughly "Tchaïkovskian" work, "Eugene Onegin," music which, in the composer's own words, "proceeded in the most literal sense from my inmost being." The famous "letter aria" contains the essence of all that is best in Tchaïkovsky's natural musical thought. One might open the score of "Eugene Onegin" at almost any page and find music more typical of the

real Tchaïkovsky than anything in the "Pathétique." How he loves to slip into dance measures!
He must have revelled in the opportunities of the
ball scene. One hardly needs to be told that
"Eugene Onegin" was written at the same time as
the Fourth Symphony. Tchaïkovsky was then in
full command of his resources; his melodic flow was
never fuller or more spontaneous; and, except in the
one instance of "Francesca da Rimini," he had not
yet begun to strain after the sensational. But there
is nothing subtle about the music of "Onegin" and
the F minor Symphony; it stands on no pedestal of
remoteness and distinction. That is why one tires
of any particular work of Tchaïkovsky's; there is
nothing beneath the surface. Some of his most
characteristic melodies, the love-theme in "Romeo
and Juliet" or the G flat melody that appears on
the first violin in the *Andante funebre* of the Third
String Quartet, are as obvious as anything in good
ballet music; their value lies in their warm life, in
their absolute spontaneity.

And Tchaïkovsky's orchestration has just the
same qualities of obviousness and naturalness. We
no longer feel that his scoring is outstandingly brilliant. But on the whole, apart from his outbursts

of sheer brutal noise, it wears very well.   His high
lights are dimmed beside those of Rimsky-Korsakov and later men, but some of his warm, delicate
effects are still unsurpassed in their rather luscious
way.   (I am thinking especially of many pages of
" Onegin " and of " The Sleeping Beauty.")   Here
again, it is the " ballet " effects—the fluttering accompaniments, the simple lines of pizzicato scale
drawn across a melody, the little demisemiquaver
rushes of wood-wind trimmngs—which always seem
to be the most characteristic of Tchaïkovsky's
orchestral mannerisms.

What can one conclude from all this?   A great
melodic gift and a wonderful flair for orchestration ;
a mediocre harmonic sense ; a certain ability to mes-
merise by persistent rather than subtle rhythms ;
little power of development or genuine architecture,
but a marvellous power of filling a big canvas with
living music.   These are not the qualifications of a
first-rate symphonic composer.   Together with
Tchaïkovsky's almost unrivalled power of rhetoric,
of telling a tale of little meaning with strong words,
they seem to point to the theatre as his proper
sphere.   But in opera, as in the symphony, Tchaïkovsky had a fatal weakness, inability to escape

from himself and his own feelings. "Onegin" suc-
ceeds *because* it is subjective. The composer could
see something of himself in each of Pushkin's two
chief characters, in Tatyana and in Eugene himself.
Both in opera and in the big instrumental forms
which he needed for the deployment of his ideas,
he was hampered by conventions. He was not
master enough to find a natural-seeming compromise between his ideas and the conventions (to
invert Goethe's phrase, Tchaïkovsky's lack of mastery shows itself in his inability to accept limitations), and not strong enough to hammer out new
conventions for himself. The obvious way out, the
symphonic poem, suited Tchaïkovsky no better than
the symphony; it only substituted one kind of
"given" framework for another. He laid out sections of music to fit a vague literary programme in
precisely the same way that he laid them down to
fit into the outline of sonata-form. It was not until
the "Pathétique" that he broke through to freedom, to a form which arose naturally from the development of his ideas, and even then the break
through was emotional rather than artistic. We
hear an excited man throwing off restraint rather
than an artist conquering his difficulties. But that

does not matter to those who find an artist more interesting than his art. Tchaïkovsky will always be ranked higher by them than by those who care immensely for art and very much less for artistic personalities.

INDEX

CATALOGUE OF
BOOKS ON MUSIC

Literature covering every branch
of Music, Biographical and Critical
Studies of Composers, Histories of
Musical Instruments, also valuable
Textbooks and Tutors for Teachers
and Students of the Piano, Organ,
Violin, Cello, Theory, Singing, etc.

All prices are net and postage extra

Published by
WILLIAM REEVES Bookseller Limited
1a Norbury Crescent, London, S.W.16

Telephone: POLlards 2108

BOOKS ABOUT MUSIC

ÆSTHETICS OF MUSICAL ART, or The Beautiful in Music. By DR. FERDINAND HAND. Translated from the German by WALTER E. LAWSON, *Mus.Bac. Cantab, etc.* Third Edition. Crown 8vo, cloth, 16/-.

THE BOWED HARP. A Study of the History of Early Musical Instruments. By OTTO ANDERSSON, *Ph.D., President of the Swedish University at Abo.* From the Original Swedish Edition, revised by the Author. The Translation Edited with additional footnotes by KATHLEEN SCHLESINGER. 116 Illustrations, Bibliography and Index. 340 pages, 8vo, cloth, 35/-.

CATECHISM OF MUSICAL HISTORY AND BIOGRAPHY. With Especial Reference to the English School. By F. J. CROWEST. 187 pages. Post 8vo, cloth, 5/-; paper, 2/6.

CHAMBER MUSIC AND ITS MASTERS IN THE PAST AND IN THE PRESENT. By DR. N. KILBURN. New Edition, revised, and with additional chapters by GERALD ABRAHAM. With Plates and Music Illustrations. Crown 8vo, cloth, 21/-.

CHRONOMETRICAL CHART OF MUSICAL HISTORY. Presenting a Bird's Eye View from the Pre-Christian Era to the XXth Century. By C. A. HARRIS, *A.R.C.O.,* etc. 5/-

THE DEEPER SOURCES OF THE BEAUTY AND EXPRESSION OF MUSIC. By JOSEPH GODDARD. With many Musical Examples. Crown 8vo, cloth, 10/-.

ELIZABETHAN VIRGINAL MUSIC AND ITS COMPOSERS. By M. H. GLYN. Second Edition, Revised, 1934. Demy 8vo, cloth, 21/-.
The author has studied all virginal manuscripts and collated a considerable part of their contents. A full index of these manuscripts is included, together with detailed references as to where they are located. Besides accounts of the lives of Byrd, Bull, Gibbons and Farnaby, there are notes concerning 26 lesser-known composers for the virginals. An explanation of Elizabethan music terms forms part of the book.

THE GIPSY IN MUSIC. By FRANZ LISZT. Translated by EDWIN EVANS.
    Gipsy and Jew, Two Wandering Races.
    Gipsy Life in Relation to Art.
    Gipsy Music and Musicians.
The result of the Author's long Experience and Investigations of the Gipsies and their Music. With Portraits of the Author etc. Demy 8vo, cloth, 35/-.

HISTORY OF THE HARP. From the Earliest Period. By JOHN THOMAS (*Pencerdd Gwalia*). 8vo, paper covers, 6/-.

HISTORY OF THE TRUMPET OF BACH AND HANDEL. By WERNER MENKE. Translated by GERALD ABRAHAM. 5 Plates and a Supplement of Music. Crown 8vo, cloth, 18/-.

This history of the trumpet from its earliest use as an artistic instrument, gives special reference to its employment by Bach and Handel. The correct modern performance of the old parts is discussed, and a description of a new instrument invented by the author for this purpose is included.

HOW TO LISTEN TO GOOD MUSIC and Encourage the Taste in Instrumental and Vocal Music. With many useful Notes for Listener and Executant. By K. BROADLEY GREENE. Complete, cloth, 8/6, or in two books, paper, 2/6 each.

INTRODUCTORY SKETCH OF IRISH MUSICAL HISTORY. By W. H. GRATTAN FLOOD. A compact Record of the Progress of Music in Ireland during 1,000 Years. Portraits. Crown 8vo, cloth, 10/6.

MUSIC IN THE HIRSCH LIBRARY (Part 53 of the Catalogue of Printed Music in the British Museum), by A. HYATT KING and C. HUMPHRIES, 1951. Published for the Trustees of the British Museum. This catalogue, prepared by the Museum staff, lists also a considerable number of works which were either not included in the original four volume catalogue by P. Hirsch, or were acquired later. 4to, cloth, 42/-.

MUSIC OF THE MOST ANCIENT NATIONS, particularly of the Assyrians, Egyptians and Hebrews, with special reference to Discoveries in Western Asia and Egypt. By CARL ENGEL, 1864 (reprinted 1929). About 100 illustrations and many music examples. Demy 8vo, cloth, 42/-.

MUSICAL DEVELOPMENT, or Remarks on the Spirit of the Principal Musical Forms. An Æsthetical Investigation, in which an Attempt is made to show the Action in Music of certain Laws of Human Expression; to point out what are the Spiritual Aims of the Chief Forms of Composition, and the Broad Principles upon which they should be Constructed. By JOSEPH GODDARD. 8vo, cloth, 10/-.

NATIONAL MUSIC OF THE WORLD. By H. F. Chorley. Edited by H. G. Hewlett. Many Music Examples. Third Edition. Crown 8vo, cloth, 15/-.

OPERA STORIES OF TODAY AND YESTERDAY. Retold Act by Act (including Wagner's Ring). By E. Duncan. Crown 8vo, cloth, 6/6.

PAN PIPES, THE SPIRIT OF MUSIC in Nature, Art and Legends, from East to West. Sixteen Articles for General Reading, with Drawings of Eastern Musical Instruments. By G. P. Green. Crown 8vo, cloth, 7/6.

THE PLACE OF SCIENCE IN MUSIC. By H. Saint-George. For Advanced Students of Harmony. With music examples. 8vo, 2/6.

POLISH MUSIC AND CHOPIN, ITS LAUREATE. A Historical Account from 995 to the Present Time, including Chopin and his Works. By E. Rayson. Four Portraits. Square 8vo, boards, 6/-, paper covers, 3/6.

RISE AND DEVELOPMENT OF MILITARY MUSIC. By Dr. H. G. Farmer. With Illustrations of Early Instruments and Music Examples, and Short Biographical Notices of all the Staff Bandmasters. Crown 8vo, cloth, 16/-.

RISE AND DEVELOPMENT OF OPERA. Embracing a Comparative View of the Art in Italy, Germany, France and England. By Joseph Goddard. Showing the Cause of the Falling Back of the English School in the Modern Period, and the Compensation which that Involved. Numerous Music Examples, Portraits and Facsimiles. Crown 8vo, cloth, 18/-.

SOME ASPECTS OF CHINESE MUSIC AND SOME THOUGHTS AND IMPRESSIONS ON ART PRINCIPLES IN MUSIC. By G. P. Green. Post 8vo, cloth, 6/-, paper covers, 3/6.

SOME ASPECTS OF GIPSY MUSIC. By D. C. Parker. Post 8vo, cloth, 6/-, paper covers, 3/6.

SOME FAMOUS SYMPHONIES, How to Understand Them. With their Story and Simple Analysis. Numerous Portraits. By J. F. Porte. Dealing with Symphonies of Beethoven, Berlioz, Borodin, Brahms, Chausson, Dvořák, Elgar, César Franck, Haydn, Mendelssohn, Mozart, Schubert, Stanford and Tchaïkovsky. Complete in cloth, 8/-, or in 2 separate parts, paper, 2/6 each.

THE SOURCES OF KEYBOARD MUSIC IN ENGLAND. By CHARLES VAN DEN BORREN, translated by J. E. Matthew. 378 pages, 237 music examples. Crown 8vo, cloth, 21/–.

A standard European work of musical scholarship and one which is of vital interest to all students of keyboard music of the 16th and early 17th centuries.

The collection of keyboard music which naturally provides the basis for this study is the Fitzwilliam Virginal Book, and detailed treatment, copiously illustrated with music examples, is given to the various figures—melodic, rhythmic, and harmonic—in this music and to the forms and styles cultivated by composers for the Virginal. Originally published in England in 1915, this book remains the only thorough study of its type, illuminating a most important branch of English and European music.

TREATISE ON BYZANTINE MUSIC. By S. G. HATHERLEY. 208 Music Examples. 162 pages, 4to, cloth, 25/–.

There are upwards of 50 unabbreviated musical pieces, ancient and modern, from Greek, Russian, Turkish and Egyptian sources, given and fully analysed.

TRIBAL MUSIC AND DANCING IN THE SOUTHERN SUDAN, at Social and Ceremonial Gatherings. A descriptive account of the music, rhythm, etc., from personal observation. By Dr. A. N. TUCKER. 5 illustrations, 61 music examples illustrating the dances, songs and rhythm. 57 pages, demy 8vo, cloth, 10/6.

THE TROUBADOUR AS MUSICIAN, Past and Present. By C. A. HARRIS. 2/6.

THE WORLD'S EARLIEST MUSIC. Traced to its Beginnings in Ancient Lands. By collected Evidences of Relics, Records, History and Musical Instruments, from Greece, Etruria, Egypt, China, through Assyria and Babylonia to the Primitive Home, the Land of Akkad and Sumer. By HERMANN SMITH. With sixty-five Illustrations, nearly 400 pages. Crown 8vo, cloth, 25/–.

BOOKS ABOUT MUSICIANS AND THEIR WORKS

FROM MENDELSSOHN TO WAGNER. Being the Memoirs of J. W. Davison, forty years Music Critic of *The Times*, compiled by his son, HENRY DAVISON, from Memoranda and Documents. With 52 portraits of Musicians and Important Letters (previously unpublished) of Mendelssohn, Berlioz, Gounod, Jullien, Macfarren, Sterndale Bennett, etc. Index, 539 pages, 8vo, cloth, 42/–.

MUSIC AND MUSICIANS. Essays and Criticisms, by ROBERT SCHUMANN. Translated, Edited and Annotated by F. R. RITTER. Two volumes, crown 8vo, cloth, 35/– each.

Schumann's literary gifts and interests almost equalled his musical ones. From boyhood he was drawn to literary expression, and his writings on music belong to the best among the romantic literature of the 19th century. The same fire, poetry, directness of expression, the same inventiveness we love in his compositions, also animates his prose.

MUSICAL MEMORIES. By WILLIAM SPARK, *Mus.Doc.* (*late Organist of the Town Hall, Leeds*). Third Edition. With sixteen Portraits. Thick crown 8vo, cloth, 10/–.

REEVES' DICTIONARY OF MUSICIANS. Biographical Accounts of about 2,500 Noteworthy Musicians of the Past and Present. Edited by EDMUNDSTOUNE DUNCAN and Others. Crown 8vo, cloth, 7/6, paper covers, 4/–.

SKETCHES OF ENGLISH GLEE COMPOSERS. Historical, Biographical and Critical. From about 1735–1866. By D. BAPTIE. Post 8vo, cloth, 10/–.

SOME MUSICAL RECOLLECTIONS OF FIFTY YEARS. By RICHARD HOFFMAN. With Memoir by MRS. HOFFMAN. Illustrated with many Portraits. Crown 8vo, cloth, 10/–.

An interesting book of reminiscences by a prominent Anglo-American pianist and composer (1831–1909). He studied under Pleyel, Moscheles, Rubinstein and Liszt, and became a concert pianist in New York, and also toured with Jenny Lind. Hoffman composed and published many pianoforte pieces of the brilliant kind in vogue at the time.

STUDIES IN RUSSIAN MUSIC. Critical Essays on the most important of Rimsky-Korsakov's operas, Borodin's "Prince Igor," Dargomïzhsky's "Stone Guest," etc.; with chapters on Glinka, Mussorgsky, Balakirev and Tschaïkovsky. By GERALD ABRAHAM. 92 music examples. 350 pages, demy 8vo, cloth, 25/-.

ON RUSSIAN MUSIC. Critical and Historical Studies of Glinka's Operas, Balakirev's Works, etc. With chapters dealing with Compositions by Borodin, Rimsky-Korsakov, Tchaïkovsky, Mussorgsky, Glazunov, and various other Aspects of Russian Music. By GERALD ABRAHAM. With Frontispiece and 88 Music Examples. Demy 8vo, cloth, 21/-.

The above two books complement one another, and together form a valuable survey of Russian music of the period 1836 to 1910. The operas of Rimsky-Korsakov are studied fully, also Borodin's "Prince Igor", Glinka's operas and Balakirev's music. Gerald Abraham is Professor of Music at Liverpool University, and is the chief English authority on Russian music.

THE SYMPHONY WRITERS SINCE BEETHOVEN. Critical Essays on Schubert, Schumann, Götz, Brahms, Tchaïkovsky, Brückner, Berlioz, Liszt, Strauss, Mahler, Mendelssohn, Saint-Saëns, etc. By FELIX WEINGARTNER. Translated by A. BLES. Twelve Portraits. *Second Impression.* With Chapter added by D. C. PARKER on Weingartner's Symphony No. 5. Crown 8vo, cloth, 16/-.

WITH THE GREAT COMPOSERS. A Series of Pen Pictures, exhibiting in the form of Interviews the Personal Characteristics as Artists of the World's great Tone Poets. By GERALD CUMBERLAND. Portraits. Cr. 8vo, cloth, 10/-.

Deals with Chopin, Haydn, Mendelssohn, Paganini, Beethoven, Handel, Rossini, Schubert, Liszt, Berlioz, Mozart, Wagner Tchaïkovsky, Cherubini, Wolf, Borodin, Schumann, Sullivan.

HOW TO PLAY BACH'S 48 PRELUDES AND FUGUES. A Guide Book for the use of Piano Students as an aid to the Unravelling and Interpretation of these Masterpieces, ensuring a more Intelligent Keyboard Rendering. By C. W. WILKINSON. Crown 8vo, cloth, 10/-.

BALFE, HIS LIFE AND WORK. By WM. ALEXANDER BARRETT. Over 300 pages. Crown 8vo, cloth, 21/-.

BEETHOVEN. By RICHARD WAGNER. With a Supplement from the Philosophical Works of Arthur Schopenhauer. Translated by EDWARD DANNREUTHER. Third Edition. Crown 8vo, cloth, 18/–.

BEETHOVEN AND HIS PIANO WORKS (Sonatas, Concertos, Variations, etc.). Descriptive and Analytic Aid to their Understanding and Rendering. By HERBERT WESTERBY. With list of Principal Editions and Bibliography. 3 illustrations, 45 music examples. Crown 8vo, cloth, 10/–.

BEETHOVEN'S PIANOFORTE SONATAS Explained for the Lovers of the Musical Art. By ERNST VON ELTERLEIN. Translated by E. HILL, with Preface by ERNST PAUER. Revised Edition (the Seventh issue). With Portrait, and View of Beethoven's House. Crown 8vo, cloth, 10/–.

NOTES ON THE INTERPRETATION OF 24 FAMOUS PIANO SONATAS BY BEETHOVEN. By J. ALFRED JOHNSTONE. Portrait, crown 8vo, cloth, 12/6.

BEETHOVEN'S PIANO SONATAS. A Descriptive Commentary on the Sonatas in the light of Schnabel's Interpretations; giving an æsthetic Appreciation of each Sonata, with an Outline of the Development of the Sonata Form in Beethoven's hands. With a Biographical Sketch of Schnabel and an account of his activity as an executant, composer and teacher. By RUDOLF KASTNER. Translated by GERALD ABRAHAM. 55 pages, post 8vo, paper, 3/6.

A CRITICAL STUDY OF BEETHOVEN'S NINE SYMPHONIES, with a Few Words on His Trios and Sonatas, a Criticism of "Fidelio" and an Introductory Essay on Music. By HECTOR BERLIOZ. Translated from the French by EDWIN EVANS. Portrait. Crown 8vo, cloth, 21/–.

BEETHOVEN'S NINE SYMPHONIES Fully Described and Analysed. A complete Account of Thematic Material and auxiliary Motives, an Analytical Chart of each Movement, full Technical Descriptions of Developments, Particulars of Formal and Rhythmic Features, Epitomical Tables, etc. Illustrated by 637 Musical Examples. By EDWIN EVANS. Cloth, Vol. I (Nos. 1 to 5), 21/–. Vol. II (Nos. 6 to 9), out of print.

BEETHOVEN'S SYMPHONIES Critically Discussed by ALEXANDER TEETGEN. With Preface by JOHN BROADHOUSE. Second Edition. Post 8vo, cloth, 6/6.

THE CRITICAL WRITINGS OF HECTOR BERLIOZ

A CRITICAL STUDY OF BEETHOVEN'S NINE SYM-PHONIES, with a few Words on his Trios and Sonatas, and a Criticism of Fidelio. Portrait. Crown 8vo, cloth, 21/–.

GLUCK AND HIS OPERAS, with an Account of their Relation to Musical Art. Portrait. Crown 8vo, cloth, 21/–.

MOZART, WEBER AND WAGNER, with various other Essays on Musical Subjects Crown 8vo, cloth, 21/–.

The above three books form a full and readable translation by Edwin Evans of the justly celebrated critical writings of Hector Berlioz issued under the title of "A Travers Chant."

BORODIN THE COMPOSER AND HIS MUSIC. A Descriptive and Critical Analysis of his Works and a Study of his Value as an Art Force. With many references to the Russian Kouchka Circle of Five—Balakirev, Moussorgsky, César Cui, Rimsky-Korsakov, and Borodin. By GERALD ABRAHAM. With music examples and 5 Portraits. Crown 8vo, cloth, 25/–.

LIFE OF JOHANNES BRAHMS. By FLORENCE MAY. Second Edition, Revised. Two Volumes, demy 8vo, cloth, 42/–.

This work still remains the most comprehensive single work on the composer published. It is based on material gathered at first hand during the course of several visits to the Continent, and its value as a personal document is enhanced by the author's own recollections and impressions of Brahms, which were the result of personal contact with and actual study under the great master.

VOCAL WORKS OF BRAHMS. In the Order of their Opus Number with Biographical, Analytical and other explanatory details, Review of Criticism, Special Translations and copious Information. By EDWIN EVANS. Demy 8vo, cloth, 42/–. (The companion volumes on the Piano, Organ and Chamber and Orchestral Works are out of print.)

LIFE OF CHERUBINI. By F. J. CROWEST. (Great Musicians Series.) Crown 8vo, cloth, 6/–.

CHOPIN'S GREATER WORKS (Preludes, Ballads, Nocturnes, Polonaises, Mazurkas). How they should be Understood. By J. KLECZYNSKI. Including Chopin's Notes for a "Method of Methods." Translated by N. JANOTHA. Second Edition. With music examples. Crown 8vo, cloth, 10/–.

HOW TO PLAY CHOPIN. The Works of Chopin, their Proper Interpretation. By J. KLECZYNSKI. Translated by A. WHITTINGHAM. Sixth Edition. Music Illustrations. Crown 8vo, cloth, 7/6.

Contains the cream of Chopin's instructions to his own pupils. To admirers of Chopin and players of his music we should say this book is indispensable.

FREDERIC CHOPIN, Critical and Appreciative Essay. By J. W. DAVISON. 8vo, 3/6.

CHOPIN THE COMPOSER AND HIS MUSIC. An Analytic Critique of Famous Traditions and Interpretations, as exhibited in the Playing of Great Pianists, Past and Present. By JOHN F. PORTE. With portrait. 193 pages, crown 8vo, cloth, 10/6.

HANDBOOK TO CHOPIN'S WORKS. A Detailed Account of all the Compositions of Chopin. Short Analyses for Piano Student and Critical Quotations from Writings of Well-known Musical Authors. Chronological List of Works, etc. By G. C. A. JONSON. Second Edition. Crown 8vo, cloth, 18/–.

"Here in one compact volume is all that is necessary to know about Chopin and his works except by the leisured enthusiast."

HANDEL'S MESSIAH. The Oratorio and its History. A Handbook of Hints and Aids to its Public Performance, with useful Notes on each Movement, as well as Numerous References and much Original Information. By J. ALLANSON BENSON. Boards, 6/6; paper, 4/–.

LISZT, COMPOSER, AND HIS PIANO WORKS. Descriptive Guide and Critical Analysis, written in a popular and concise style. By HERBERT WESTERBY, *Mus.Bac., Lon., etc.* 5 illustrations, 24 music examples. 336 pp., crown 8vo, cloth, 21/–.

ANALYSIS OF MENDELSSOHN'S ORGAN WORKS. A Study of their Structural Features. By JOSEPH W. G. HATHAWAY, *Mus.B. Oxon.* 127 Music Examples. Portrait and Facsimiles. Crown 8vo, cloth, 12/6.

HOW TO INTERPRET MENDELSSOHN'S "SONGS WITHOUT WORDS" (the celebrated "Lieder ohne Worte"). A Readable and Useful Guide for All. Gives the Piano Students helpful Insight into the first Principles of Form in Music. By CHARLES W. WILKINSON. With portrait and facsimile of MS. Crown 8vo, cloth, 6/-; paper, 3/6.

MOZART: a Commemorative Address read before the Positivist Society. By V. LUSHINGTON. 8vo, 3/-.

Mozart and Religion.

THE SONATA: Its Form and Meaning, as Exemplified in the Piano Sonatas by Mozart. A Descriptive Analysis, with Musical Examples. By F. HELENA MARKS. 8vo, cloth, 18/-.

QUESTIONS ON MOZART'S SONATAS. By F. HELENA MARKS. Aid and Companion to the Study of the Author's work, "The Sonata: Its Form and Meaning as Exemplified in the Piano Sonatas by Mozart." Paper covers, 2/6.

RACHMANINOFF. An Exhilarating Biographical Study of this Genius of the Keyboard. By WATSON LYLE. Preface by LEFF POUISHNOFF. Two Portraits and List of Works. Crown 8vo, cloth, 18/-.

FRANZ SCHUBERT, Man and Composer. A Vivid Story of a Charming Personality. By C. WHITAKER-WILSON. With Original Translations into English of eight Well-known Schubert Songs, together with the Music for the Voice. Portraits and Illustrations of Schubert and his Friends. Crown 8vo, cloth, 15/-.

HENRY SMART'S ORGAN COMPOSITIONS ANALYSED. By J. BROADHOUSE. Crown 8vo, cloth, 7/6.

WAGNER'S TEACHINGS BY ANALOGY. His Views on Absolute Music and of the Relations of Articulate and Tonal Speech, with Special Reference to "Opera and Drama." By EDWIN EVANS. Crown 8vo, cloth, 6/-; paper, 3/6.

WAGNER'S Ring des Nibelungen. The Story of Wagner's "Ring" for English Readers. By N. KILBURN, *Mus.Bac.*, *Cantab.* Crown 8vo, paper, 2/–.

HOW TO UNDERSTAND WAGNER'S "RING OF THE NIBELUNG." Being the Story and a Descriptive Analysis of the "Rheingold," the "Valkyr," "Siegfried" and the "Dusk of the Gods." With Musical Examples of the Leading Motives of Each Drama. By GUSTAVE KOBBE. Together with a Sketch of Wagner's Life. By N. KILBURN, *Mus.Bac. Cantab.* Seventh Edition. Crown 8vo, cloth, 12/6.

Description and analysis go hand in hand with the narration of the story. Musical examples are given as aids to the identification of the leading motives and an index makes it easy for any reader to turn up any particular motive instantly.

WIT AND MIRTH: OR PILLS TO PURGE MELANCHOLY. Edited by THOMAS D'URFEY. Introduction by CYRUS L. DAY. A facsimile reproduction of the 1876 reprint of the original edition of 1719-20. This is a famous collection of songs, poems and ballads, all with music, a few dating from the Elizabethan period, but the majority from the second half of the 17th century. Three Volumes, £8.

OUT-OF-PRINT BOOKS.

Positive Microfiches can be supplied of the following books where the printed editions are out of print They must be used in conjunction with a reader (usually found in large libraries).

HISTORY OF THE VIOLONCELLO, Viola da Gamba, etc., with Biographies of all the Most Eminent Players, 1915. By E. VAN DER STRAETEN, 50/–.

ORCHESTRAL

THE CONDUCTOR, THE THEORY OF HIS ART. By HECTOR
BERLIOZ. Translated by J. BROADHOUSE. With 41 Diagrams
and Examples. Crown 8vo, cloth, 8/6; paper covers, 5/-.

INSTRUMENTS AND ART OF THE ORCHESTRA. An Introductory Study. With Table showing Range of each Instrument. By P. W. DE COURCY-SMALE, *Mus.Bac.* 8vo, boards, 6/-.

METHOD OF INSTRUMENTATION. How to Write for the
Orchestra and Arrange an Orchestral or Band Score. Illus-
trated with Music Examples and various large folding Charts
and Index. By EDWIN EVANS. Demy 8vo, cloth, two volumes.
Vol. I. How to Write for Strings, Arrangement of Scoring and
Preparation of Parts. With Charts. 10/-.
Vol. II. How to Write for Wood, Brass and Drums, and
Arrange a Band Score. With large folding Charts. 10/-.

NOTES ON CONDUCTORS AND CONDUCTING. By T. R.
CROGER, *F.R.G.S.*, *F.Z.S.*, also the Organising and Conducting of Amateur Orchestras, with three full-page Illustrations of the various "Beats" and Plan of the Orchestra.
Revised and Enlarged. Crown 8vo, paper covers, 3/6.

ON CONDUCTING. By RICHARD WAGNER. Translated by E.
DANNREUTHER. Crown 8vo, boards, 12/6.

ORCHESTRAL AND BAND INSTRUMENTS. A Short Account
of the Instruments used in the Orchestra, and in Brass and
Military Bands. By G. F. BROADHEAD, *Mus.B. Dunelm,*
L.Mus.T.C.L. With 24 Illustrative Music Examples. Post
8vo, cloth, 5/-, paper covers, 3/-.

ORCHESTRAL WIND INSTRUMENTS, Ancient and Modern
Being an Account of the Origin and Evolution of Wind
Instruments from the Earliest Times. By U. DAUBENY, 11
plates illustrating 61 Instruments or Parts. 8vo, cloth, 25/-.

PRACTICAL GUIDE FOR THE CONDUCTOR and Useful
Notes for the Orchestra. By F. W. DE MASSI-HARDMAN. With
Music Examples and Diagrams. 3/-.

ORGAN

ART OF ORGAN ACCOMPANIMENT IN THE CHURCH SERVICES. What to Do and what to Avoid: being a Guide to the Organist in the effective rendering of the Music. By WALTER L. TWINNING, *F.R.C.O.* Boards, 3/6.

THE CHURCH ORGAN. An Introduction to the Study of Modern Organ Building. By NOEL A. BONAVIA-HUNT. With 40 diagrams. A reprint of the well-known book first published in 1920. Demy 8vo, cloth, 25/–.

THE EARLY ENGLISH ORGAN BUILDERS and their Works, from the Fifteenth Century to the Period of the Great Rebellion By DR. E. F. RIMBAULT. Post 8vo, boards, 12/–.

THE INFLUENCE OF THE ORGAN IN HISTORY. By DUDLEY BUCK. Crown 8vo, boards, 4/–; paper covers, 2/–.

INTERNATIONAL REPERTOIRE GUIDE (Historical, Educational and Descriptive) to Foreign, British and American Works. By HERBERT WESTERBY. 4to, cloth, 25/–.

Describes the best Organ Music of foreign countries as well as of Britain and America.

A large and beautifully presented quarto work, fully illustrated by thirty-six plates on fine art paper, comprising seven English and sixteen foreign organs, thirty-one portraits, and illustrations of the houses of Bach and Handel.

LECTURE ON THE PEDAL ORGAN. Its History, Design and Control. By THOMAS CASSON. With folding Diagram. 8vo boards, 8/6.

MODERN ORGAN BUILDING. By WALTER & THOMAS LEWIS (Organ Builders). Practical Explanation and Description of Organ Construction with especial regard to Pneumatic Action and Chapters on Tuning, Voicing, etc. Third Edition, Revised. 116 Illustrations, including 76 Drawn to Scale and Reproduced from actual Working Drawings. 4to, cloth, 42/–.

MODERN ORGAN TUNING, The How and Why, Clearly Explaining the Nature of the Organ Pipe and the System of Equal Temperament, together with an Historic Record of the Evolution of the Diatonic Scale from the Greek Tetrachord. By HERMANN SMITH. Crown 8vo, cloth, 15/–.

NEW ORGAN PRINCIPLES AND THEIR INTERPRETATION. A Guide to and Suggestions on Phrasing and Registration with a view to improved Organ Playing. By TERENCE WHITE. With 54 music examples. Demy 8vo, paper covers, 4/–.

THE ORGAN FIFTY YEARS HENCE. A Study of its Development in the Light of its Past History and Present Tendencies. By FRANCIS BURGESS, *F.S.A.*, *Scot.*, 1908. Demy 8vo, 3/6.

ORGAN OF THE ANCIENTS FROM EASTERN SOURCES (Hebrew, Syriac and Arabic). By HENRY GEORGE FARMER, *M.A.*, *Ph.D.*, *Carnegie Research Fellow.* Foreword by CANON F. W. GALPIN. With numerous Illustrations. 8vo, cloth, 42/–.

REFORM IN ORGAN BUILDING. By THOMAS CASSON. Demy 8vo, 3/–.

SOME CONTINENTAL ORGANS and their Makers. With Specifications of many of the fine Examples in Germany and Switzerland. By JAMES I. WEDGWOOD. Post 8vo, boards, 8/6.

TECHNICS OF ORGAN TEACHING. A Handbook which treats of Special Points in Organ Teaching Examinations, together with Test Questions. By R. A. JEVONS. Boards, 3/6.

TECHNICS OF THE ORGAN. An Illuminative Treatise on many Points and Difficulties connected therewith. Special Treatment of Rhythm, Minimisation of the Use of Accessories, Extemporisation, Expressive Regulation of Organ Tone and Accompaniment. By EDWIN EVANS, *F.R.C.O.* With over 100 Music Examples. 4to, 15/–.

PIANO

THE APPROACH TO LISZT. A Course of Modern Tonal-Technique for the Piano, in the form of Graded Studies from the Moderately Difficult to the Master Stage. By HERBERT WESTERBY, *Mus.Bac. Lond., F.R.C.O., etc.* Folio, 5/6.

Preliminary Studies in Touch and Phrasing in all Keys. Based on the Scales and Broken Chords.

Intermediate Studies in Sequential, Wrist and Preparatory Arpeggio Work in the Black and White Key Positions.

Advanced Sequential Studies on the Black Keys, with Sixteen Excerpts from Liszt's Piano Works. The Master Works: Fifty-eight Excerpts from Liszt.

THE ART OF TUNING THE PIANOFORTE. A New Comprehensive Treatise to enable the Musician to Tune his Piano upon the System founded on the Theory of Equal Temperament. By HERMANN SMITH. New Edition, Revised. Crown 8vo, boards, 8/6.

THE ARTIST AT THE PIANO. Essays on the Art of Musical Interpretation. By GEORGE WOODHOUSE. 8vo, cloth, 6/–.

The celebrated pianist, Paderewski, after reading the manuscript of this stimulating volume, wrote: "The booklet is quite a remarkable work and a really valuable contribution to the philosophy of pianistic art."

THE BYRD ORGAN BOOK, for Piano or Organ. A Collection of 21 Pieces (Pavans, Galliards, etc.), by William Byrd, 1543–1623, edited from the Virginal MSS., and now first published in Modern Notation. By M. H. GLYN. 7/6.

DELIVERY IN THE ART OF PIANOFORTE PLAYING, On Rhythm, Measure, Phrasing, Tempo. By C. A. EHREN-FECHTER. Crown 8vo, cloth, 6/–.

THE DEPPE FINGER EXERCISES for Rapidly Developing an Artistic Touch in Pianoforte Playing, Carefully Arranged, Classified and Explained by AMY FAY (Pupil of Tausig, Kullak, Liszt and Deppe). Folio, English or Continental Fingering, 2/–.

EXTEMPORISING AT THE PIANO MADE EASY. A Manual for Beginners in Musical Composition. Hints and Aids for the "From Brain to Keyboard" Composer. By REV. E. H. MELLING, *F.R.C.O.* 8vo, 2/–.

HOW TO ACCOMPANY AT THE PIANO. By EDWIN EVANS. (Plain Accompaniment, Figurated Accompaniment and Practical Harmony for Accompanists.) 172 Music Examples. Crown 8vo, cloth, 7/6.

HOW TO PLAY 110 FAVOURITE PIANO SOLOS. Being the 4 Series complete in 1 vol. of "Well-Known Piano Solos: How to Play them with Understanding, Expression and Effect." By CHARLES W. WILKINSON. Crown 8vo, cloth, 12/6.

HOW TO STUDY THE PIANOFORTE WORKS OF THE GREAT COMPOSERS. By HERBERT WESTERBY, *Mus.Bac.* Handel, Bach, Haydn, Scarlatti, Mozart, Clementi, C. P. E. Bach, Beethoven. With 123 Musical Examples. Crown 8vo, cloth, 12/6.

The following issued singly, paper covers:
HANDEL, 1/–; D. SCARLATTI, 1/–; J. S. BACH, 1/6; C. P. E. BACH AND HAYDN, 1/–; CLEMENTI, 1/–; MOZART, 1/6.

INDIVIDUALITY IN PIANO TOUCH. By ALGERNON H. LINDO and J. ALFRED JOHNSTONE. Crown 8vo, 2/6.

INTRODUCTION TO RUSSIAN PIANO MUSIC. By HERBERT WESTERBY, *Mus.Bac.Lond.*, *F.R.C.O.*, *L.Mus.T.C.L.*, 1/–.

NATURAL TECHNICS IN PIANO MASTERY. A Complete and authoritative Manual, covering every Phase of Piano Playing and Study—tracing in simple Steps for the Student's Guidance the aesthetic Steps as well as the technical Problems leading from Beginning Stages to Concert Artistry. By JACOB EISENBERG. 55 illustrations. Crown 8vo, cloth, 12/6.

PIANOFORTE TEACHER'S GUIDE. By L. PLAIDY. Translated by F. R. RITTER. Crown 8vo, boards. 3/–; paper, 2/–.

REEVES' VAMPING TUTOR. Art of Extemporaneous Accompaniment, or Playing by Ear on the Pianoforte, Rapidly Enabling anyone having an Ear for Music (with or without any Knowledge of Musical Notation) to Accompany with Equal Facility in any Key. Practical Examples. By FRANCIS TAYLOR. Folio, 2/–.

THE STUDENT'S GUIDE TO THE ART OF TEACHING THE PIANOFORTE. By CYRIL R. H. HORROCKS, *L.R.A.M.*, *L.T.C.L.*, *A.R.C.M.* With an Extensive and Carefully Graded List of Studies and Course of the Great Masters. Numerous Musical Examples. Second edition, Revised. Crown 8vo, cloth, 10/–.

A SYSTEM OF STUDY OF SCALES AND CHORDS. Being Chapters on the Elements of Pianoforte Technique. By B. VINE WESTBROOK, *F.R.C.O.* Numerous Examples. Revised edition. 8vo, 3/–.

B

TECHNICAL STUDY IN THE ART OF PIANOFORTE PLAY-ING (Deppe's Principles). By C. A. EHRENFECHTER. With numerous music examples. Fourth Edition. Crown 8vo, cloth, 6/-.

CONTENTS: Position—Arm—Wrist—Fingers; Touch (Tone Production); Legato; Equality of Tone; Tension and Contraction; Five Finger Exercises; Skips; The Scale; Arpeggio Chords; Firm Chords; High Raising of the Arm; Melody and its Accompaniment; Connection of Firm Chords; The Tremolo; The Shake (Trill); The Pedal; Fingering.

TOUCH, PHRASING AND INTERPRETATION. By J. ALFRED JOHNSTONE. Crown 8vo, cloth, 7/6.

TECHNICAL AND THEORETICAL

THE ART OF MODULATING. A Series of Papers on Modulating at the Pianoforte. By HENRY C. BANISTER. With 62 Music Examples. Crown 8vo, cloth, 6/–; paper covers, 3/6.

THE ART OF MODULATION. A Handbook showing at a Glance the Modulations from one Key to any other in the Octave, consisting of 1,008 Modulations. For the Use of Organists and Musical Directors. Edited by CARLI ZOELLER. 4to, paper covers, 5/–.

COMPEND OF MUSICAL KNOWLEDGE. By PERCY BAKER, *F.R.C.O.*, *L.Mus.T.C.L.* Being a Guide with Notes, Hints and Articles on the Study of Examination Questions. Crown 8vo, cloth, 6/–; paper, 3/6.

ELEMENTARY MUSIC. A Book for Beginners. By DR. WESTBROOK. With Questions and Vocal Exercises. Crown 8vo, cloth, 4/–; paper, 2/–.

ESSENTIALS IN MUSIC STUDY FOR EXAMINATIONS. A Helpful Guide both for the General Student and Candidates for Junior and Intermediate Examinations. By REV. E. H. MELLING, *F.R.C.O.* Cloth, 5/–; paper covers, 2/6.

EXAMINATION CANDIDATE'S GUIDE to Scale and Arpeggio Piano Playing (with Tests). All that is required for the Various Exams. By WILSON MANHIRE, *L.R.A.M.* 3/–.

EXAMINATION TEST QUESTIONS. Containing spaces for the Pupils' Written Answers. By WALTER L. TWINNING, *F.R.C.O.* No. 1, Musical Notation and Time; No. 2, Formation of Scales; No. 3, Ornaments; No. 4, Intervals, 9d. each.

EXERCISES IN FIGURED BASS AND MELODY HARMONIZATION. By JAMES LYON, *Mus.Doc.* 4to, 3/6.

EXAMPLES OF FOUR-PART WRITING FROM FIGURED BASSES AND GIVEN MELODIES. By JAMES LYON, *Mus.Doc.* 4to, 5/6.
These exercises are printed in open score so as to be of use in score reading tests. This volume forms a key to "Exercises in Figured Bass" by the same author (see above).

EXERCISES ON GENERAL ELEMENTARY MUSIC. A Book for Beginners. By K. PAIGE. Part I, 1/6; Part II, 2/–.

GUIDE FOR THE YOUNG COMPOSER. Hints on the Art of Composition, with Examples of Easy Application. By REV. E. H. MELLING, *F.R.C.O.* 2/6

HANDBOOK OF MUSICAL FORM. For Instrumental Players and Vocalists. By E. VAN DER STRAETEN. With Musical Examples, 205 pages. Crown 8vo, boards, 8/6; paper, 4/-.

THE HARMONISING OF MELODIES. A Textbook for Students and Beginners. By H. C. BANISTER. Third Edition, with numerous Music Examples. Crown 8vo, limp cloth, 5/-.

HARMONY, EASILY AND PROGRESSIVELY ARRANGED. Presenting in a Simple Manner the Elementary Ideas as well as the Introduction to the Study of Harmony. With about 300 Music Examples and Exercises. By PAUL COLBERG. Crown 8vo, cloth 7/6; paper covers, 3/6.

HOW TO COMPOSE WITHIN THE LYRIC FORM. By EDWIN EVANS, *F.R.C.O.* Described for the General Reader, Practically Exemplified for the Musician and Reduced to Precept for the Student. With 60 Music Examples. Crown 8vo, cloth, 6/-.

HOW TO HARMONIZE MELODIES. With Hints on Writing for Strings and Pianoforte Accompaniments. By J. HENRY BRIDGER, *Mus.Bac.* With Music Examples. Crown 8vo, cloth, 6/-.

HOW TO MEMORISE MUSIC. By C. F. KENYON. With numerous Music Examples. Crown 8vo, cloth, 6/-.

HOW TO PLAY FROM SCORE. Treatise on Accompaniment from Score on the Organ or Piano. By F. FETIS. Translated by A. WHITTINGHAM. With forty pages of Examples. Crown 8vo, cloth, 7/6.

This popular and useful book might have been entitled "The Art of Making Arrangements for the Organ or Pianoforte from Full Orchestral and Other Scores." It contains all that is necessary to know upon this subject.

THE MODAL ACCOMPANIMENT OF PLAIN CHANT. A Practical Treatise. By EDWIN EVANS, Senior, *F.R.C.O.* Part I, Theoretical; Part II, Practical School of Plain Chant Accompaniment, consisting of 240 Exercises, with an Appendix of Notes. Crown 8vo, cloth, 12/-.

MODERN CHORDS EXPLAINED. (The Tonal Scale in Harmony.) By ARTHUR G. POTTER. Music Examples from Debussy, Strauss and Bantock. 8vo, cloth, 4/-; paper covers, 2/-.

MUSICAL ACOUSTICS. (Student's Helmholtz), or the Phenomena of Sound as Connected with Music. By JOHN BROADHOUSE. With more than 100 Illustrations. Fifth Impression. Crown 8vo, cloth, 21/–.

MUSICAL ANALYSIS. A Handbook for Students. By H. C. BANISTER. With Music Examples. Crown 8vo, limp cloth, 5/–; paper covers, 2/6.

MUSICAL EXPRESSIONS, PHRASES AND SENTENCES, with their Corresponding Equivalents in French, German and Italian. By F. BERGER. 8vo, cloth, 5/6.

MUSICAL PRONOUNCING DICTIONARY. By DR. DUDLEY BUCK. Eighth Edition, with the Concise Explanation and Pronunciation of each Term. Edited and Revised by A. WHITTINGHAM. Crown 8vo, 1/6.

PRIMARY COURSE IN THE RUDIMENTS OF MUSIC, With Hints on Answering Questions (Written Work) for All Examinations in the Primary, Elementary and Preparatory Grades. By WILSON MANHIRE, *L.R.A.M.*, etc. 2/–.

THE RUDIMENTS OF GREGORIAN MUSIC. By FRANCIS BURGESS, *F.S.A.*, *Scot.* Crown 8vo, limp cloth, 2/6; paper, 1/6.

RUDIMENTS OF MUSIC, Set forth in Graded QUESTIONS with ANSWERS, for Use of Candidates preparing for the Examinations of R.A.M., R.C.M. and T.C.L. By B. HOWARTH, *L.R.A.M.* and *A.R.C.M.* Crown 8vo, 2/–.
The Answers are always on the right hand page and can be covered over if desired, the Questions being on the corresponding left hand pages.

SCHUMANN'S RULES AND MAXIMS FOR YOUNG MUSICIANS. Sewed, 6d.

STEPS IN HARMONY. With Copious Explanatory Examples and Graded Test Exercises. A Handbook for Students. By DR. CHURCHILL SIBLEY. With Music Examples throughout. Crown 8vo, boards, 6/–.

THE STUDENT'S BOOK OF CHORDS. With an Explanation of their Inversions and Resolutions. By PASCAL NEEDHAM. Crown 8vo, 1/6.

STUDIES IN HISTORICAL FACTS AND MUSICAL FORM. Being a Guide and Note Book for a more Systematic Preparation of the General Knowledge Papers now set at the Universities and Colleges of Music. By PERCY BAKER. Crown 8vo, 3/-.

STUDIES IN MODULATION for Practical and Theoretical Purposes. By PERCY BAKER, *F.R.C.O.*, etc. 3/-.

102 TEST QUESTIONS ON THE GENERAL RUDIMENTS OF MUSIC. In Groups of Six each Lesson, for Written or Oral Use. By WILSON MANHIRE, *L.R.A.M.* 6d.

THEORY OF MUSIC FOR YOUNG MUSICIANS. With Answers given to all the Questions, and a Dictionary of necessary Musical Terms. By MARY SHARP. 1/6.

TRANSPOSITION AT SIGHT. For Students of the Organ and Pianoforte. By H. E. NICHOL. Fourth Edition, with numerous Musical Exercises. Crown 8vo, 2/-.

The practice of transposing upon the lines here laid down develops the "mental ear," quickens the musical perception and gives ease in sight reading; as it is evident that, if the student can *transpose* at sight, he will not have much difficulty in merely *playing* at sight. Free use is made of the tonic sol-fa as well as the standard notation in many musical examples.

VIOLIN AND STRINGED INSTRUMENTS

ADVICE TO VIOLIN STUDENTS. Containing Information of the Utmost Value to every Violinist. By WALLACE RITCHIE. Crown 8vo, cloth, 7/6; paper, 5/–.

AIDS TO ELEMENTARY VIOLIN PLAYING. By JEFFREY PULVER. Crown 8vo, cloth, 12/6.

ART OF HOLDING THE VIOLIN AND BOW AS EXEMPLIFIED BY OLE BULL. His Pose and Method proved to be based on true Anatomical Principles. By A. B. CROSBY, *M.D., Professor of Anatomy.* Portrait, Diagrams and Illustrations. 8vo, cloth, 6/–.

ART OF VIOLONCELLO PLAYING. Tutor in Three Books. By E. VAN DER STRAETEN. Text in English and French. 4to. Book I, 3/6; Book II, 4/–; Book III, unpublished.

BIOGRAPHICAL DICTIONARY OF FIDDLERS. Including Performers on the Violoncello and Double Bass. By A. MASON CLARKE. 9 Portraits. Post 8vo, cloth, 25/–.

BOW INSTRUMENTS, their Form and Construction. Practical and Detailed Investigation and Experiments regarding Vibration, Sound Results, and Construction. By J. W. GILTAY. Numerous Diagrams. 8vo, cloth, 16/–.

CHATS WITH VIOLINISTS. By WALLACE RITCHIE. Crown 8vo, cloth, 10/6.

GERMAN VIOLIN MAKERS. By FRIDOLIN HAMMA. A Critical Dictionary of German Violin Makers with a Series of Plates Illustrating Characteristic and Fine Examples of their Work. Translated by Walter Stewart. 64 pages of text and 80 plates in half-tone, 12 × 10 inches, cloth, 105/–.

This book is written by one of the most prominent experts in Europe, this status assuring the importance of his contribution to violin connoisseurship.

About 80 fine German instruments are represented in the plates of this book, the majority by two views, whilst many are extra-illustrated by separate scroll pictures. Good, representative examples of the German masters were selected for the purpose of providing the most informative illustrations, and a short descriptive general treatment accompanies each maker's name in the text. The arrangement of the text is on an alphabetical plan.

Fridolin Hamma's book is one of the most important contributions of our time to violin literature, a work which no connoisseur or maker should miss.

THE HISTORY OF THE VIOLIN and other Instruments Played on with the Bow from the Remotest Times to the Present. Also an Account of the Principal Makers. Coloured Frontispiece and numerous Illustrations and Figures. By W. SANDYS, *F.S.A.*, and S. A. FORSTER. Demy 8vo, cloth, 35/-.

This well-known book, first published in 1864, is especially valuable in connection with the instrument makers of the English school, and is the chief literary source of information concerning our old native craftsmen. It is good to bear in mind that as Simon Forster was a skilled and experienced instrument worker, the technical notes to be discovered in the pages of this book in which he collaborated are worthy of attention.

HOW TO BECOME A PROFESSIONAL VIOLINIST. By OSCAR CREMER. Preface by CHARLES WOODHOUSE. Crown 8vo, cloth, 8/6.

HOW TO MAKE A VIOLIN. By J. BROADHOUSE. Revised Edition. Folding Plates and many Diagrams, Figures, etc. Crown 8vo, cloth, 12/6.

CONTENTS: Introduction—The Parts of the Violin—On the Selection of Wood—The Tools required—The Models—The Mould—The Side-pieces and Side Linings—The Back—Of the Belly—The Thickness of the Back and Belly—The Bass Bar—The Purfling—The Neck—The Finger-board—The Nut and String Guard—Varnishing and Polishing—Varnishes and Colouring Matter—The Varnish—A Mathematical Method of Constructing the Outline—The Remaining Accessories of the Violin.

HOW TO PLAY THE FIDDLE. For Beginners on the Violin. By H. W. and G. GRESSWELL. Eighth Edition. Crown 8vo, 2 parts, paper covers, 1/6 each.

HOW TO REPAIR VIOLINS and other Musical Instruments. By ALFRED F. COMMON. With Diagrams. Crown 8vo, cloth, 8/6.

AN IMPORTANT LESSON TO PERFORMERS ON THE VIOLIN. By the Celebrated TARTINI. Portrait. Translated by DR. BURNEY, issued originally in 1779, together with the original Italian. 8vo, boards, 7/6.

INFORMATION FOR PLAYERS, Owners, Dealers and Makers of Bow Instruments, also for String Manufacturers. Taken from Personal Experiences, Studies and Observations. By WILLIAM HEPWORTH. Crown 8vo, cloth, 8/6.

A MUSICAL ZOO. Twenty-four Illustrations displaying the Ornamental Application of Animal Forms to Musical Instruments (Violins, Viol da Gambas, Guitars, Pochette, Serpent, etc.). Drawn from the Carved Examples by HENRY SAINT-GEORGE. Cloth, 6/-; paper, 3/6.

NOTABLE VIOLIN SOLOS: How to Play Them. Three Series (consisting of 44 descriptive Articles in all). By E. VAN DER STRAETEN. 2/6 each series. Also complete in boards, with Portraits, 15/-.

NOTICE OF ANTHONY STRADIVARI. With a Theoretical Analysis of the Bow and Remarks on Tourte. By F. J. FETIS. Demy 8vo, cloth, 21/-.

First published in 1864, this book is of particular value because the facts and ideas contained in it were given to the author by the great violin maker Vuillaume.

OLD VIOLINS AND VIOLIN LORE, Famous Makers of Cremona and Brescia, and of England, France and Germany (with Biographical Dictionary), Famous Players, and Chapters on Varnish, Strings and Bows, with 13 full-page plates. By H. R. HAWEIS. Demy 8vo, cloth, 25/-.

A delightful informal account of famous makers, players and collectors. In matters pertaining to old violins, the author is known as a specialist and, moreover, one who writes in a pleasant flowing style, which cannot be said of all specialists. He discourses about Italian, French and English violins, about varnish, strings, bows, violin dealers, collectors and amateurs. There are some fine plates, a dictionary of violin makers and a bibliography. This book is one for reading, and also for reference, and in its lighter pages for recreation.

PLAYING AT SIGHT FOR VIOLINISTS and Others in an Orchestra. Valuable Hints and Aids for its Mastery. By SYDNEY TWINN. Post 8vo, 3/6.

70 PREPARATORY VIOLIN EXERCISES for Beginners in the First Position, carefully Graduated, Supplementary to the First Instruction Book. By WILSON MANHIRE, *L.R.A.M.*, *A.R.C.M.*, *etc.* 2/6.

ROYSTON'S PROGRESSIVE VIOLIN TUTOR (with Illustrations giving Correct Position for Hand, Wrist and Fingers). Folio, 3/-.

SKETCHES OF GREAT PIANISTS AND GREAT VIOLINISTS. Biographical and Anecdotal, with Account of the Violin and Early Violinists. Viotti, Spohr, Paganini, De Beriot, Ole Bull, Clementi, Moscheles, Schumann (Robert and Clara), Chopin, Thalberg, Gottschalk, Liszt. By G. T. FERRIS. Third Edition. Crown 8vo, cloth, 12/6.

TONAL SCALES AND ARPEGGIOS FOR VIOLIN. Introductory to the Unusual Intonation and Finger-grouping of Advanced Modern Music. By SYDNEY TWINN. Folio, 3/-.

TREATISE ON THE STRUCTURE AND PRESERVATION OF THE VIOLIN and all other Bow Instruments. By JACOB AUGUSTUS OTTO. Together with an Account of the most Celebrated Makers and of the Genuine Characteristics of their Instruments. Translated by JOHN BISHOP. Fourth Edition. Crown 8vo, cloth, 12/6.

VIOLIN AND CELLO BUILDING AND REPAIRING. By ROBERT ALTON. With 82 diagrams and 2 plates. Crown 8vo, cloth, 16/-.
Robert Alton gave forty years to the study of the violin and its construction and was in close touch with makers, both amateur and professional, all over the world. He invented several tools by reason of actual experience at the bench, and has proved that they are entirely satisfactory for the work required of them. He has carried out innumerable repairs to violins, bows and cellos, and is entirely practical.

THE VIOLIN AND OLD VIOLIN MAKERS. Being a Historical and Biographical Account of the Violin. By A. MASON CLARKE. With Facsimile of Labels used by Old Masters. Crown 8vo, cloth, 10/-.

VIOLIN HARMONICS. What They Are and How to Play Them. By C. E. JACOMB. Crown 8vo, cloth, 6/-.

THE VIOLIN HUNTER. The Life Story of Luigi Tarisio, the Great Collector of Violins. By W. A. SILVERMAN. Demy 8vo, cloth, 30/-.
Luigi Tarisio had a fascinating career in the early 19th century discovering Cremona violins in Italy where they had lain forgotten and gathering dust for years, and bringing them to the dealers and collectors of Paris and London. In this book on violin romance and history, the author tells Luigi Tarisio's life story for the first time.

VIOLIN MANUFACTURE IN ITALY and its German Origin. By DR. E. SCHEBEK. Translated by W. E. LAWSON. Second Edition. Square 12 mo, cloth, 6/-

VIOLIN TECHNICS, or How to Become a Violinist. Exact Instructions, Step by Step, for its Accomplishment with or without a Teacher. By "FIRST VIOLIN." 3/6.

VIOLINIST'S ENCYCLOPÆDIC DICTIONARY. Containing the Explanation of about 4,000 Words, Phrases, Signs, References, etc., Foreign, as well as English, used in the Study of the Violin, and also by String Players generally, by F. B. EMERY, *M.A.* New and enlarged edition. 246 pp., crown 8vo. Cloth, 15/-

WELL-KNOWN VIOLONCELLO SOLOS. How to Play Them. Three Series. By E. VAN DER STRAETEN. 2/5 each series. Also complete in cloth, with Portraits, 18/-.

VOCAL

THE AMATEUR VOCALIST. A Guide to Singing. With Useful Hints on Voice Production, Song Preparation, etc. By WALTER L. TWINNING, *F.R.C.O.* Post 8vo, limp cloth, 2/–.

THE ART OF VOCAL EXPRESSION. A Popular Handbook for Speakers, Singers, Teachers and Elocutionists. By the REV. CHAS. GIB. Crown 8vo, cloth, 5/–; paper, 2/6.

THE CENTRAL POINT IN BEAUTIFUL VOICE PRODUC-TION. By H. TRAVERS ADAMS, *M.A.* 2/6.

ELEMENTARY LESSONS ON SIGHT SINGING. Combining the Staff and Tonic Sol-fa Notations. With Music Examples throughout. By J. W. ROSSINGTON, *L.R.A.M.* Cloth, 3/6; paper, 2/–.

HOW TO ATTAIN THE SINGING VOICE, or Singing Shorn of its Mysteries. A Popular Handbook for those desirous of winning Success as Singers. By A. RICHARDS BROAD. Crown 8vo, boards, 6/–.

HOW TO SING AN ENGLISH BALLAD. By E. PHILP. Eighth Edition. Crown 8vo, paper, 1/–.

HOW TO TEACH CLASS SINGING, and a Course of Outline Lessons which illustrate the psychological principles upon which successful tuition is based. By GRANVILLE HUMPHREYS, Professor of the Art of Teaching, Voice Production, etc., at the T.S.-F.C.; late Lecturer in Class Singing at the Training School for Music Teachers. Numerous Music Illustrations. Cloth, 10/–.

OBSERVATIONS ON THE FLORID SONG. Or Sentiments on the Ancient and Modern Singers. By P. F. TOSI. Translated by Mr. Galliard. With music examples. A reprint of this celebrated book, first published in 1743. Crown 8vo, 25/–.

SIMPLICITY AND NATURALNESS IN VOICE PRODUC-TION. A Plea and an Argument. By EDWIN WAREHAM. Crown 8vo, cloth, 2/6.

SPEECH DISTINCT AND PLEASING, or Why not Learn to Speak Correctly? A clear description of the mental and physical qualities on which the art of good speaking is founded. By FRANK PHILIP. 162 pages, Crown 8vo, cloth, 7/–; paper covers, 4/–.

SUCCESS IN AMATEUR OPERA. Instructions on Auditions, Equipment of the Society and the Conductor, Allocation of Rôles, Rehearsals, Training of Soloists, Diction, Conducting, etc. By HUBERT BROWN. Including a Section on Stage Management, by H. G. TOY. Crown 8vo, cloth, 6/-.

TEXTBOOK OF VOCAL TRAINING AND PREPARATION FOR SONG INTERPRETATION. With a Section showing how to Determine Accurately by Pitch and Curve Graphs the special Suitability of Songs selected for particular Vocal Requirements. Music Illustrations and Descriptive Diagrams. By FRANK PHILIP. 8vo, cloth, 15/-.

THE THROAT IN ITS RELATION TO SINGING. By WHITFIELD WARD, *A.M.*, *M.D.* Illustrations. Crown 8vo, cloth, 5/-.

TREATISE ON THE TRAINING OF BOYS' VOICES. With Examples and Exercises and Chapters on Choir-Organization. Compiled for the Use of Choirmasters. By GEORGE T. FLEMING. Crown 8vo, cloth, 5/-; paper, 2/6.

TWELVE LESSONS ON BREATHING AND BREATH CONTROL for Singers, Speakers and Teachers. By GEORGE E. THORP. Crown 8vo, paper covers, 3/-.

TWENTY LESSONS ON THE DEVELOPMENT OF THE VOICE. For Singers, Speakers and Teachers. By G. E. THORP. Crown 8vo, limp cloth, 2/6.

THE VOICE AND SINGING. Practically Explained, Condensed but Comprehensive Treatise, designed principally for Students and Amateurs, by an Experienced Singer and Teacher (C. W. PALMER). Cloth, 5/-; paper, 2/6.

VOCAL SCIENCE AND ART. Hints on Production of Musical Tone. By REV. CHAS. GIB. The Boy's Voice, Muscular Relaxation, Art of Deep Breathing, Elocution for Ordination Candidates. Crown 8vo, cloth, 6/-.

VOCAL SUCCESS, or Thinking and Feeling in Speech and Song, including a Chapter on Ideal Breathing for Health. By the REV. CHAS. GIB. Crown 8vo, cloth, 5/-; paper covers, 2/6.

VOICE PRODUCTION FOR ELOCUTION AND SINGING. By REV. E. H. MELLING. Music Examples. 31 pages, f'cap 8vo, cloth, 4/-; paper covers, 2/-.

Printed in Great Britain by
Lowe and Brydone (Printers) Limited, London, N.W.10

66 a